P9-CLH-993

[☞ *SECOND EDITION.—GREATLY ENLARGED.*]

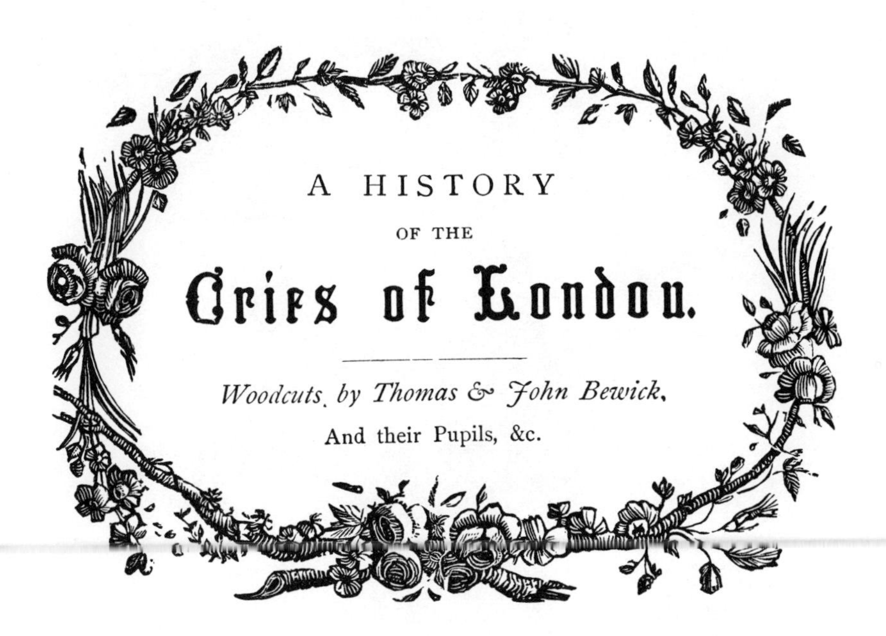

A HISTORY

OF THE

Cries of London.

Woodcuts, by Thomas & John Bewick,

And their Pupils, &c.

HOGARTH'S PIEMAN.

"We frequently meet with the pieman in old prints; and, in Hogarth's 'March to Finchley,' there he stands in the very centre of the crowd, grinning with delight at the adroitness of one robbery, while he is himself the victim of another. We learn from this admirable figure by the greatest painter of English life, that the pieman of the last century perambulated the streets in professional costume; and we gather further, from the burly dimensions of his wares, that he kept his trade alive by the laudable practice of giving 'a good pennyworth for a penny.' Justice compels us to observe that his successors of a later generation have not been very conscientious observers of this maxim"

A HISTORY

OF THE

CRIES OF LONDON.

Ancient and Modern.

*"Let none despise the merry, merry Cries
Of famous London Town."*

SECOND EDITION.

GREATLY ENLARGED AND CAREFULLY REVISED

BY

CHARLES HINDLEY, Esq.,

Editor of "The Old Book Collector's Miscellany; or, a Collection of Readable Reprints of Literary Rarities,' "Works of John Taylor—the Water Poet," "The Roxburghe Ballads," "The Catnach Press," "The Curiosities of Street Literature," The Book of Ready Made Speeches," "Life and Times of James Catnach, late of the Seven Dials, Ballad Monger,' "Tavern Anecdotes and Sayings," etc.

London:
CHARLES HINDLEY
[THE YOUNGER,]
BOOKSELLERS' ROW, ST. CLEMENT DANES,
STRAND, W.C.
1884

Detroit: Reissued by Singing Tree Press, Book Tower, 1969

Library of Congress Catalog Card Number 67–23948

TO

HORATIO NOBLE PYM, Esq.,

OF

HARLEY STREET, CAVENDISH SQUARE,

AS

A TESTIMONIAL OF ESTEEM

For His Private Worth,

AND AS

A PATRON OF LITERATURE:

A HISTORY OF THE CRIES OF LONDON,

Ancient and Modern,

Is Respectfully Dedicated by

Charles Hindley

Rectory Road, Stoke Newington,
London, N.

NOTICE.
On or about
LADY DAY, 1885,
will be published
for the same
Author,
THE HISTORY OF
The Catnach Press.
To be followed
by a
New Edition
of the
CURIOSITIES OF
STREET LITERATURE

Oh, dearly do I love "Old Cries,"
Your "Lilies all a'blowing!"
Your blossoms blue, still wet with dew,
"Sweet Violets all a'growing!"
Eliza Cook.

The idea of printing and publishing "A History of the Cries of London—Ancient and Modern," somewhat in the manner and style here presented to the public, was first suggested to me by the late Rev:—

Thomas Hugo

Author of "The Bewick Collector," 1866. The Supplement to same, 1868, and "Bewick's Woodcuts," 1870, etc., and at the time, Rector of West Hackney Church, Stoke Newington, London, N., in the year 1876.

While actively engaged in preparing for publication "The Life and Times of

James Catnach

late of Seven Dials: Ballad Monger,"—to which the present work may be considered a sequel, and the completion of the series on the subject of the—

"CURIOSITIES OF STREET LITERATURE,"

I had frequently to consult the pages of "The Bewick Collector," and other works of a kindred character for information respecting the elder Catnach, who, by himself, and afterwards in conjunction with his partner, and subsequently his successor, William Davison, employed Thomas Bewick, the famous English artist who imparted the first impulse to the art of wood engraving, for several of their Alnwick publications. This led to my communicating with the Rev. Thomas Hugo, wherein I informed him of my plans, and of the object I had in view with regard to the publication I was then preparing for the press: at the same time soliciting his co operation, especially in reference to the loan of some of the Bewick wood-cuts, formerly possessed by the elder Catnach, while he was in business as a printer, in Narrowgate Street, Alnwick, an ancient borough and market-town in Northumberland.

In answer to my application, I received the letters that follow:—

THE RECTORY,
WEST HACKNEY,
STOKE NEWINGTON,
LONDON,
N.

21*st* *August*, 1876.

DEAR SIR,

I shall be glad to aid you in any way. I must ask you to see me on some *morning*, between nine and eleven o'clock, and to make a previous appointment, as I am a working man, with plenty to do.

Yours sincerely,

Thomas Hugo.

CHARLES HINDLEY, ESQ.,
76, Rose Hill Terrace,
Brighton.

West Hackney Rectory,

Amhurst Road, West,

Stoke Newington, N.

Tuesday Night. [13*th September*, 1876.]

Dear Sir,

I have been expecting you for the last ten days. In a few hours I am leaving town for my holiday; I shall not return till far on in October.

As Brighton is but a short way off, I shall hope to see you on my return. You shall be welcome to the loan of some Blocks. You had better examine my folio volume, called "Bewick's Woodcuts," in the British Museum, and give me the numbers of the cuts, when I will see what I can do for you.

Yours sincerely,

Thomas Hugo.

Mr. C. Hindley, Senr.,
(of Brighton,)
8, Booksellers' Row,
Strand, W.C.

West Hackney Rectory,

Amhurst Road, West,

Stoke Newington, N.

8th Nov., 1876.

Dear Sir,

I can see you between 9.30 and 10.30 on *Friday* Morning.

Be so good as to advise me beforehand *what* you wish to see.

Yours sincerely,

Thomas Hugo.

C. Hindley, Esq.,
(of Brighton,)
8, Booksellers' Row,
Strand, W.C.

The proposed interview took place at the Rectory-house, on the 10th of November, and was of a very delightful and intellectual character. The reverend gentleman found me an apt scholar in all matters with respect to his favourite "Hobby-horse," viz:—the Brothers Bewick and their Works. All the rich and rare Bewickian gems were placed before me for inspection, and all the desired assistance I needed at his hands was freely offered and ultimately carried out. During our conversation the learned Rector said:—

"I look upon it as a curious fact that you should have been of late occupying your leisure in working out your own ideas of Catnach and his Times, because, while I was in the office at Monmouth-court, where I went several times to look out all the examples of Bewick I could find, and which I afterwards purchased of Mr. Fortey—the person who has succeeded to the business of the late James Catnach, I one day caught nearly the same notion, but it was more in reference to OLD LONDON CRIES: as I possess a fairly large collection of nicely engraved wood-blocks on the subject, that I met with in 'Canny Newcassel,'—in some of which it is asserted, and can hardly be denied, that Thomas Bewick had a hand. I have since used the set in my 'BEWICK'S WOODCUTS.' But, alas!—*Tempus fugit*, and all thoughts on the subject got—by reason of my having so much to do and think of—crowded out of my memory. Now, sir, as you seem to have much more leisure time than myself, I shall be happy to turn the subject-matter over to you and to assist in every way in my power."

I thanked the rev. gentleman, at the same time promising to bear the suggestion in mind for a future day.

West Hackney Rectory, Amhurst Road, West,
Stoke Newington, N., 14*th* *Nov.*, 1876.

Dear Sir,

Accept my best thanks for your letter, books, and promises of future gifts, all of which I cordially accept.

To-morrow, if all be well, I shall have time to look out the Blocks, and they shall be with you soon afterwards.

Very truly yours,

Thomas Hugo.

C. Hindley, Esq., Rose Hill Terrace,
Brighton.

W. H. R. 29*th* *Nov.* [1876.]

Dear Sir,

Herewith the Block. I have made a few corrections (of fact) in your proof.

Yours sincerely,
T. H.

C. Hindley, Esq., 76, Rose Hill Terrace,
Brighton.

The somewhat sudden and unexpected death of the Rev. Thomas Hugo on the last day of the year 1876 is now a matter of history.

In Memoriam.

The Rev. T. HUGO, M.A.

Rector of West Hackney Church.

Departed this life, Sunday, December 31st, 1876.

On Christmas Day, before the altar kneeling,
Taking that Food by which our souls are fed ;
Around us all a solemn silence stealing,
And broken only by the priests' slow tread.

Yes, he was there, our good and earnest Rector,
And firmly strove his weakness to withstand,
Giving the cup, he, the pure Faith's protector—
That cup of blessing with a trembling hand.

His church, for which he felt such admiration,
Was deck'd with flow'rs and evergreens that morn,
In praise to Christ, who died for our salvation,
And deign'd as a weak infant to be born.

Ah ! little did we think that happy morning—
So truly, bravely kept he at his post—
When next a Sabbath came, to us his warning
And kind, yet noble, presence would be lost.

That solemn sound, which tells of souls departed,
Took the glad place of that which calls to prayer,
And his loved people, shocked and broken-hearted,
Could hardly enter, for *he* was not there.

But when they heard it was his last desire
That they should meet at midnight as was said,
They met by thousands, mov'd with holy fire,
And spoke in whispers of their shepherd—*dead.*

No, no, not dead, but calm in Jesus sleeping ;
Free from all sorrow, all reproach, all pain :
And though he leaves a congregration weeping
Their earthly loss is his eternal gain.

He loved the weak, and all the mute creation,
In generous deeds he ever took his part ;
At Death, the *thrice*-repeated word *Salvation*
Showed the firm trust of that true, tender heart.

. . . .

Again we meet : they come his coffin bringing
Midst solemn chant, and deck'd with purest flowers,
And feel, whilst we his own sweet hymn are singing,
The joy is *his*, the sad rememberance *ours.*

Mrs. HILDRETH.

At the sale of the HUGO COLLECTION, I purchased among many others :—

LOT 405. London Cries, also used in Newcastle and York Cries, two very pretty series of early Cries, some with back-grounds, from Hodgson's office, and R. Robinson, Newcastle—[51 *blocks*],

To carry out the suggestion before-mentioned, and to utilize the very pretty series of fifty-one woodcuts as above, and other Bewick, Bewickiana, and *ultra anti*-Bewickian woodcut blocks I possess, formed and accumulated by reason of my published works: "The Catnach Press," 1868. "Curiosities of Street Literature," 1871. And "Life and Times of James Catnach," 1878.

In collecting information on the subject of "The Cries of London—Ancient and Modern," I have availed myself of all existing authorities within reach, and therefore, to prevent the necessity of continual reference, here state that I have drawn largely from Charles Knight's "London." Mayhew's "London Labour and the London Poor." Hone's "Every-Day Book." An article on Old London Cries, in "Fraser's Magazine." "Cuthbert Bede." Mr. Edwin Goadby's "The England of Shakespeare,"—an excellent Text Book, forming one of Cassell's Popular Shilling Library. "Our Milk Supply," from the columns of *The Daily Telegraph*. Charles Manby Smith's "Curiosities of London Life," and his "Little World of London." And what from various other sources was suitable for my purpose.

To the one lady, and many gentlemen friends who have responded to my enquiries for advice, material, and assistance, and by which they have so greatly enriched the contents of this volume, I beg to express my best thanks. I must in a more particular manner mention the names of—the one lady first—

Mrs. Rose Hildreth; then Mr. John Furbor Dexter, Mr. William Mansell; next Messrs. W. H. & L. Collingridge, the Proprietors of *The City Press*, Aldersgate-street, London, for the use of the following woodcuts that have appeared in the pages of their ever-entertaining work, "Ye OLD CITY," by Aleph.: 1.—Shakespeare's London; 2.—Aldersgate; 3.—Cheapside Cross; 4.—Old Stage Waggon; 5.—Baynard's Castle; 6.—Old London Shop; 7—St. Pauls Cathedral. I have also to express my cordial thanks to Messrs. Longman, Green & Co., who kindly allowed the use of 1.—Colebrook Cottage; 2.—The Old Queen's Head; and 3.—Canonbury Tower. From Howitt's "Northern Heights of London." Messrs. Chatto & Windus, Piccadilly: 1.—Charles Lamb's House, Enfield; 2—House at Edmonton, where Charles Lamb died; 3.—Edmonton Church. Messrs. Marks and Sons, Publishers of all kinds of Fancy Stationery, Toy-books, Valentines, &c., 72, Houndsditch, for the eight blocks used in their "Cries of London," at pages 351 to 358. Messrs. Goode, Toy-book Manufacturers, Clerkenwell Green. Mr. John W. Jarvis, Mr. William Briggs, Mr. G. Skelly, Alnwick, and Dr. David Morgan, Brighton.

SECOND EDITION.

The rapid sale of the whole of the First Edition of this work—about one half of which went Due-North, that is to say, in and round about "Canny Newcassel" (the home-land of the Brothers Bewick), America taking the remainder,—will sufficiently explain the re-appearance of "A History of the Cries of London" in its new, and, the Author ventures to think, improved form.

RECTORY ROAD, STOKE NEWINGTON,
LONDON, N.

Lady-Day, 1884.

CATALOGUE

OF THE

CHOICE AND VALUABLE COLLECTION

OF

BOOKS, WOOD ENGRAVINGS,

AND

ENGRAVED WOODCUT BLOCKS,

Manuscripts, Autograph Letters & Proof Impressions,

BY OR RELATING TO

THOMAS AND JOHN BEWICK,

AND THEIR PUPILS,

GLEANED FROM EVERY AVAILABLE SOURCE BY THE LATE

REV. THOMAS HUGO,

M.A., F.S.A.,

AUTHOR OF

"THE BEWICK COLLECTOR," 1866;

"SUPPLEMENT TO SAME," 1868;

AND

"BEWICK WOODCUTS," (folio) 1870.

WHICH WILL BE SOLD BY AUCTION,

BY MESSRS.

SOTHEBY, WILKINSON & HODGE,

Auctioneers of Literary Property & Works illustrative of the Fine Arts,

At their House, No. 13, Wellington Street, Strand, W.

On WEDNESDAY, 8th of AUGUST, 1877, and following Day,

AT ONE O'CLOCK PRECISELY.

May be Viewed Two Days prior, and Catalogues had.

Dryden Press: J. Davy and Sons. 137, Long Acre.

GOLDSMITH AND PARNELL POEMS: Published by William Bulmer, *Shakespeare Printing Office*, London, 1795. Embellished with thirteen designs on wood. Most of the cuts were drawn by Robert Johnson and John Bewick, and all were engraved by Thomas Bewick, except the vignettes on the title-pages, and the large cut of "The Sad Historian," and the tail-piece at the end of the volume, which was done by John Bewick.

The most magnificent result of the efforts of the wood-engraver, type-founder, paper-maker, and printer, "that ever was produced in any age, or in any country." Bulmer realized, after paying all expenses, a profit of £1,500 on the work these exquisite blocks adorned.

[*John Bewick, del. et Sculp.*]

THE SAD HISTORIAN.

Published January 1, 1795, by William Bulmer, at the Shakespeare Printing Office, Cleveland Row.

[2.

John Johnson, del.] [*T. Bewick, Sculp.*

THE HERMIT AT HIS MORNING DEVOTIONS.

Published January 1, 1795, by William Bulmer, at the Shakespeare Printing Office, Cleveland Row.

R Johnson, del.] [*T. Bewick, Sculp.*

———o———

THE HERMIT, ANGEL, AND GUIDE.

Published January 1, 1795, by William Bulmer, at the Shakespeare Printing Office, Cleveland Row.

John Bewick, del] [*T. Bewick, sculp.*

THE CHASE.

A POEM

BY

WILLIAM SOMERVILE, ESQ.

LONDON:
Printed by W. BULMER & Co.,
Shakespeare Printing Office, Cleveland Row.

1796.

John Bewick, del.] [*T. Bewick, sculp.*

SOMERVILE'S CHASE.

This work contains the best specimens of John Bewick's abilities as a designer ; all the cuts were drawn by him except one, but none of them were engraved by him. Shortly after he had finished the drawings on the blocks, he left London and returned to the North in consequence of ill-health. They were engraved by Thomas Bewick, with the exception of the tail-piece at the end of the volume, which was engraved by Charles Nesbit, one of his pupils.

John Bewick, del.] [*T. Bewick, sculp*

SOMERVILE'S CHASE.

The cuts in the Chase, on the whole, are superior in point of execution to those in the Poems of Goldsmith and Parnell. Many conceive it impossible that such delicate effects could be produced from blocks of wood, and his late Majesty (George III.) ordered his bookseller, Mr. George Nicolls, to procure the blocks for his inspection, that he might convince himself of the fact.

John Bewick, del.] [*T. Bewick, sculp.*

SOMERVILE'S CHASE.

Speaking of the death of John Bewick, which took place at Ovingham on the 5th of December, 1795,—aged 35, a writer in the *Gentleman's Magazine* says, "The works of this young artist will be held in estimation, and the engravings to 'Somervile's Chase' will be a monument of fame of more celebrity than marble can bestow."

THE PEACOCK.

(*Pavo cristatus*, Linn. —— *Le Paon*, Buff,)

(From Bewick's Land Birds.)

THE COMMON SANDPIPER.
(Bewick's Water Birds).

THE WATER OUZEL.
(Bewick's Water Birds.)

THE SNIPE.
(Bewick's Water Birds.)

THE REDSTART.
(Bewick's Water Birds.)

FIRST STATE!

"THE LITTLE HOUSE" and PIG, &c.

> "Snug in an English garden's shadiest spot
>   A structure stands, and welcomes many a breeze;
> Lonely and simple as a ploughman's cot!
>   Where monarchs may unbend who wish for ease."
>
> COLMAN'S—*Broaa Grins.*

Among the very many and all much admired Tail-pieces drawn and engraved by Bewick himself, the above, which, in its—*First state*! is at page 285 of vol. i. of 'A History of British Birds,' 1797, has obtained by far the greatest notoriety.

SECOND STATE!!

It appears that soon after publication, it was pointed out to Bewick that the nakedness of a prominent part of his subject required to be a little more covered—*draped!* So one of his apprentices was employed to blacken over with ink all the copies then remaining unsold. But by the time Bewick received the 'gentle hint,' a goodly number had been delivered to local subscribers and the London agents—Messrs. G. G. and J. Robinson. It is these '*not inked!*' copies that are now so readily sought after by all "Bewick Collectors."

THIRD STATE!!!

For the next, and all subsequent editions a plug was inserted in the block, and the representation of two bars of wood engraved upon it, to hide the *part!* However, it seems that before the block was thus altered and amended, many impressions on various papers were taken of the—*First state!* The late Rev. Hugo possessed several of such, one of which—*Proof on paper*—he gave me on the 10th of November, 1876.—C.H.

The Water Rail.

(Bewick's Water Birds.)

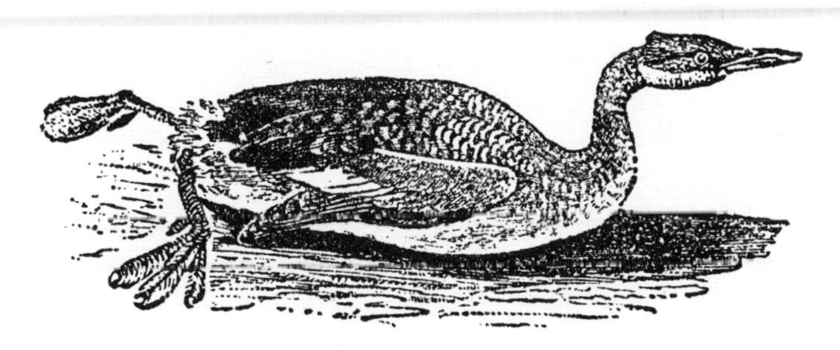

The Red necked Grebe.

(Bewick's Water Birds.)

THE CHILLINGHAM WILD BULL.

Used in Richardson's Table Book, Vol. vi p. 15.

*** Attributed to T. Bewick.

T. Bewick.

GIN AND BITTERS.

The Sportsman's Cabinet, 1803.

"WILLIE BREW'D A PECK O'MAUT."

The Poetical Works of Robert Burns. Engravings on Wood by Bewick, from designs by Thurston. Alnwick: Printed by Catnach and Davison, 1808." And London: Printed for T. Cadell and Davis, Strand, 1814. With cuts previously used in Davison's publications.

"Many of the engravings produced for Burns' Poems, are of a very superior class, and cannot be too highly commended."—*Hugo.*

"*And for whole days would wander in those places where she had been used to walk with Henry.*"

THE HISTORY OF CRAZY JANE.

By Sarah Wilkinson.

With a Frontispiece by Bewick.

ALNWICK: Printed by W. DAVISON, 1813.

JACKSON'S: A TREATISE ON WOOD ENGRAVING.

See Hugo's "Bewick Collector."—The Supplement.

THE REPOSITORY OF SELECT LITERATURE.

Adorned with beautiful Engravings by Bewick.

ALNWICK: Printed by W. DAVISON, 1808.

ARMS OF NEWCASTLE.
(*Signed* Bewick, *Sculpt.*)

BULL PURSUING A MAN.

THE POETICAL WORKS OF ROBERT FERGUSON, with his Life.

Engravings on Wood by BEWICK.

"SANDIE AND WILLIE."

THE POETICAL WORKS OF ROBERT FERGUSON.

Alnwick: Printed by W. DAVISON.—1814.

SCOTTISH BALLADS AND SONGS.

Printed and Sold by G. NICHOLSON,
Poughnill, Near Ludlow.

G. NICHOLSON, PRINTER,
Poughnill, near Ludlow.

G. Nicholson, Printer,
Poughnill, near Ludlow.

G. Nicholson, Printer.

" *Not to return, how painful the remembrance*
Of joys departed,"

BLAIR'S GRAVF.

Alnwick : Printed by CATNACH and DAVISON,—1808.

FROM NEWCASTLE.
HUGO'S Bewick's Woodcuts, No. 1333.

View of Strawberry Hill.

With Shield of Arms of the Hon. Horace Walpole.

Mr. Bigge's cut of the

Figure of Liberty.

TYNE-SIDE SCENE,
With Shield of Arms.

A CHURCHYARD MEMORIAL CUT.

THE SPORTSMAN'S CALENDER. 1818.

Hugo's "*Bewicks Woodcuts,*" No. 1309.

THE DOG IN THE MANGER.

HASTIE'S READING EASY.

From Angus's Office, where the book was printed.

"Bewick cut for Mrs. Angus, twenty-four figures for the Alphabet :—The Fox and Grapes, the Crow and Pitcher, the Foolish Stag, Joseph and his Brethren, etc. All of them excellent cuts. The fortieth edition was printed in 1814, and the seventy-third in 1839, so that they must have been done in his early days."

MS. Note of the late Mr. John Bell, of Newcastle." See Hugo's *Bewick's Woodcuts*. No. 240–276.

Fox and the Grapes.

The Crow and Pitcher.

The Foolish Stag.

Joseph and his Brethren.

T. Bewick.—Sculpt.

T. Bewick.—Sculpt.

[*R. Johnson, del.* *Charlton Nesbit, sculpt.*]

Cut to the memory of ROBERT JOHNSON.

Bewick's favourite Pupil.

On the South side of Ovingham Church there is this tablet—

In Memory of

ROBERT JOHNSON,

PAINTER AND ENGRAVER,

A NATIVE OF THIS PARISH.

Who died at Kenmore in Perthshire,

The 29*th*, *of October*, 1796.

IN THE 26th, YEAR OF HIS AGE.

THOMAS BEWICK.

Thomas Bewick died at his house on the Windmill-Hills, Gateshead, November the 8th, 1828, in the seventy-sixth year of his age, and an the 13th he was buried in the family burial-place at Ovingham, where his parents, wife, and brother were interred.

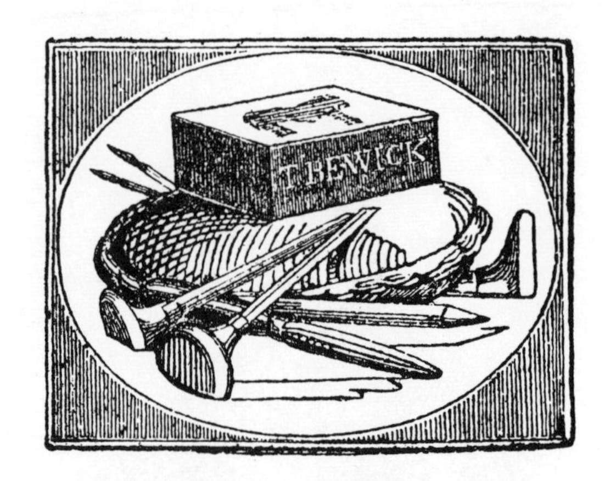

"O death, where is thy sting? O grave, where is thy victory?"

A HISTORY

OF THE

CRIES OF LONDON.

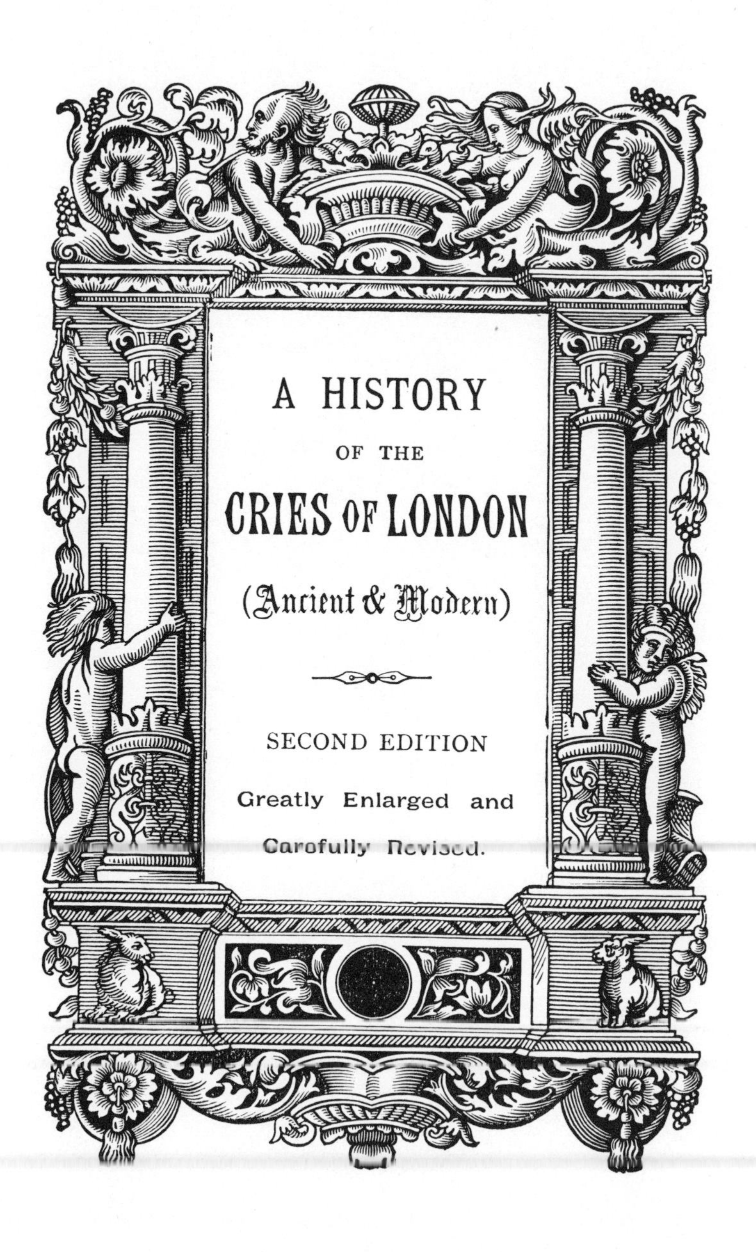

A HISTORY

OF THE

CRIES OF LONDON

(Ancient & Modern)

SECOND EDITION

Greatly Enlarged and

Carefully Revised.

NOTE

Due to a most regretable error on the part of a Victorian compositor page numbers 307 through 336 do not exist.

HISTORY

OF THE

CRIES OF LONDON.

> "Let none despise the merry, merry cries
> Of famous London Town" :—*Rox. Ballad.*

THE CRIES OF LONDON have ever been very popular, whether as broadsides, books, ballads, or engravings. Artists of all countries and times have delighted to represent those peculiarities of costume and character which belong to the history of street-cries, and the criers thereof. Annibale Carracci—1560-1609—has immortalized the cries of Bologna; and from the time of Elizabeth to that of Queen Victoria, authors, artists and printers combined, have presented the Cries and Itinerant Trades of London, in almost numberless forms, and in various degrees of quality, from the roughest and rudest wood-cut-blocks to the finest of copper and steel plate engravings, or skilfully wrought etchings. While many of the early English dramatists often introduced the subject, eminent composers were wont to "set to music" as catch, glee, or roundelaye, all the London Cries then most in vogue,—"They were, I ween, ryght merrye songs, and the musick well engraved."

The earliest mention of London trade-cries is by Dan John Lydgate (1370—1450), a Monk of the Benedictine Abbey of Bury St. Edmund's, the friend and immediate follower of Geoffrey Chaucer, and one of the most prolific writers of his age

B

this country has produced. To enumerate Lydgate's pieces would be to write out the catalogue of a small library. No poet seems to have possessed a greater versatility of talents. He moves with equal ease in every mode of composition; and among his minor pieces he has left us a very curious poem entitled "London Lyckpeny," *i.e.*, *London Lackpenny*: this has been frequently printed; by Strutt, Pugh, Nicolas, and partly by John Stow in "A Survey of London," 1598. There are two copies in the British Museum, Harl. MSS., 367 and 542. We somewhat modernize the text of the former and best of these copies, which differ considerably from each other.

> "O Mayster Lydgate! the most dulcet sprynge
> Of famous rethoryke, with balade ryall
> The chefe orygynal."
>
> "*The Pastyme of Plasure*," *by Stephen Hawes*, 1509.

In "London Lackpenny" we have a most interesting and graphic picture of the hero coming to Westminster, in term time, to obtain legal redress for the wrong he had sustained, and explain to a man of law his case—"*How my goods were defrauded me by falsehood*," but being without the means to pay even the preliminary fee, he was sent—"from pillar to post," that is from one Law-court to another, but although he "*crouched*, *kneeled*, *prayed for God's sake*, *and Mary's love*, he could not get from one the—*mum of his mouth*." So leaving the City of Westminster—minus his hood, he walked on to the City of London, which he tells us was crowded with peripatetic traders, but tempting as all their goods and offers were, his *lack-of-money* prevented him from indulging in any of them—But, however, let *Lackpenny*, through the ballad, speak for himself:—

LONDON LACKPENNY.

To London once my steps I bent,
  Where truth in no wise should be faint,
To Westminster-ward I forthwith went,
  To a man of law to make complaint,
  I said, "for Mary's love, that Holy saint!
Pity the poor that would proceed,"
But, for lack of money, I could not speed.

And as I thrust the *prese* among, [crowd]
By froward chance my hood was gone,
Yet for all that I stayed not long,
Till to the King's Bench I was come,
Before the Judge I kneeled anon,
And prayed him for God's sake to take heed;
But, for lack of money, I might not speed.

Beneath them sat Clerks a great rout,
Which fast did write by one assent,
There stood up one and cryed about,
Richard, Robert, and John of Kent.
I wist not well what this man meant,
He cried so thick there indeed,
But he that lacked money, might not speed.

Unto the Common-place *I yode thoo*, [I went then]
Where sat one with a silken hood;
I did him reverence, for I ought to do so,
And told him my case as well as I could,
How my goods were defrauded me by falsehood.
I gat not a mum of his mouth for my meed,
And, for lack of money, I might not speed.

Unto the Rolls I gat me from thence,
Before the clerks of the Chancery,
Where many I found earning of pence,
But none at all once regarded me,
I gave them my plaint upon my knee;
They liked it well, when they had it read:
But, lacking money, I could not speed.

In Westminster Hall I found out one,
Which went in a long gown of *ray*; [velvet]
I crouched and kneeled before him anon,
For Mary's love, of help I him pray.
"I wot not what thou meanest" gan he say:

To get me thence he did me bede,
For lack of money, I could not speed.

Within this Hall, neither rich nor yet poor
  Would do for me ought, although I should die:
Which seeing, I gat me out of the door,
  Where Flemings began on me for to cry:
  "Master, what will you *copen or buy*? [chap or exchange]
Fine felt hats, or spectacles to read?
Lay down your silver, and here you may speed."

Spectacles to read before printing was invented must have had a rather limited market; but we must bear in mind where they were sold. In Westminster Hall there were lawyers and rich suitors congregated,—worshipful men, who had a written law to study and expound, and learned treatises diligently to peruse, and titles to hunt after through the labyrinths of fine and recovery. The dealer in spectacles was a dealer in hats, as we see; and the articles were no doubt both of foreign manufacture. But lawyers and suitors had also to feed, as well as to read with spectacles; and on the Thames side, instead of the coffee-houses of modern date, were tables in the open air, where men every day ate of "*bread, ribs of beef, both fat and full fine*," and drank jollily of "*ale and wine*," as they do now at a horse-race:—

Then to Westminster Gate I presently went,
  When the sun was at high prime:
Cooks to me, they took good intent,
  And proffered me bread, with ale and wine,
  Ribs of beef, both fat and full fine;
A fair cloth they gan for to spread,
But, wanting money, I might not there speed.

Passing from the City of Westminster, through the village of Charing and along Strand-side, to the City of London, the cries of food and feeding were first especially addressed to those who preferred a vegetable diet, with dessert and "*spice, pepper, and saffron*" to follow. "*Hot peascod one began to cry,*" Peascod being the shell of peas; the *cod* what we now call the *pod*:—

> "Were women as little as they are good,
> A peascod would make them a gown and hood."

"*Strawberry ripe, and cherries in the rise.*" Rise—branch, twig, either a natural branch, or tied on sticks as we still see them.

> Then unto London I did me hie,
> Of all the land it beareth the prize;
> Hot peascods! one began to cry;
> Strawberry ripe, and Cherries in the rise!
> One bade me come near and buy some spice;
> Pepper and saffron they gan me *bede*; [offer to me]
> But, for lack of money, I might not speed.

In Chepe (Cheapside) he saw "*much people*" standing, who proclaimed the merits of their "*velvets, silk, lawn, and Paris thread.*" These, however, were shopkeepers; but their shops were not after the modern fashion of plate-glass windows, and carpeted floors, and lustres blazing at night with a splendour that would put to shame the glories of an eastern palace. They were rude booths, the owners of which bawled as loudly as the itinerants; and they went on bawling for several centuries, like butchers in a market, so that, in 1628, Alexander Gell, a bachelor of divinity, was sentenced to lose his ears and to be degraded from the ministry, for giving his opinion of Charles I., that he was fitter to stand in a Cheapside shop with an apron before him, and say "What do ye lack, what do ye lack? What lack ye?" than to govern a kingdom.

> Then to the Chepe I began me drawn,
> Where much people I saw for to stand;
> One offered me velvet, silk, and lawn;
> Another he taketh me by the hand,
> "Here is Paris thread, the finest in the land."
> I never was used to such things indeed;
> And, wanting money, I might not speed.
>
> Then went I forth by London Stone,
> Throughout all Canwyke Street:
> Drapers much cloth me offered anon;
> Then comes in one crying "Hot sheep's feet;"
> One cried mackerel, rushes green, another gan greet;
> One bade me buy a hood to cover my head;
> But, for want of money, I might not speed.

The London Stone, the *lapis milliaris* (mile stone) of the Romans, has never failed to arrest the attention of the "Countryman in Lunnun." The Canwyke Street of the days of John Lydgate, is the Cannon Street of the present. "*Hot sheep's feet*," which were cried in the streets in the time of Henry V., are now sold *cold* as "sheep's trotters," and vended at the doors of the lower-priced theatres, music-halls, and public-houses. Henry Mayhew in his "London Labour and the London Poor," estimates that there are sold weekly 20,000 sets, or 80,000 feet. The wholesale price at the "trotter yard" is five a penny, which gives an outlay by the street sellers of £3,033 6s. 8d. yearly. The cry which is still heard and tolerated by law, that of *Mackerel* rang through every street. The cry of *Rushes-green* tells us of by-gone customs. In ages long before the luxury of carpets was known in England, the floors of houses were covered with rushes. The strewing of rushes in the way where processions were to pass is attributed by our poets to all times and countries. Thus at the coronation of Henry V., when the procession is coming, the grooms cry—

"More rushes, more rushes."

Not worth a rush became a common comparison for anything worthless; the rush being of so little value as to be trodden under foot. *Rush-lights*, or candles with rush wicks, are of the greatest antiquity.

> Then I hied me into East-chepe,
> One cries ribs of beef, and many a pie;
> Pewter pots they clattered on a heap;
> There was harp, pipe, and minstrelsy;
> "Yea by Cock! Nay by Cock!" some began cry;
> Some sung of Jenkin and Julian for their meed;
> But, for lack of money, I might not speed.

Eastcheap, this ancient thoroughfare, originally extended from Tower-street westward to the south end of Clement's-lane, where Cannon-street begins. It was the Eastern Cheap or Market, as distinguished from Westcheap, now Cheapside. The site of the Boar's Head Tavern, first mentioned *temp.* Richard II., the scene of the revels of Falstaff and Henry V., when Prince of Wales, is very nearly that of the statue of King William IV. *Lackpenny* had presented to him several of the real Signs of the Times and of Life in London with "*ribs of beef—many a pie—pewter pots—music and singing*"—*strange oaths*, "*Yea by Cock*" being a vulgar corruption for a profane oath. Our own taverns still supply us with ballad-singers—"*Buskers*"—who will sing of "*Jenkin and Julian*"—Ben Block; or, She Wore a Wreath of Roses, "*for their meed*."

Then into Cornhill anon I *yode*, [went]
  Where was much stolen gear among;
I saw where hung mine own hood
  That I had lost among the throng;
  To buy my own hood I thought it wrong;
I knew it well, as I did my creed;
But, for lack of money, I could not speed.

The manners and customs of the dwellers in Cornhill in the time of John Lydgate, when a stranger could have his hood stolen at one end of the town and see it exposed for sale at the other, forcibly reminds us of Field-lane and the Jew Fagin, so faithfully sketched in pen and ink by Charles Dickens of our day. Where "a young man from the country" would run the risk of meeting with an Artful Dodger, to pick his pocket of his silk handkerchief at the entrance of the Lane, and it would be offered him for sale by a Jew fence at the end, not only "Once a Week" but "All the Year Round." However, when Charles Dickens and Oliver Twist came in, Field-lane and Fagin went out.

At length the Kentish man being wearied, falls a prey to the invitation of a taverner, who with a cringing bow, and taking him by the sleeve:—"*Sir*," saith he, "*will you our wine assay?*" Whereupon *Lackpenny*, coming to the safe conclusion that "*a penny can do no more than it may*," enters the tempting and hospitable house of entertainment, and there spends his only penny, for which he is supplied with a pint of wine:—

The taverner took me by the sleeve,
  "Sir," saith he, "will you our wine assay?"
I answered "That cannot be much grieve,
  A penny can do no more than it may;"
  I drank a pint, and for it did pay;
Yet, sore a-hungered from hence I *yode*, [went]
And, wanting money, I could not speed.

Worthy old John Stow supposes this interesting incident to have happened at the Pope's Head, in Cornhill, and bids us enjoy the knowledge of the fact, that :—"Wine one pint for a pennie, and bread to drink it was given free in every taverne." Yet Lydgate's hero went away "*Sore-a-hungered*," for there was no eating at taverns at this time beyond a crust to relish the wine, and he who wished to dine before he drank had to go to the cook's.

Wanting money, *Lackpenny* has now no choice but to return to the country, and applies to the watermen at Billingsgate :—

Then hied I me to Billingsgate,
  And one cried "Hoo! go we hence!"
I prayed a bargeman, for God's sake,
  That he would spare me my expense,
  "Thou scap'st not here, quod he, under two-pence,
I list not yet bestow any almes deed."
Thus, lacking money, I could not speed.

We have a corroboration of the accuracy of this picture in Lambarde's "Perambulation of Kent." The old topographer informs us that in the time of Richard II. the inhabitants of Milton and Gravesend agreed to carry in their boats, from London to Gravesend, a passenger with his truss or fardel [burden] for twopence.

Then I conveyed me into Kent;
  For of the law would I meddle no more;
Because no man to me took entent,
  I *dyght* [prepared] me to do as I did before.
  Now Jesus, that in Bethlem was bore,
Save London, and send true lawyers their meed!
For whoso wants money, with them shall not speed.

The poor Kentish suitor, without two-pence in his pocket to pay the Gravesend bargemen, whispers a mild anathema against London lawyers, then takes his solitary way on foot homeward —a sadder and a wiser man.

With unpaved streets, and no noise of coaches to drown any particular sound, we may readily imagine the din of the great London thoroughfares of four centuries ago, produced by all the vociferous demand for custom. The chief body of London retailers were then itinerant,—literally pedlars; and those who had attained some higher station were simply stall-keepers. The streets of trade must have borne a wonderful resemblance to a modern fair. Competition was then a very rude thing, and the loudest voice did something perhaps to carry the customer.

THE LONDON STONE.

In the old play entitled :—"A ryght excellent and famous Comedy called the *Three Ladies of London*, wherein is Notable declared and set fourth, how by the meanes of Lucar, Love and Conscience is so corrupted, that the one is married to Dissimulation, the other fraught with all abhomination. A Perfect Patterne of All Estates to looke into, and a worke ryght worthie to be marked. Written by R. W. ; as it hath been publiquely played. At London, Printed by Roger Warde, dwelling neere Holburne Conduit at the sign of the Talbot, 1584," is the following poetical description of some London cries :—

Enter CONSCIENCE, with brooms, singing as followeth : –

New broomes, green broomes, will you buy any ?
Come maydens, come quickly, let me take a penny.
My brooms are not steeped,
But very well bound :
My broomes be not crooked,
But smooth cut and round.
I wish it would please you,
To buy of my broome :
Then would it well ease me,
If market were done.

Have you any olde bootes,
Or any old shoone :
Pouch ringes, or buskins,
To cope for new broome ?
If so you have, maydens,

I pray you bring hither;
That you and I, friendly,
May bargin together.
New broomes, green broomes, will you buy any?
Come maydens, come quickly, let me take a penny.

CONSCIENCE *speaketh.*

Thus am I driven to make a virtue of necessity;
And seeing God Almighty will have it so, I embrace it thankfully,
Desiring God to mollify and lesson Usury's hard heart,
That the poor people feel not the like penury and smart.
But Usury is made tolerable amongst Christians as a necessary thing,
So that, going beyond the limits of our law, they extort, and to many misery bring.
But if we should follow God's law we should not receive above what we lend;
For if we lend for reward, how can we say we are our neighbour's friend?
O, how blessed shall that man be, that lends without abuse,
But thrice accursed shall he be, that greatly covets use;
For he that covets over-much, insatiate is his mind:
So that to perjury and cruelty he wholly is inclined:
Wherewith they sore oppress the poor by divers sundry ways,
Which makes them cry unto the Lord to shorten cut-throats' days.
Paul calleth them thieves that doth not give the needy of their store,
And thrice accurs'd are they that take one penny from the poor.
But while I stand reasoning thus, I forget my market clean;
And sith God hath ordained this way, I am to use the mean.

Sings again.

Have ye any old shoes, or have ye any boots? have ye any buskins, or will ye buy any broome?
Who bargins or chops with Conscience? What will no customer come?

Enter USURY.

USURY.

Who is that cries brooms? What, Conscience, selling brooms about the street?

CONSCIENCE.

What, Usury, it is a great pity thou art unhanged yet.

USURY.

Believe me, Conscience, it grieves me thou art brought so low.

CONSCIENCE.

Believe me, Usury, it grieves me thou wast not hanged long ago,
For if thou hadst been hanged, before thou slewest Hospitality,
Thou hadst not made me and thousands more to feel like Poverty.

By another old comedy by the same author as the preceding one, which he entitles :—"The pleasant and Stately Morall of the *Three Lords and Three Ladies of London.* With the great Joye and Pompe, Solemnized at their Marriages: Commically interlaced with much honest Mirth, for pleasure and recreation, among many Morall observations, and other important matters of due regard. By R. W., London. Printed by R. Ihones, at the Rose and Crowne, neere Holburne Bridge, 1590," it appears that woodmen went about with their beetles and wedges on their backs, crying "*Have you any wood to cleave?*" It must be borne in mind that in consequence of the many complaints against coal as a public nuisance, it was not in common use in London until the reign of Charles I., 1625.

There is a character in the play named *Simplicity*, a poor Freeman of London, who for a purpose turns ballad-monger, and in answer to the question of "What dainty fine ballad have you now to be sold?" replies :—"I have '*Chipping-Norton*,' '*A mile from Chapel o' th' Heath*'—'*A lamentable ballad of burning of the Pope's dog;*' '*The sweet ballad of the Lincolnshire bagpipes;*' and '*Peggy and Willy: But now he is dead and gone; Mine own sweet Willy is laid in his grave.*'"

SHAKESPEARE'S LONDON.

"City of ancient memories! Thy spires
Rise o'er the dust of worthy sons; thy walls,
Within their narrow compass, hold as much
Of Freedom as the whole wide world beside."

The London of Shakespeare, Ben Jonson and Co.,—*Limited* as it was within its great wall, occupied very much the same space as that now covered by the City proper; its streets were narrow and winding, yet there were still left many open spaces; it was covered with people; its river was full of shipping; it was rich, prosperous, and possessed of a considerable amount of

ALDERSGATE.

liberty. The great wall of London, broad and strong, with towers at intervals, was more than two miles long, from end to end, beginning at the Tower of London on the east, and ending at the Fleet River and the Thames on the west.

As regards the gates, there were anciently only four—namely, Aldersgate, Aldgate, Ludgate, and Bridgegate—that is to say, one for each of the cardinal points. Then other gates and posterns were added for the convenience of the citizens: Bishopsgate, for those who had business in the direction of Norfolk, Suffolk, or Cambridgeshire; Moorgate, for those who would practice archery, or take their recreation in Moor Fields; Cripplegate, more ancient than the two preceding, had a prison for debtors attached to it; and there was also a postern for the Convent of Grey Friars, now Christ's Hospital. At Newgate was a small, incommodious, and fever-haunted prison for criminals; and at Ludgate was another prison, appropriated to debtors, trespassers, and those who committed contempt of Court. Along the river-side were several water-gates, the chief of which were Blackfriars, Greenhithe, Dowgate and Billingsgate.

Within the narrow space of the City Walls there rose a forest of towers and spires. The piety of Merchants had erected no fewer than a hundred and three churches, which successive citizens were continually rebuilding, beautifying, or enlarging. They were filled with the effigies and splendid tombs, the painted and gilded arms, of their founders and benefactors, for whose souls masses were continually said.

"London was divided into Wards, and was perhaps as catholic in its commercial and industrial pursuits then as now. Every kind of trade was carried on within its walls, just as every kind of merchandise was sold. The combination of fellows of the same craft began in very early times, guilds were formed for the protection of trade and its followers; the guild-brothers met once a month to consider the interests of the craft, regulating prices, recovering debts and so forth. But the London of the period was not so gay as Paris, nor so bustling and prosperous as Antwerp, nor so full of splendour and intellectual life as Venice.* Yet to the Englishman of the day it was an ever-

* "The England of Shakespeare," by E. Goadby—Cassell, Petter, Galpin & Co., London, E.C.

CHEAPSIDE CROSS.

lasting wonder. Its towers and palaces, its episcopal residences and gentlemen's inns, the bustle of its commerce, the number of its foreigners, the wealth of its Companies, and the bravery of its pageants, invested it with more poetry than can be claimed for it at the present time, unless Wealth be our deity, Hurry our companion, and Progress our muse. The rich were leaving their pleasant country mansions to plunge into its delights. At the law terms there was a regular influx of visitors, who seemed to think more of taking tobacco than of winning a lawsuit. Ambitious courtiers, hopeful ecclesiastics, pushing merchants, and poetic dreamers, were all caught by the fascinations of London. Site, antiquity, life, and, above all, abundance of the good things that make up half its charm, in the shape of early delicacies, costly meats, and choice wines, combined to make it a miraculous city in the eyes of the Elizabethan."

"The external appearance of the City was certainly picturesque. Old grey walls threw round it the arm of military protection. Their gates were conspicuous objects, and the white uniforms of the train-bands on guard, with their red crosses on the back, fully represented the valour which wraps itself in the British flag and dies in its defence. To the north were the various fields whose names survive, diversified by an occasional house, and Dutch-looking windmills, creaking in the breeze. Finsbury was a fenny tract, where the City archers practised; Spitalfields, an open, grassy place, with grounds for artillery exercise and a market cross; and Smithfield, or Smoothfield, was an unenclosed plain, where tournaments were held, horses were sold, and martyrs had been burnt. To the east was the Tower of London, black with age, armed with cannon and culverin, and representing the munificence which entertained royalty as well as the power which punished traitors. Beyond it was Wapping, the Port of London, with its narrow streets, its rope-walks and biscuit shops. Black-fronted taverns, with low doorways and leaden framed windows, their rooms reeking with smoke and noisy with the chatter of ear-ringed sailors, were to be found in nearly every street. Here the merchant adventurer came to hire his seamen, and here the pamphleteer or the ballad-maker could any night gather materials for many a long-winded yarn about Drake and the Spanish main, negroes, pearls, and palm-groves.

"To the west, the scene was broken with hamlets, trees, and country roads. Marylebone and Hyde Park were a royal hunting-ground, with a manor house, where the Earls of Oxford lived in later times. Piccadilly was 'the road to Reading,' with

OLD STAGE WAGGON.

foxgloves growing in its ditches, gathered by the simple dealers of Bucklersbury, to make anodynes for the weary-hearted. Chelsea was a village ; Pimlico a country hamlet, where pudding-pies were eaten by strolling Londoners on a Sunday. Westminster was a city standing by itself, with its Royal Palace, its Great Hall for banquets and the trial of traitors, its sanctuary, its beautiful Abbey, and it famous Almonry. St. James's Park was walled with red brick, and contained the palace Henry VIII. had built for Anne Boleyn. Whitehall Palace was in its glory. The Strand, along which gay ladies drove in their

SMITH'S ARMS, BANKSIDE.*

'crab-shell coaches,' had been recently paved, and its streams of water diverted. A few houses had made their appearance on the north side of the Strand, between the timber house and its narrow gateway, which then formed Temple Bar, the boundary between London and Westminster, and the church of St. Mary-le-Strand. The southern side was adorned with noble episcopal residences, and with handsome turreted mansions, extending to the river, rich with trees and gardens, and relieved by flashes of sparkling water.

* For the use of the woodcut blocks representing the "Smith Arms," and the Globe Theatre, we are indebted to our friend Mr. John W. Jarvis, author of "Musee-Phusee-Glyptic: A Scrap Book of Jottings from Stratford-on-Avon, and Elsewhere," London, 1875, who introduces them into the pages of his work thus:—

"Not long since, after a pleasing and interesting walk, one fine morning on Bankside, and standing near the still existing Cardinal Cap Alley, with the aid of an artist friend, we drew up a fancy picture of what Bankside was in Shakespeare's day.—Here a small creek with craft and busy life around; a small bridge, with road leading to the Globe, the

"To the south, Lambeth, with its palace and church, and Faux Hall, were conspicuous objects. Here were pretty gardens and rustic cottages. The village of Southwark, with its prisons, its public theatres, its palace, and its old Tabard Inn, had many charms. It was the abode of Shakespeare himself, as he resided in a good house in the Liberty of the Clink, and was assessed in the weekly payment of 6d., no one but Henslowe, Alleyn, Collins, and Barrett, being so highly rated. That part of the Borough of Southwark known as Bankside was not only famous in Shakespeare's time for its Theatres, but also as the acknowledged retreat of the warmest of the *demi-monde!*

> "'And here, as in a tavern, or a stew,
> He and his wild associates spend their hours.'"
>
> —*Ben Jonson.*

"We fear our best zeal for the drama will not authorise us to deny that Covent-garden and Drury-lane have succeeded to the *Bank-side* in every species of fame!

---

famous theatre afterwards to be so widely known. The sunshiny time of our literature and life, making a red-letter period in happy old England's history. We were interrupted by a kindly-faced, round-shouldered man of the bargee type, who asked us 'if it was Shakespeare, him as writ plays, we was a torkin' on; if so be it were, he could show us the wery 'ouse he used, least ways, all as is left on it.' After a twisting tramp through Cardinal Cap Alley, we were brought out opposite the public-house known by the name of the 'Smith Arms,' which had just then only escaped entire demolition from fire by a very near chance—(the damage done has since necessitated the rebuilding; so the sketch stands as a bit of rescued old London.)

"Our informant assured us that—'Shakespeare as had a playus nigh there, used to use that wery 'ouse; him as writ the Merchant of Venice, Money, and the Forest of Bondy.' Our kind friend was interrupted by a companion, who said, 'Not Bondy: him didn't write that.' 'I won't give up Money, because the Merchant of Venice is all about Money. You better say he didn't write Richard the Third and Richard the Fourth.'

"We gladly retired before our historic doubts were confirmed by this traditional scholar, about this double Gloucester. His companion, as we thought rather aptly, but churlishly remarked, 'cheese it,' for they were both getting grumpy, and after this duplicate, we were fearful a fifth or a sixth might appear. But the house itself, one among the oldest in Southwark, we considered worthy a sketch, and, as our guide told us, ought to be '*perpetrated*.' He said he could pull a bit, but draw he couldn't; but he did—that is, four-pence for beer."

THE GLOBE THEATRE.

"We must not forget the river Thames. It was one of the sights of the time. Its waters were pure and bright, full of delicate salmon, and flecked by snowy swans, 'white as Lemster wool.' Wherries plied freely on its surface. Tall masts clustered by its banks. Silken-covered tiltboats, freighted with ruffed and feathered ladies and gentlemen, swept by, the watermen every now and then breaking the plash of the waves against their boats by singing out, in their bass voices, 'Heave and how, rumbelow.' At night, the scene reminded the travelled man of Venice. All the mansions by the water-side had river-terraces and steps, and each one its own tiltboat, barge, and watermen. Down these steps, lighted by torches and lanterns, stepped dainty ladies, in their coloured shoes, with masks on their faces, and gay gallants, in laced cloaks, by their side, bound for Richmond or Westminster, to mask and revel. Noisy parties of wits and Paul's men crossed to Bankside to see *Romeo and Juliet, or Hamlet the Dane*, or else 'The most excellent

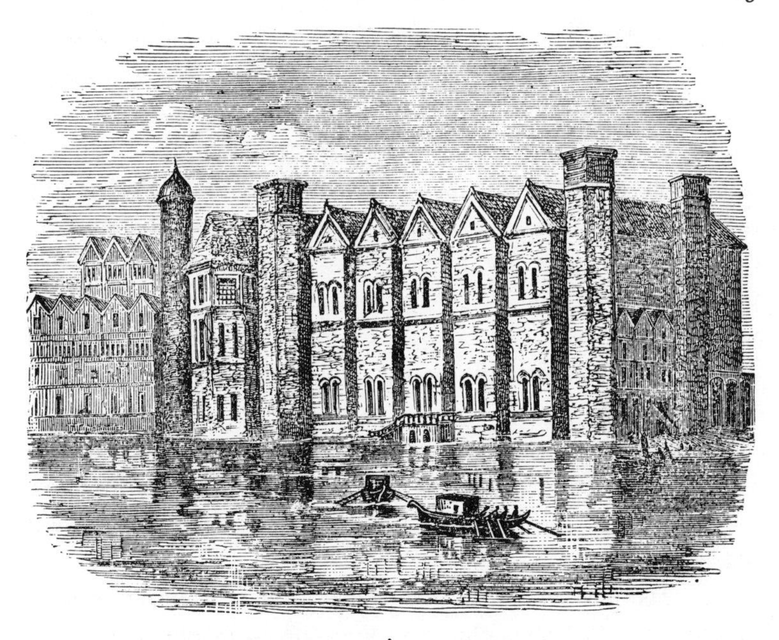

BAYNARD'S CASTLE.

historie of the *Merchant of Venice,* with the extreme crueltie of *Shylocke*, the Jewe, towards the sayd merchant, in cutting a just pound of his flesh, and obtaining of Portia by the choyse of three caskets, as it hath diverse times been acted by the Lord Chamberlain, his servants. Written by William Shakespeare.'

"From Westminster to London Bridge was a favourite trip. There was plenty to see. The fine Strand-side houses were always pointed out—Northumberland House, York House, Baynard's Castle, the scene of the secret interview between the Duke of York and the Earls of Salisbury and Warwick, was singled out, between Paul's Wharf and Puddle Dock. Next to the Temple, and between it and Whitefriars, was the region known as Alsatia. Here safe from every document but the writ of the Lord Chief Justice and the Lords of the Privy Council, in dark dwellings, with subterranean passages, narrow streets, and trap-doors that led to the Thames, dwelt all the rascaldom of the time—men who had been 'horned' or outlawed, bankrupts, coiners, thieves, cheaters at dice and cards, duellists, homicides, and foreign bravoes, ready to do any desperate deed. At night the contents of this kingdom of villany were sprayed out over London, to the bewilderment of good-natured Dogberries, and country gentlemen, making their first visit to town.

"Still further down the river was the famous London Bridge. It consisted of twenty arches; its roadway was sixty feet from the river; and the length of the bridge from end to end was 926 feet.

"It was one of the wonders that strangers never ceased to admire. Its many shops were occupied by pin nacres, just beginning to feel the competition with the Netherland pin-makers, and the tower at its Southwark end was adorned with three hundred heads, stuck on poles, like gigantic pins, memorials of treachery and heresy.

"The roar of the river through the arches was almost deafening. 'The noise at London Bridge is nothing near her,' says one of the characters in Beaumont and Fletcher's *Woman's Prize.* Shakespeare, Ben Jonson & Co., must have crossed the bridge many a time on their visits to the City, to 'gather humours of men daily,' as Aubrey quaintly expresses it."

The name of Ben Jonson reminds us that in *The Silent Woman*,—one of the most popular of his Comedies,—we have presented to us a more vivid picture than can elsewhere be found of the characteristic noises, and street-cries of London more than two centuries ago. It is easy to form to ourselves a general idea of the hum and buzz of the bees and drones of this mighty hive, under a state of manners essentially different from our own; but it is not so easy to attain a lively conception of the particular sounds that once went to make up this great discord, and so to compare them in their resemblances and their differences with the roar which the great Babel *now* "sends through all her gates." We propose, therefore, to put before our readers this passage of Jonson's comedy; and then, classifying what he describes, illustrate our fine old dramatic painter of manners by references to other writers, and by the results of our own observation.

The principal character of Jonson's *Silent Woman* is founded upon a sketch by a Greek writer of the fourth century, Libanius. Jonson designates this character by the name of

"Morose;" and his peculiarity is that he can bear no kind of noise, not even that of ordinary talk. The plot turns upon this affectation; for having been entrapped into a marriage with the 'Silent Woman," she and her friends assail him with tongues the most obstreperous, and clamours the most uproarious, until, to be relieved of this nuisance, he comes to terms with his nephew for a portion of his fortune and is relieved of the "Silent Woman," who is in reality a boy in disguise. We extract the dialogue of the whole scene; the speakers being "Truewitt," "Clerimont," and a "Page":—

"*True.* I met that stiff piece of formality, Master Morose, his uncle, yesterday, with a huge turban of night-caps on his head, buckled over his ears.

"*Cler.* O! that's his custom when he walks abroad. He can endure no noise, man.

"*True.* So I have heard. But is the disease so ridiculous in him as it is made? They say he has been upon divers treaties with the fish-wives and orange-women; and articles propounded between them: marry, the chimney-sweepes will not be drawn in.

"*Cler.* No, nor the broom-men: they stand out stiffly. He cannot endure a costard-monger; he swoons if he hear one.

"*True.* Methinks a smith should be ominous.

"*Cler.* Or any hammer-man. A brasier is not suffer'd to dwell in the parish, nor an armourer. He would have hang'd a pewterer's 'prentice once upon a Shrove-Tuesday's riot, for being of that trade, when the rest were quit.

"*True.* A trumpet should fright him terribly, or the hautboys.

"*Cler.* Out of his senses. The waits of the City have a pension of him not to come near that ward. This youth practised on him one night like the bellman, and never left till he had brought him down to the door with a long sword; and there left him flourishing with the air.

"*Page.* Why, sir, he hath chosen a street to lie in, so narrow at both ends that it will receive no coaches, nor carts, nor any of these common noises; and therefore we that love him devise to bring him in such as we may now and then, for his exercise, to breathe him. He would grow resty else in his cage; his virtue would rust without action. I entreated a bearward, one day, to come down with the dogs of some four parishes that way, and I thank him he did; and cried his games under Master Morose's window; till he was sent crying away, with his head made a most bleeding spectacle to the multitude. And, another time, a fencer marching to his prize had his drum most tragically run through, for taking that street in his way at my request.

"*True.* A good wag! How does he for the bells?

"*Cler.* O! In the queen's time he was wont to go out of town every Saturday at ten o'clock, or on holiday eves. But now, by reason of the sickness, the perpetuity of ringing has made him devise a room with double walls and treble ceilings; the windows close shut and caulk'd; and there he lives by candlelight."

The first class of noises, then, against which "Morose" protected his ears by "a huge turban of night-caps," is that of the ancient and far-famed London Cries. We have here the very loudest of them—fish-wives, orange-women, chimney-sweepers, broom-men, costard-mongers. But we might almost say that there were *hundreds* of other cries; and therefore, reserving to ourselves some opportunity for a special enumeration of a few of the more remarkable of these cries, we shall now slightly group them, as they present themselves to our notice during successive generations.

We shall not readily associate any very agreeable sounds with the voices of the "fish-wives." The one who cried "*Mackerel*" in Lydgate's day had probably no such explanatory cry as the "*Mackerel alive, alive ho!*" of modern times. In the seventeenth century the cry was "*New Mackerel.*" And in the same way there was:—

New Wall-Fleet Oysters.

New Flounders.

New Whiting.

New Salmon.

The freshness of fish must have been a considerable recommendation in those days of tardy intercourse. But quantity was also to be taken into the account, and so we find the cries of "*Buy my dish of Great Smelts;*" "*Great Plaice;*" "*Great Mussels.*" Such are the fish-cries enumerated in Lauron's and various other collections of "London Cries."

BUY GREAT SMELTS.

BUY GREAT PLAICE.

BUY GREAT MUSSELS.

BUY GREAT EELS.

But, we are forgetting "Morose," and his "turban of night-caps." Was Hogarth familiar with the old noise-hater when he conceived his own:—

ENRAGED MUSICIAN.

In this extraordinary gathering together of the producers of the most discordant sounds, we have a representation which may fairly match the dramatist's description of street noises. Here we have the milk-maid's scream, the mackerel-seller's shout, the sweep upon the house-top,—to match the fish-wives and orange-women, the broom-men and costard-mongers. The smith, who was "ominous," had no longer his forge in the busy streets of Hogarth's time; the armourer was obsolete: but Hogarth can rival their noises with the pavior's hammer, the sow-gelder's horn, and the knife-grinder's wheel. The waits of the city had a pension not to come near "Morose's" ward; but it was out of the power of the "Enraged Musician" to avert the terrible discord of the blind hautboy-player. The bellman who frightened the sleepers at midnight, was extinct; but modern London had acquired the dustman's bell. The bear-ward no longer came down the street with the dogs of four parishes, nor did the fencer march with a drum to his prize; but there was the ballad-singer, with her squalling child, roaring worse than bear or dog; and the drum of the little boy playing at soldiers was a more abiding nuisance than the fencer. "Morose" and the "Enraged Musician" had each the church bells to fill up the measure of discord.

The fish-wives are no longer seen in our great city of London thoroughfares. In Tottenham Court-road, Hoxton, Shoreditch,

Kingsland, Whitechapel, Hackney-road, and many other suburban districts, which still retain the character of a street-market, they stand in long rows as the evening draws in, with paper-lanterns stuck in their baskets on dark nights; and there they vociferate as loudly as in the olden time.

The "costard-monger" whom Morose dreaded, still lives amongst us, and is still noisy. He bawls so loud even to this day, that he puts his hand behind his ear to mitigate the sensation which he inflicts upon his own tympanum. He was originally an apple-seller, whence his name; and, from the mention of him in the old dramatists, he appears to have been frequently an Irishman. In Jonson's "Bartholomew Fair," he cries "*pears.*" Ford makes him cry "*pippins.*" He is a quarrelsome fellow, according to Beaumont and Fletcher :—

> "And then he'll rail like a rude costermonger,
> That schoolboys had cozened of his apple,
> As loud and senseless."

The costermonger is now a travelling shopkeeper. We encounter him not in Cornhill, or Holborn, or the Strand: in the neighbourhood of the great markets and well-stored shops he travels not. But his voice is heard in some silent streets stretching into the suburbs; and there, with his donkey and hampers stands at the door, as the servant-maid cheapens a bundle of cauliflowers. He has monopolized all the trades that were anciently represented by such cries as "*Buy my artichokes, mistress;*" "*Ripe cowcumbers;*" *White onions, white St. Thomas' onions;*" "*White radish;*" "*Ripe young beans;*" "*Any baking pears;*" "*Ripe sparrowgrass.*" He would be indignant to encounter such petty chapmen interfering with his wholesale operations. He would rail against them as the city shopkeepers of the sixteenth and seventeenth centuries railed against itinerant traders of every denomination. In the days of Elizabeth, they declare by act of common council, that in ancient times the open streets and lanes of the city have been used, and ought to be used, as the common highway only, and not for hucksters, pedlars, and hagglers, to stand or sit to sell their wares in, and to pass from street to street hawking and offering their wares. In the seventh year of Charles I. the same authorities denounce the oyster-wives, herb-wives, tripe-wives, and the like, as "unruly people;" and they charge them somewhat unjustly, as it must appear, with "framing to themselves a way whereby to live a more easy life than by labour."

"How busy is the man the world calls idle!"

The evil, as the citizens term it, seems to have increased; for in 1694 the common council threatened the pedlars and petty chapmen with the terrors of the laws against rogues and sturdy beggars, the least penalty being whipping, whether for male or female. The reason for this terrible denunciation is very candidly put: the citizens and shopkeepers are greatly hindered and prejudiced in their trades by the hawkers and pedlars. Such denunciations as these had little share in putting down the itinerant traders. They continued to flourish, because society required them; aud they vanished from our view when society required them no longer. In the middle of the last century they were fairly established as rivals to the shopkeepers. Dr. Johnson, than whom no man knew London better, thus writes in the "Adventurer:"—"The attention of a new-comer is generally first struck by the multiplicity of cries that stun him in the streets, and the variety of merchandise and manufactures which the shopkeepers expose on every hand." The shopkeepers have now ruined the itinerants—not by putting them down by fiery penalties, but by the competition amongst themselves to have

NEW BROOMS FOR OLD SHOES!

every article at hand for every man's use, which shall be better and cheaper than the wares of the itinerant. Whose ear is now ever deafened by the cries of the broom-man? He was a sturdy fellow in the days of old "Morose," carrying on a barter which in itself speaks of the infancy of civilization. His cry was "*Old Shoes for some Brooms.*" Those proclamations for barter no doubt furnished a peculiar characteristic of the old London Cries. The itinerant buyers were as loud, though not so numerous, as the sellers.

OLD CLOWZE, ANY OLD CLO', CLO'.

The familiar voice of "*Old Clowze, any old Clo' Clo,*" has lasted through some generations; but the glories of Monmouth-street were unknown when a lady in a peaked bonnet and a laced stomacher went about proclaiming "*Old Satin, old Taffety, or Velvet.*" And a singular looking party of the Hebrew persuasion, with a cocked hat on his head, and a bundle of rapiers and sword-sticks under his arm, which he was ready to barter for:—

OLD CLOAKS, SUITS, OR COATS.

HATS OR CAPS—BUY, SELL, OR EXCHANGE.

While another of the tribe proclaimed aloud from east to west—and back again, "From morn to noon, from noon to dewy eve," his willingness to "*Buy, sell, or exchange Hats or Caps.*"

Why should the Hebrew race appear to possess a monopoly in the purchase and sale of dilapidated costumes? Why should their voices, and theirs alone, be employed in the constant iteration of the talismanic monosyllables "Old Clo'?" Is it because Judas carried the bag that all the children of Israel are to trudge through London streets to the end of their days with sack on shoulder? Artists generally represent the old clothes-man with three, and sometimes four, hats, superposed one above the other. Now, although we have seen him with many hats in his hands or elsewhere, we never yet saw him with more than one hat on his head. The three-hatted clothesman, if ever he existed, is obsolete. According to Ingoldsby, however, when "Portia" pronounced the law adverse to Shylock":

> "Off went his three hats, and he look'd as the cats
> Do, whenever a mouse has escaped from their claw."

There was trading then going forward from house to house, which careful housewifery and a more vigilant police have

Any Kitchen-Stuff have you Maids?

banished from the daylight, if they have not extirpated it altogether. Before the shops are open and the chimneys send forth their smoke, there may be now, sometimes, seen creeping up an area a sly-looking beldam, who treads as stealthily as a cat. Under her cloak she has a pan, whose unctuous contents will some day assist in the enlightenment or purification of the world, in the form of candles or soap. But the good lady of the house, who is a late riser, knows not of the transformation that is going forward. In the old days she would have heard the cry of a maiden, with tub on head and pence in hand, of "*Any Kitchen-stuff have you Maids?*" and she probably would have dealt with her herself, or have forbidden her maids to deal.

So it is with the old cry of "*Any Old Iron take Money for?*" The fellow who then went openly about with sack on back was a thief, and an encourager of thieves; he now keeps a marine-store.

Any Old Iron take Money for?

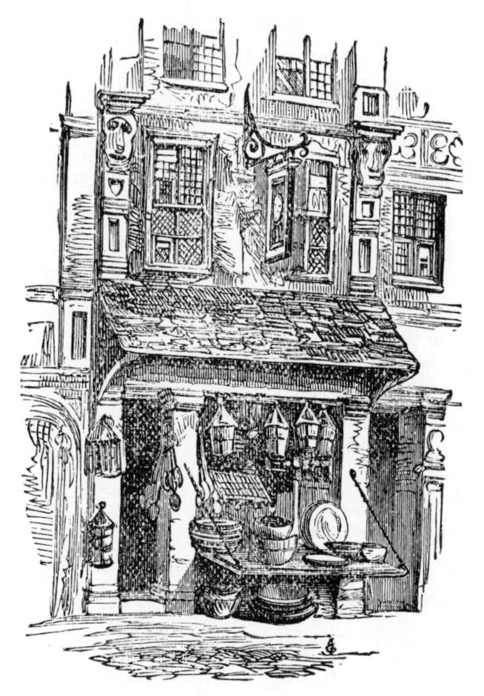

OLD LONDON SHOP.

Sir Walter Scott, in his *Fortunes of Nigel*, has left us a capital description of the shop of a London tradesman during the reign of King James in England, the shop in question being that of David Ramsay, maker of watches and horologes, within Temple-bar—a few yards eastward of St. Dunstan's church, Fleet-street, and where his apprentice, Jenkin Vincent—abbreviated to Jin Vin, when not engaged in 'prentices-riots—is crying to every likely passer-by :—

"What d'ye lack?—What d'ye lack?—Clocks—watches—barnacles?—What d'ye lack?—Watches—clocks—barnacles?—What d'ye lack, sir? What d'ye lack, madam?—Barnacles—watches—clocks? What d'ye lack, noble sir ?—What d'ye lack, beauteous madam ?—God bless your reverence, the Greek and Hebrew have harmed your reverence's eyes. Buy a pair of David Ramsay's barnacles. The king, God bless his sacred Majesty ! never reads Hebrew or Greek without them. What d'ye lack ? Mirrors for your toilets, my pretty madam ; your head-gear is something awry—pity, since it so well fancied. What d'ye lack ? a watch, Master Sargeant ?—a watch that will go as long as a lawsuit, as steady and true as your own eloquence ? a watch that shall not lose thirteen minutes in a thirteen years' lawsuit—a watch with four wheels and a bar-movement—a watch that shall tell you, Master Poet, how long the patience of the audience will endure your next piece at the Black Bull."

The verbal proclaimers of the excellence of their commodities, had this advantage over those who, in the present day, use the public papers for the same purpose, that they could in many cases adapt their address to the peculiar appearance and apparent taste of the passengers. This direct and personal mode of invitation to customers became, however, a dangerous temptation to the young wags who were employed in the task of solicitation during the absence of the principal person interested in the traffic ; and, confiding in their numbers and civic union, the 'prentices of London were often seduced into taking liberties with the passengers, and exercising their wit at the expense of those whom they had no hopes of converting into customers by their eloquence. If this were resented by any act of violence, the inmates of each shop were ready to pour forth in succour ; and in the words of an old song which Dr. Johnson was used to hum,—

> " Up then rose the 'prentices all,
> Living in London, both proper and tall."

Desperate riots often arose on such occasions, especially when the Templars, or other youths connected with the aristocracy, were insulted, or conceived themselves so to be.

ST. PAUL'S CATHEDRAL.

Upon such occasions, bare steel was frequently opposed to the clubs of the citizens, and death sometimes ensued on both sides. The tardy and inefficient police of the time had no other resource than by the Alderman of the ward calling out the householders, and putting a stop to the strife by overpowering numbers, as the Capulets and Montagues are separated upon the stage.

It must not be imagined that these 'prentices of the City of London were of mean and humble origin. The sons of freemen of the City, or country boys of good and honourable families, alone were admitted to the seven years' apprenticeship. The common people—the *ascripti glebæ*—the poor rustics who were bound to the soil, had little or no share in the fortunes of the City of London. Many of the burgesses were as proud of their descent as of their liberties.

A Street at Night—Shakespeare's London.

Once apprenticed, and having in a few weeks imbibed the spirit of the place, the lad became a Londoner. It is one of the characteristics of London, that he who comes up to the City from the country speedily becomes penetrated with the magic of the golden pavement, and falls in love with the great City. And he who has once felt that love of London can never again be happy beyond the sound of Bow Bells, which could formerly be heard for ten miles and more. The greatness of the City, its history, its associations, its ambitions, its pride, its hurrying crowds— all these things affect the imagination and fill the heart. There is no place in the world, and never has been, which so stirs the heart of her children with love and pride as the City of London.

A year or two later on, the boy would learn, with his fellow-'prentices that he must betake himself to the practice of bow and arrow, "pellet and bolt," with a view to what might happen. Moorfields was convenient for the volunteers of the time. There was, however, never any lack of excitement and novelty in the City of London. But this is a digression.

Amongst the earliest of the Cries of London we must class the "cry" of the City watchman; although it essentially differed from the "cries" of the shopkeepers and the hawkers; for they, as a rule, had something to exchange or sell—*copen or buy?* as Lydgate puts it—then the watchmen were wont to commence their "cry" at, or about, the hour of night when all others had finished for the day. After that it was the business of the watchman to make his first call, or cry after the manner inscribed over the figure here given.

He had to deal with deaf listeners, and he therefore proclaimed with a voice of command, "Lanthorn!" but a lanthorn alone was a body without a soul; and he therefore demanded "a *whole* candle." To render the mandate less individually oppressive, he went on to cry, "Hang out your Lights!" And, that even the sleepers might sleep no more, he ended with "Heare!" It will be seen that he carries his staff and lanthorn with the air of honest old Dogberry about him,—"A good man and true, "and" the most desartless man to be constable."

The making of lanthorns was a great trade in the early times. We clung to King Alfred's invention for the preservation of light with as reverend a love, during many centuries, as we bestowed upon his civil institutions. The horn of the favoured utensil was a very dense medium for illumination, but science had substituted nothing better; and, even when progressing people carried about a neat glass instrument with a brilliant reflector, the watchman held to his ponderous and murky relic of the past, making "night hideous" with his voice, to give news of the weather, such as: "Past eleven, and a starlight night;" or "Past one o'clock, and a windy morning;" in fact, disturbed your rest to tell you "what's o'clock."

We are told by the chroniclers that, as early as 1416, the mayor, Sir Henry Barton, ordered lanthorns and lights to be hanged out on the winter evenings, betwixt Allhallows and Candlemass. For three centuries this practice subsisted, constantly evaded, no doubt through the avarice or poverty of individuals, sometimes probably disused altogether, but still the custom of London up to the time of Queen Anne. The cry of the watchman, "Hang out your Lights," was an exhortation to the negligent, which probably they answered only by snores, equally indifferent to their own safety and the public preservation. A worthy mayor in the time of Queen Mary provided the watchman with a bell, with which instrument he accompanied the music of his voice down to the days of the Commonwealth. The "Statutes of the Streets," in the time of Elizabeth, were careful enough for the preservation of silence in some things. They prescribed that, "no man shall blow any horn in the night, or whistle after the hour of nine o'clock in the night, under pain of imprisonment;" and, what was a harder thing to keep, they also forbade a man to make any "sudden outcry in the still of the night, as making any affray, or beating his wife." Yet a privileged man was to go about knocking at doors and ringing his alarum—an intolerable nuisance if he did what he was ordered to do.

THE WATCH—SHAKESPEARE'S LONDON.

But the watchmen were, no doubt, wise in their generation. With honest Dogberry, they could not "see how sleeping should offend;" and after the watch was set, they probably agreed to "go sit upon the church bench till two, and then all to bed."

THE BELLMAN—FROM DEKKER, 1608.

We have observed in our old statutes, and in the pages of authors of various kinds, that separate mention is made of the Watchman and the Bellman. No doubt there were several degrees of office in the ancient Watch and Ward system, and that part of the office of the old Watch, or Bellman, was to bless the sleepers, whose door he passed, which blessing was often sung or said in verse—hence Bellman's verse. These verses were in many cases, the relics of the old incantations to keep off elves and hobgoblins. There is a curious work by Thomas Dekker — otherwise Decker, — entitled: "The Bellman of London. Bringing to light the most notorious Villanies that are now practised in the Kingdom, Profitable for Gentlemen, Lawyers, Merchants, Citizens, Farmers, Masters of Households and all sortes of servants to Marke, and delightful for all men to Reade, *Lege, Perlege, Relege.*" Printed at London for Nathaniel Butter, 1608. Where he describes the Bellman as a person of some activity—"the child of darkness; a common nightwalker; a man that had no man to wait upon him, but only a dog; one that was a disordered person, and at midnight would beat at men's doors, bidding them (in mere mockery) to look to their candles, when they themselves were in their dead sleeps." Stow says that in Queen Mary's day one of each ward "began to go all night with a bell, and at every lane's end, and at the ward's end, gave warning of fire and candle, and to help the poor and pray for the dead." Milton, in his "Il Penseroso," has:—

> "Far from the resort of mirth,
> Save the cricket on the hearth,
> Or the bellman's drowsy charm,
> To bless the doors from nightly harm."

In "A Bellman's Song" of the same date, we have:—

> "Maidens to bed, and cover coal,
> Let the mouse out of her hole,
> Crickets in the chimney sing,
> Whilst the little bell doth ring;
> If fast asleep, who can tell
> When the clapper hits the bell?"

Herrick, also, has given us a verse of Bellman's poetry in one of the charming morsels of his "Hesperides:"—

"From noise of scare-fires rest ye free,
From murders Benedicite;
From all mischances that may fright
Your pleasing slumbers in the night,
Mercy secure ye all, and keep
The goblin from ye while ye sleep.
Past one o'clock, and almost two,
My masters all, 'Good day to you!'"

But, with or without a bell, the real prosaic watchman continued to make the same demand as his predecessors for lights through a long series of years; and his demand tells us plainly that London was a city without lamps. But though he was a prosaic person, he had his own verses. He addressed himself to the "maids." He exhorted them to make their lanthorns "bright and clear." He told them how long their candles were expected to burn. And, finally, like a considerate lawgiver, he gave reason for his edict: —

"That honest men that walk along,
May see to pass safe without wrong."

Formerly it was the duty of the bellman of St. Sepulchre's parish, near Newgate, to rouse the unfortunates condemned to death in that prison, the night before their execution, and solemnly exhort them to repentance with good words in bad rhyme, ending with

"When St. Sepulchre's bell to-morrow tolls,
The Lord above have mercy on your souls."

It was customary for the bellman to present at Christmas time to each householder in his district "A Copy of Verses," and he expected from each in return some small gratuity. The execrable character of his poetry is indicated by the contempt with which the wits speak of "Bellman's verses" and the comparison they bear to "Cutler's poetry upon a knife," whose poesy was—"*Love me, and leave me not.*" On this subject there is a work entitled—"The British Bellman. Printed in the year of Saint's Fear, Anno Domini 1648, and reprinted in the *Harleian Miscellany*." "The Merry Bellman's Out-Cryes, or the Cities O Yes! being a mad merry Ditty, both Pleasant and Witty, to be cry'd in Prick-Song* Prose, through Country and City. Printed in the year of Bartledum Fair, 1655." Also—"The Bell-man's Treasury, containing above a Hundred several Verses fitted for all Humours and Fancies, and suited to all Times and Seasons. London, 1707." It was from the riches of this "treasury" that the predecessors of the present parish Bellman mostly took their *own* (!) "Copy of Verses."

In the Luttrell Collection of Broadsides (Brit. Mus.) is one dated 1683-4, entitled, "A Copy of Verses presented by Isaac Ragg, Bellman, to the Masters and Mistresses of Holbourn Division, in the Parish of St. Giles's-in-the-Fields." It is headed by a woodcut representing Isaac in his professional accoutrements, a pointed pole in his left hand, and in the right a bell, while his lanthorn hangs from his jacket in front; below is a series of verses, the only specimen worth giving here being the expression of Mr. Ragg's official duty; it is as follows:—

"Time Masters, calls your bellman to his task,
To see your doors and windows are all fast,
And that no villany or foul crime be done
To you or yours in absence of the sun.
If any base lurker I do meet,
In private alley or in open street,
You shall have warning by my timely call,
And so God bless you and give rest to all."

---

* PRICK-SONG, music pricked or noted down, full of flourish and variety.—*Halliwell.*

In a similar, but unadorned broadside, dated 1666, Thomas Law, Bellman, greets his Masters of "St. Giles, Cripplegate, within the Freedom," in twenty-three dull stanzas, of which the last may be subjoined :—

"No sooner hath St. Andrew crowned November,
But Boreas from the North brings cold December,
And I have often heard a many say
He brings the winter month Newcastle way;
For comfort here of poor distressed souls,
Would he had with him brought a fleet of coals."

We have in our possession a "copy of verses," coming down to our own time. It is a folio broadside, and contains in addition to a portrait of the Bellman of the Parish and his dog on their rounds, fifteen smaller cuts, mostly Scriptural. It is entitled :—

A COPY OF VERSES FOR 1839,
HUMBLY PRESENTED TO ALL MY WORTHY MASTERS AND MISTRESSES, OF THE PARISH OF SAINT JAMES, WESTMINSTER,
By Richard Mugeridge, 20, Marshall Street, Golden Square.

The "Verses" all contain allusions to the prominent events of the past year, and have various headings--first we have the :—

Prologue.

My Masters and Mistresses, pray lend an ear,
While your Bellman recounts some events of the year ;
For altho' its commencement was rather distressing,
We've had reason to thank it for more than one blessing,
'Tis true that Canadian proceedings were strange,
And a very sad fire was the Royal Exchange ;
Yet the first, let us hope, is no serious matter,
And we'll soon have a new one in lieu of the latter.
Our rulers have grappled with one of our crosses,
While for beauty and fitness the other no loss is.
And still more to make up for these drawbacks vexatious,
Dame Fortune has been on the whole, pretty gracious.
We've had peace to get wealth, which of war is the sinews,
Grant us wit to make hay while the sunshine continues.
Then, the Bear of the North, that insatiate beast,
Has been check'd in his wily attempts on the East ;
And his further insidious advances forbidden
By the broadsword of Auckland, which warns him from Eden.
While our rulers, in earnest, apply to the work,
And a treaty concludes with the Austrian and Turk,
Which, when next the fell Monster is tempted to roam,
May provide him some pleasant employment at home.

To the Queen.

Whilst the high and the noble in gallant array,
Assemble around her, their homage to pay ;
While the proud Peers of Britain with rapture, I ween,
Place her crown on the brow of their peerless young Queen ;
While by prince and by peasant her sceptre is blest ;
Why may not the Bellman chime in with the rest ?
Tho' alas ! my poor muse would long labour in vain,
To express our delight in Victoria's reign,
Long may we exult in her merciful sway,
May her moments speed blithely and sweetly as May,
And her days be prolonged till her glories efface
The last maiden lady's, who sate in her place.

THE GREAT WESTERN.

WELL, despite of some thousand objections pedantic,
The "Great Western" has cross'd and *re-cross'd* the Atlantic,
Nor is *this* the first time—to the foe's consternation—
That the deeds of our tars have defied calculation.
Though few of our learned professors did dream
That our seamen in steamers would reach the gulf stream,
Yet a fortnight's vibration, from Bristol or Cork,
Will now set us down with our friends at New York ;
And a closer acquaintance bind firmer than ever,
A friendship which nothing on earth ought to sever.

* * * * * *

* * * * * *

EPILOGUE.

Now having conducted his well-meant effusion
Thus far on its way to a happy conclusion,
Your Bellman, tho' not quite so fresh as at starting,
Would still have a word with his patrons at parting,
Just by way of a cordial and kindly farewell,
For his heart, altho' softer, is sound as his bell,
And he cannot say more for himself or his strains,
Than, whatever his success, he has not spared pains ;
And that blest in their kindness, and countenance steady,
His song and his services always are ready ;
So he bids them adieu till next season appears—
May their wealth and their virtues increase with their years ;
May they always have more than they ever can spend,
With the soul to help on a less fortunate friend ;
And their Bellman continue to cudgel his brain,
For their yearly amusement, again and again.

Cheap and Expeditious Printing by Steam Machinery, executed by C. REYNELL, 16, *Little Pulteney Street, Golden Square.*—First printed in 1735.

There is a very rare sheet of woodcuts in the Print-room of the British Museum, containing twelve cries, with figures of the "Criers" and the cries themselves beneath. The cuts are singularly characteristic, and may be assigned with safety, on the authority of Mr. John Thomas Smith, the late keeper of the prints and drawings, as of the same date as Ben Jonson's "fish-wives," "costard-mongers," and "orange women."

No. 1 on the sheet, is the "Watch;" he has no name, but carries a staff and a lanthorn, is well secured in a good frieze gabardine, leathern-girdle, and wears a serviceable hat to guard against the weather. The worthy here depicted has a most venerable face and beard, showing how ancient was the habit of parish officers to select the poor and feeble for the office of watchman, in order to keep them out of the poor-house. The "cry" of the "watch" is as follows:—

"A light here, maids, hang out your light,
And see your horns be clear and bright,
That so your candle clear may shine,
Continuing from six till nine;
That honest men that walk along,
May see to pass safe without wrong."

No. 2 is the "Bellman"—Dekker's "Bellman of London and Dog." (as at page 49.) He carries a halberd lanthorn, and bell, and his "cry" is curious:—

"Maids in your smocks, look to your locks,
Your fire and candle-light;
For well 'tis known much mischief's done
By both in dead of night;
Your locks and fire do not neglect,
And so you may good rest expect."

No. 3 is the "Orange Woman," a sort of full-grown Nell Gwynne, if we can only fancy *Nelly*, the favourite mistress of King Charles the Second, grown up in her humble occupation. She carries a basket of oranges and lemons under her arm, and seeks to sell them by the following "cry":—

> "Fine Sevil oranges, fine lemmons, fine;
> Round, sound, and tender, inside and rine,
> One pin's prick their vertue show:
> They've liquor by their weight, you may know."

No. 4 is the "Hair-line Man," with a bundle of lines under his arm, and a line in his hand. Clothes-pegs was, perhaps, a separate "cry." Here is his:—

> "Buy a hair-line, or a line for Jacke,
> If you any hair or hemp-cord lack,
> Mistris, here's good as you need use;
> Bid fair for handsel, I'll not refuse."

No. 5 is the "Radish and Lettuce Woman."—Your fine "goss" lettuce is a modern cry:—

> "White raddish, white young lettis,
> White young lettis white;
> You hear me cry, come mistris, buy,
> To make my burden light."

No. 6 is the man who sells "Marking Stones," now, unless we except slate-pencils, completely out of use:—

> "Buy marking-stones, marking-stones buy,
> Much profit in their use doth lie;
> I've marking-stones of colour red,
> Passing good, or else black lead."

No. 7 is the "Sausage Woman," holding a pound of sausages in her hand:—

"Who buys my sausages, sausages fine?
I ha' fine sausages of the best;
As good they are as ere was eat;
If they be finely drest.
Come, mistris, buy this daintie pound,
About a capon roast them round."

No. 8 is a man with "Toasting-forks and Spice-graters':—

"Buy a fine toasting-fork for toast,
Or fine spice-grater—tools for an hoast;
If these in winter be lacking, I say,
Your guests will pack, your trade decay."

No. 9 is the "Broom Man," and here we have a "cry" different from the one we have already given. He carries a pair of old boots in his hand:—

"Come buy some brooms, come buy of me:
Birch, Heath, and green,—none better be;
The staves are straight, and all bound sure;
Come, maids, my brooms will still endure.
Old boots or shoes I'll take for brooms,
Come buy to make clean all your rooms!"

No. 10 is a woman with a box of "Wash balls":—

"Buy fine washing-balls, buy a ball,
Cheaper and dearer, greater and small;
For scouring none do them excel,
Their odour scenteth passing well;
Come buy rare balls, and trial make,
Spots out of clothes they quickly take."

No. 11 sells Ink and Pens.—He carries an ink-bottle hung by a stick behind him, and has a bunch of pens in his hand :—

> "Buy pens, pens, pens of the best,
> Excellent pens and seconds the least ;
> Come buy good ink as black as jet,
> A varnish like gloss on writing 'twill set."

The twelfth and last is a woman with a basket of Venice Glasses, such as a modern collector would give a great deal to get hold of :—

> "Come glasses, glasses, fine glasses buy ;
> Fine glasses o' the best I call and cry.
> Fine Venice-glasses,—no chrystal more clear,
> Of all forms and fashions buy glasses here,
> Black pots for good ale I also do cry ;
> Come therefore quickly before I pass by."

In the same collection, is a series of three plates, "Part of the Cries in London," evidently belonging to the same set, though only one has got a title. Each plate contains thirty-six criers, with the addition of a principal "Crier" in the centre. These were evidently executed abroad, as late, perhaps, as the reign of Charles II. No. 1 (with the title page) is ornamented in the centre with the "Rat-Catcher," carrying an emblazoned banner of rats, and attended by a boy. The leather investment of the rat-catcher of the present day is a pleasant memorial of the banner of the past. Beneath the rat-catcher, the following lines occur :—

> "Hee that wil have neither
> Ratt nor Mowssee
> Lett him pluck of the tillies
> And set fire of his hows."

Proving, evidently that the rat-catcher courted more to his banner than his poetry. Then follow the thirty-six cries, some of which, it will be seen, are extremely curious. The names are given beneath the cuts, but without any verse or peculiarity of cry.

Cooper	Alminake	Olde Iron
Ende of Golde	Coonie skine	Aqua vitæ
Olde Dublets	Mussels	Pens and Ink
Blackinge man	Cabeches	Olde Bellows
Tinker	Kitchen stuff	Herrings
Pippins	Glasses	Buy any Milke
Bui a Matte	Cockels	Piepin Pys
Cooles	Hartti chaks	Osters
Chimnie swepes	Mackrill	Shades
Bui Brumes	Oranges, Lemens	Turneps
Camphires	Lettice	Rosmarie Baie
Cherry ripe	Place	Onions.

"Haie ye any work for John Cooper?" is the title of one of the Martin Marprelate pamphlets. "Haie ye ani gold ends to sell?" is mentioned as a "cry," in "Pappe with a Hatchet" (*cir.* 1589). "Camphires," means Samphires. The "Alminake" man has completely gone, and "Old Dublets" has degenerated into "Ogh Clo," a "cry" which teased Coleridge for a time, and occasioned a ludicrous incident, which we had reserved for a place somewhat later in our history, had not "Old Dublets" brought it, not inopportunely, to mind. "The other day," said Coleridge, "I was what you would call *floored* by a Jew. He passed me several times crying out for old clothes, in the most nasal and extraordinary tone I ever heard. At last I was so provoked, that I said to him, 'Pray, why can't you say 'old clothes' in a plain way, as I do?' The Jew stopped, and looking very gravely at me, said in a clear and even accent, 'Sir, I can say 'old clothes' as well as you can; but if you had to say so ten times a minute, for an hour together, you would say *Ogh Clo* as I do now;' and so he marched off." Coleridge was so confounded with the justice of the retort that he followed and gave him a shilling—the only one he had.

The principal figure on the second plate is the "Bellman," with dog, bell, halberd, and lanthorns. His "cry" is curious, though we have had it almost in the same form before, at page 56:—

"Mayds in your Smocks, Looke
Wel to your lock—your fire
And your light, and God
Give you good night. At
One a Clock."

The cries around him deserve transcription:—

Buy any Shrimps	Buy a Purs	Buy any Marking Stones
Buy some Figs	Buy a dish a Flounders	The Bear bayting
Buy a Tosting Iron	Buy a Footestoole	Buy any blew Starch
Lanterne candellyht	Buy a fine Bowpot	Buy any Points
Buy any Maydes	Buy a pair a Shoes	New Hadog
The Water bearer	Buy any Garters	Yards and Ells
Buy a whyt Pot	Featherbeds to dryue	Buy a fyne Brush
Bread and Meate	Buy any Bottens	Hote Mutton Poys
Buy a Candelsticke	Buy any Whiting maps	New Sprats new
Buy any Prunes	Buy any Tape	New Cod new
Buy a Washing ball	Worcestershyr Salt	Buy any Reasons
Good Sasages	Ripe Damsons	P. and Glasses to mend

On the third plate, the principal figure is the "Crier," with his staff and keys:—

"O yis, any man or woman that
Can tell any tydings of a litle
Mayden Childe of the age of 24
Yeares. Bring worde to the cryer,
And you shal be pleased for
Your labor
And God's blessinge."

The figures surrounding the Common Crier are in the same style of art, and their cries characteristic of bygone times :—

Buy any Wheat	Buy a Hair Lyne	Hats or Caps to dress
Buy al my Smelts	Buy any Pompeons	Wood to cleave
Quick Periwinckels	Whyt Scalions	Pins of the maker
Rype Chesnuts	Rype Walnuts	Any sciruy Grass
Payres fyn	Fyn Potatos fyn	Any Cornes to pick
White Redish whyt	Hote Eele Pyes	Buy any Parsnips
Buy any Whyting	Fresh Cheese and Creame	Hot Codlinges hot
Buy any Bone lays	Buy any Garlick	Buy all my Soales
I ha rype Straberies	Buy a longe Brush	Good Marroquin
Buy a Case for a Hat	Whyt Carots whyt	Buy any Cocumber
Birds and Hens	Fyne Pomgranats	New Thornebacke
Hote Podding Pyes	Buy any Russes	Fyne Oate Cakes.

The only crier in the series who has a horse and cart to attend him is the Worcestershire salt-man. Salt is still sold from carts in poor and crowded neighbourhoods.

We have been somewhat surprised in not finding a single Thames waterman among the criers of London; but the series was, perhaps, confined to the streets of London, and the watermen were thought to belong altogether to the stairs leading to their silent highway. Three of their cries have given titles to three good old English comedies, "Northward, ho!" "Eastward, ho!" and "Westward, ho!" But our series of cries is still extremely incomplete. Every thing in early times was carried and cried, and we have seen two rare prints of old London Cries not to be found in the lists already enumerated. One is called "*Clove Water, Stomock Water,*" and the other "*Buy an new Booke.*" Others may still exist. In the Duke of Devonshire's collection of drawings, by Inigo Jones, are several cries, drawn in pen-and-ink, for the masques at court in the reigns of James I. and Charles I.

THE LIGHT OF OTHER DAYS.

In Thomas Heywood's, "*The Rape of Lucrece*, a True Roman Tragedy, acted by Her Majestie's Servants at the *Red-Bull*, 1609," is the following long list of LONDON CRIES, but called for the sake of the dramatic action of the scene, "*Cries of Rome*," which was the common practice with the old dramatists, Rome being the canting name of London. Robert Greene, in his "*Perimedes the Blacksmith*, 1588," when he wished to criticise the London *Theatre* at Shoreditch, talks of the *Theatre in Rome;* also in his "*Never too Late*, 1590," when he talks of the London actors, he pretends only to speak of Roscius and the actors of *Rome*. In the pedlar's French of the day Rome-vyle—or ville—was London, and Rome-mort the Queen [Elizabeth]. There is some humour in the classification, and if the cries were well imitated by the singer, the ballad—or as it would then be called "*jig*"—is likely to have been extremely popular in its day.

THE CRIES OF ROME [*i.e.* London.]

Thus go the cries in *Rome's* fair town,
First they go up street, and then they go down,
Round and sound all of a colour,
Buy a very fine marking stone, marking stone,
Round and sound all of a colour;
Buy a very fine marking stone, marking stone.

Thus go the cries in *Rome's* fair town,
First they go up street, and then they go down.

Bread and—meat—bread—and meat
For the—ten—der—mercy of God to the
poor pris—ners of *Newgate*, fourscore and ten—poor—prisoners.

Thus go the cries in *Rome's* fair town,
First they go up street, and then they go down.

MARKING STONE.

BREAD AND MEAT.

WORSTERSHIRE SALT.

BUY A MOUSE TRAP.

Salt—salt—white Wor—stershire Salt,

Thus go the cries in *Rome's* fair town,
First they go up street, and then they go down.

Buy a very fine Mouse—trap, or a tormentor for your Fleas.

Thus go the cries in *Rome's* fair town,
First they go up street, and then they go down.

Kitchen--stuff, maids.

Thus go the cries in *Rome's* fair town,
First they go up street, and then they go down.

I have white Radish, white hard Lettuce, white young Onions.

Thus go the cries in *Rome's* fair town,
First they go up street, and then they go down.

I have Rock—Samphire Rock—Samphire,

Thus go the cries in *Rome's* fair town,
First they go up street, and then they go down.

Buy a Mat, a Mil—Mat,
Mat or a Hassock for your pew,
A stopple for your close—stool,
Or a Pesock to thrust your feet in.

Thus go the cries in *Rome's* fair town,
First they go up street, and then they go down.

Whiting maids, Whiting.

Thus go the cries in *Rome's* fair town,
First they go up street, and then they go down.

KITCHEN STUFF, MAIDS.

WHITE RADISH LETTUCE.

ROCK SAMPIER.

MAT, A MILL MAT.

Hot fine Oat—Cakes, hot.

Thus go the cries in *Rome's* fair town,
First they go up street, and then they go down.

Small—Coals here.

Thus go the cries in *Rome's* fair town,
First they go up street, and then they go down.

Will you buy any Milk to day.

Thus go the cries in *Rome's* fair town,
First they go up street, and then they go down.

Lanthorn and Candle light here,
Maid, a light here.

Thus go the cries in *Rome's* fair town,
First they go up street, and then they go down.

Here lies a company of very poor
Women, in the dark dungeon,
Hungary, cold, and comfortless, night and day;
Pity the poor women in the dark dungeon.

Thus go the cries where they do house them,
First they come to the grate, and then they go
lowse them.

WHITING MAIDS, WHITING.

HOT FINE OAT CAKES.

SMALL COALS HERE.

ST. THOMAS' ONIONS.

From "Deuteromelia: or, the Second Part of Pleasant Roundelayes; K. H. Mirth, or Freeman's Songs, and such delightful Catches. London, printed for Thomas Adams, dwelling in Paul's Church-yard, at the sign of the White Lion, 1609."

Who liveth so merry in all this land
As doth the poor widdow that selleth the sand?
And ever shee singeth as I can guesse,
Will you buy any sand, any sand, mistress?

The broom-man maketh his living most sweet,
With carrying of brooms from street to street;
Who would desire a pleasanter thing,
Then all the day long to doe nothing but sing.

The chimney-sweeper all the long day,
He singeth and sweepeth the soote away;
Yet when he comes home altho' he be weary,
With his sweet wife he maketh full merry.

* * * * * *

Who liveth so merry and maketh such sport
As those that be of the poorest sort?
The poorest sort wheresoever they be,
They gather together by one, two, three.

And every man will spend his penny
What makes such a shot among a great many?

Thomas Morely, a musical composer, set music of four, six, eight and ten parts, to the cries in his time, among them are some used by the milliners' girls in the New Exchange, which was on the south side of the Strand, opposite the now Adelphi

Theatre, it was built in the reign of James I., and pulled down towards the end of the last century; among others are "*Italian falling Bands*," "*French Garters*," "*Robatos*," a kind of ruff then fashionable. "*Nun's Thread*," *&c.*

The effeminacy and coxcombry of a man's ruff and band are well ridiculed by many of our dramatic writers. There is a small tract bearing the following title—"A Merrie Dialogue between Band, Cuffe and Ruffe. Done by an excellent Wit, and lately acted in a Shew in the Famous Universitie of Cambridge. London, printed by W. Stansby for Miles Partrich, and are to be sold at his shop neere Saint Dunstone's Church-yard in Fleet Street, 1615." This *brochure* is a *bonne-bouche* of the period, written in dramatic dialogue form, and full of puns as any modern comedy or farcical sketch from the pen of the greatest word-twister of the day—Henry J. Byron (who, on *Cyril's Success*, *Married in Haste*, *Our Boys*, and *The Girls*,) and is of considerable value as an illustration of the history of the costume of the period. The band, as an article of ornament for the neck, was the common wear of gentlemen, though now exclusively retained by the clergy and lawyers; the cuff, as a fold at the end of a sleeve, or the part of the sleeve turned back from the hand, was made highly fantastical by means of "cut work;" the ruff, as a female neck ornament, made of plaited lawn, or other material, is well-known, but it was formerly worn by both sexes.

In a Roxburghe Ballad entitled "The Batchelor's Feast," &c., we have:—

"The taylor must be pay'd for making of her gowne,
The shoomakers for fine shoes: or else thy wife will frowne;
For *bands*, fine *ruffes*, and *cuffes*, thou must dispence as free:
O 'tis a gallant thing to live at liberty," &c.

In another, "The Lamentations of a New Married Man, briefly declaring the sorrow and grief that comes by marrying a young wanton wife":—

"Against that she is churched, a new Gowne she must have,
A daintie fine *Rebato* about her neck to brave;"

In "*Loyal Subject*," by Beaumont and Fletcher, act iii., sc. 5, we find that in the reign of James I., potatoes had become so common, that "*Potatoes! ripe Potatoes!*" were publicly hawked about the city.

POTATOES! RIPE POTATOES.

Orlando Gibbons,—1583-1625—set music in madrigals to several common cries of the day. In a play called "*Tarquin and Lucrece*," some of the music of the following occur,—"*Rock Samphire*," "*A Marking Stone*," "*Bread and Meat for the poor Prisoners*," "*Hassock for your pew*," "*Lanthorne and Candle-light*," *&c.*

In the Bridgewater library (in the possession of the Earl of Ellesmere) is a series of engravings on copper thirty-two in number, without date or engraver's name; but called, in the handwriting of the second Earl of Bridgewater, "The Manner of Crying Things in London." They are, it is said, by a foreign artist, and probably proof impressions, for on the margin of one of the engravings is a small part of another, as if it had been taken off for a trial of the plate. Curious and characteristic they certainly are, and of a date anterior to 1686; in which year the second Earl of Bridgewater died. The very titles kindle old recollections as you read them over:—

1. Lanthorne and a whole candell light: hang out your lights heare!
2. I have fresh cheese and creame.
3. Buy a brush or a table book.
4. Fine oranges, fine lemons.
5. Ells or yeards: buy yeard or ells.
6. I have ripe straw-buryes, ripe straw-buryes.
7. I have screenes, if you desier to keepe yr butey from ye fire.
8. Codlinges hot, hot codlinges.
9. Buy a steele or a tinder box.
10. Quicke peravinkells, quicke, quicke.
11. Worke for a cooper; worke for a cooper.
12. Bandestringes, or handkercher buttons.
13. A tanker bearer.
14. Macarell new: maca-rell.
15. Buy a hone, or a whetstone, or a marking stone.
16. White unions, white St. Thomas unions.
17. Mate for a bed, buy a doore mate.
18. Radishes or lettis, two bunches a penny.
19. Have you any work for a tinker?
20. Buy my hartichokes, mistris.
21. Maribones, maides, maribones.
22. I ha' ripe cowcumber, ripe cowcumber.
23. Chimney sweepe.
24. New flounders new.
25. Some broken breade and meate for ye poore prisoners; for the Lord s sake pittey the poore.
26. Buy my dish of great smelts.
27. Have you any chaires to mend?
28. Buy a cocke, or a golding.
29. Old showes or bootes: will you buy some broome?
30. Mussels, lilly white mussels.
31. Small cole a penny a peake.
32. What kitchen stuff have you, maides?

The figures, male and female, in the engravings, are all three-quarter lengths, furnished with the implements of their various trades, or with the articles in which they deal. The Watchman (one of the best) is a fine old fellow, with a broad brim to his hat, a reverential beard, a halberd in one hand, and a lanthorn in the other (after the manner of the one we have given at page 46). But perhaps the most curious engraving in the set is the "cry" called "Some broken breade and meate for ye poore prisoners: for the Lord's sake pittey the poore." This represents a poor prisoner with a sealed box in his hand, and a basket at his back—the box for alms in the shape of money, and the basket for broken bread and meat. There is also preserved a small handbill printed in 1664, and entitled, "The Humble Petition of the Poor Distressed Prisoners in Ludgate, being above an hundred and fourscore poor persons in number, against the time of the Birth of our Blessed Lord and Saviour Jesus Christ." "We most humbly beseech you," says the hand-bill "(even for God's cause), to relieve us with your charitable benevolence, and to put into this Bearers Boxe, the same being sealed with the house seale as it is figured on this Petition."

"Pity the sorrows of a poor old man,
Whose trembling limbs have borne him to your door."

To, "O, rare Ben Jonson!" we are indebted for the most perfect picture of Smithfield at "Barthol'me-tide," which he gives us, together with the popular cries in vogue at the time, in his comedy of "*Bartholomew Fair*," produced at the Hope Theatre, on the Bankside, 1614, and acted, as Jonson tells us, by the lady Elizabeth's servants.

The second act opens with "*The Fair. A number of Booths, Stalls, &c., set out.*" The characters presented are "Lanthorn Leatherhead," *a hobby-horse seller.* "Bartholomew Cokes," *an esquire of Harrow.* "Nightingale," *a ballad-singer, a costard-monger, mousetrap-man, corn cutter.* "Joan Trash," *a gingerbread woman.* "Leatherhead" calls—"What do you lack? what is't you buy? what do you lack? rattles, drums, halberts, horses, babies o' the best? fiddles o' the finest." "Joan Trash" cries, "Buy my gingerbread, gilt gingerbread!" the costard-monger, bawls out, "Buy any pears, pears, fine, very fine pears!" "Nightingale," the ballad man sings—

> "Hey, now the Fair's a filling!
> O, for a tune to startle
> The birds o' the booths here billing
> Yearly with old saint *Barile!*
> The drunkards they are wading,
> The punks and chapmen trading:
> Who'd see the *Fair* without his lading?
> Buy my ballads! new ballads!"

"What do you lack?" continues Leatherhead, "What do you lack, gentlemen? my pretty mistress, buy a fine hobby-horse for your young master; cost you but a token a week for his provender." The corn cutter cries, "Have you any corns in your feet or toes?" The tinder-box man calls, "Buy a mouse-trap, a mouse-trap, or a tormentor for a flea!" Trash cries, "Buy some gingerbread!" Nightingale bawls, "Ballads, ballads, fine new ballads!" Leatherhead repeats, "What do you lack, gentlemen, what is't you lack? a fine horse? a lion? a bull? a bear? a dog? or a cat? an excellent fine Bartholomew bird? or an instrument? what is't you lack, what do you buy, mistress? a fine hobby-horse, to make your son a tilter? a drum, to make him a soldier? a fiddle, to make him a reveller? what is't you lack? little dogs for your daughters? or babies, male and female? fine purses, pouches, pincases, pipes; what is't you lack? a pair o' smiths to wake you i' the morning? or a fine whistling bird?" A character named "Bartholomew Cokes," a silly "Esquire of Harrow," stops at Leatherhead's stall to purchase.—"Those six horses, friend, I'll have, and the three Jew's trumps; and half a dozen o' birds; and that drum; and your smiths—I like that devise o' your smiths, and four halberts; and let me see, that fine painted great lady, and her three women of state, I'll have. A set of those violins I would buy too, for a delicate young noise* I have i' the country, that are every one a size less than another, just like your fiddles." Joan Trash, invites the Esquire to buy her gingerbread, and he turns to her basket, whereupon Leatherhead says, "Is this well, Goody Joan, to interrupt my market in the midst, and call away my customers? Can you answer this at the *Pie-poudres*?"† whereto Joan Trash replies, "Why, if his master-ship have a

---

* NOISE.—A set, or company of musicians. "*These terrible noyses, with threadbare cloaks,*"—*Decker's Bellman, of London*, 1608.

† *Pie-Poudre.* A court formerly held at a fair for the rough-and-ready treatment of pedlars and hawkers, to compel them and those with whom they dealt to fulfil their contracts. This court arose from the necessity of doing justice expeditiously, among persons resorting from distant places to a fair or market. It is said to be called the court of *pie-poudre, curia, pedis pulverizate*, from the dusty feet of the suitors, or, as Sir Edward Coke says, because justice is there done as speedily as dust can fall from the feet.

mind to buy, I hope my ware lies as open as anothers; I may show my ware as well as you yours." Nightingale begins to sing:—

> "My masters and friends, and good people draw near."

Squire Cokes hears this, and says, "Ballads! hark, hark! pray thee, fellow, stay a little! what ballads hast thou? let me see, let me see myself—How dost thou call it? *A Caveat against Cut-purses!*—a good jest i' faith; I would fain see that demon, your cut-purse, you talk of;" He then shows his purse boastingly, and enquires "Ballad-man, do any cut-purses haunt hereabout? pray thee raise me one or two: begin and show me one." Nightingale answers, "Sir, this is a spell against 'em, spick and span new: and 'tis made as 'twere in mine own person, and I sing it in mine own defence. But 'twill cost a penny alone if you buy it." The Squire replies: "No matter for the price; thou dost not know me, I see, I am an old *Bartholomew*." The ballad has "pictures," and Nightingale tells him, "It was intended, sir, as if a purse should chance to be cut in my presence, now, I may be blameless though; as by the sequel will more plainly appear." He adds, "It is, to the tune of *Paggington's Pound*, sir." and he finally sings the ballad, the first and last stanzas of which follow:—

> "My masters, and friends, and good people draw near,
> And look to your purses, for that I do say;
> And though little money, in them you do bear,
> It cost more to get, than to lose in a day,
> You oft' have been told,
> Both the young and the old,
> And bidden beware of the cut-purse so bold;
> Then if you take heed not, free me from the curse,
> Who both give you warning, for, and the cut purse.
> Youth, youth, thou hadst better been starved by thy nurse,
> Than live to be hanged for cutting a purse.

* * * * * * * *

"But O, you vile nation of cut-purses all,
Relent, and repent, and amend, and be sound,
And know that you ought not by honest men's fall,
Advance your own fortunes to die above ground.
And though you go gay
In silks as you may,
It is not the highway to heaven (as they say.)
Repent then, repent you, for better, for worse;
And kiss not the gallows for cutting a purse.
Youth, youth, thou hadst better been starved by thy nurse,
Than live to be hanged for cutting a purse."

While Nightingale sings this ballad, a fellow tickles Coke's ear with a straw, to make him withdraw his hand from his pocket, and privately robs him of his purse, which, at the end of the song, he secretly conveys to the ballad-singer; who notwithstanding his "Caveat against cut-purses," is their principal confederate, and in that quality, becomes the unsuspected depository of the plunder.

In the years 1600-18, there was published a musical work, entitled "*Pammelia*—MVSICKES MISCELLANIE; *Or*, Mixed Varietie of pleasant ROVNDELAYS and delightful CATCHES. London, Printed by Thomas Snodhom, for Matthew Lownes and Iohn Browne." It was compiled by some eminent musicians, who had a practice of setting the cries of London to music, retaining only the very musical notes of them, here we find, "What Kitchen-Stuffe haue you maids," and there is a Round in six parts to the cry of "New Oysters:"—

"New Oysters, new Oysters, new Oysters new,
New Oysters, new Wall-fleet Oysters—
At a groat a pecke—each Oyster worth twopence.
Fetch vs bread and wine, that we may eate,
Let vs lose no time with such good meate—
A Banquet for a Prince—New Oysters.
New—*vt supra*—Oysters."

From "Meligmata: Musical Phantasies, fitting the Court, City, and Country Manners, to three, four and five Voices -—

> "To all delightful, except to the spiteful;
> To none offensive, except to the pensive."

"London, printed by William Stansby, for Thos. Adams, 1611," we take as follows :—

"CITTIE ROUNDS.

"Broomes for old shoes! pouch-rings, bootes and buskings!
Will yee buy any new broome?
New oysters! new oysters! new new cockles!
Cockels nye! fresh herrings! will yee buy any straw?
Hay yee any kitchen stuffe, maides?
Pippins fine, cherrie ripe, ripe, ripe!
Cherrie ripe, &c.
Hay any wood to cleaue?
Give care to the clocke!
Beware your locke!
Your fire and your light!
And God giue you good night!
One o' clocke!"

Some of the "Common Cryes i' th' City," as Oysters, Codlings, Kitchen-stuff, Matches for your Tinder-box, &c., are enumerated in Richard Brome's—The "Court Beggar, A Comedie acted at the *Cock-pit*, by His Majesties Servants, *Anno* 1632."

"The London Chanticleers, a witty Comedy full of Various and Delightful Mirth," 1659. This piece is rather an interlude than a play, and is amusing and curious, the characters being, with two exceptions, all London criers. The allusions to old usages, with the mention of many well known ballads, and some known no longer, contribute to give the piece an interest and a value of its own.

The principal *dramatis personæ* consists of:—

HEATH.—*A broom-man.* "Brooms, maids, broom! Come, buy my brooms, maids; 'Tis a new broom, and will sweep clean. Come, buy my broom, maids!"

BRISTLE.—*A brush-man.* "Come, buy a save-all. Buy a comb-brush, or a pot-brush; buy a flint, or a steel, or a tinder-box."

DITTY.—*A ballad-man.* "Come, new books, new books, newly printed and newly come forth! All sorts of ballads and pleasant books! *The Famous History of Tom Thumb* and *Unfortunate Jack*, *A Hundred Goodly Lessons* and *Alas, poor Scholar, whither wilt thou go? The second part of Mother Shipton's Prophecies, newly made by a gentleman of good quality*, foretelling what was done four hundred years ago, and *A Pleasant Ballad of a bloody fight seen i' th' air*, which, the astrologers say, portends scarcity of fowl this year. The *Ballad of the Unfortunate Lover.* I have *George of Green*, *Chivy Chase*, *Collins and the Devil; or, Room for Cuckolds*, *The Ballad of the London 'Prentice*, *Guy of Warwick*, *The Beggar of Bethnal Green*, *the Honest Milkmaid; or, I must not wrong my Dame*, *The Honest Fresh Cheese and Cream Woman.* Then I have *The Seven Wise Men of Gotham*, *A Hundred Merry Tales*, *Scoggin's Jests; or, A Book of Prayers and Graces for Young Children.* I have very strange news from beyond seas. The King of Morocco has got the black jaundice, and the Duke of Westphalia is sick of the swine-pox, with eating bacon; the Moors increase daily, and the King of Cyprus mourns for the Duke of Saxony, that is dead of the stone; and Presbyter John is advanced to Zealand; the sea ebbs and flows but twice in four-

and-twenty hours, and the moon has changed but once the last month."

BUDGET.—*A Tinker.* "Have you any work for the tinker? Old brass, old pots, old kettles. I'll mend them all with a tara-tink, and never hurt your metal."

GUM.—*A Tooth drawer.* "Have you any corns upon your feet or toes? Any teeth to draw?"

JENNITING.—*An Apple wench.* "Come buy my pearmains, curious John Apples, dainty pippins? Come, who buy? who buy?"

CURDS.—*A fresh Cheese and Cream woman.* "I have fresh cheese and cream; I have fresh cheese and cream."

THE SORROWFUL LAMENTATIONS of the PEDLARS AND PETTY CHAPMEN, For the Hardness of the Times and the Decay of Trade.

To the Tune of "My Life and my Death."

"The times are grown hard, more harder than stone,
And therefore the Pedlars may well make their moan,
Lament and complain that trading is dead,
That all the sweet golden days now are fled.
Then maidens and men, come see what you lack,
And buy the fine toys that I have in my pack!

"Come hither and view, here's choice and here's store,
Here's all things to please ye, what would you have more?
Here's points for the men, and pins for the maid,
Then open your purses and be not afraid.
Come, maidens, &c.

"Let none at a tester repent or repine:
Come bring me your money, and I'll make you fine;
Young Billy shall look as spruce as the day,
And pretty sweet Betty more finer than May.
Then, maidens, &c.

"To buy a new license your money I crave;
'Tis that which I want, and 'tis that which you have:
Exchange then a groat for some pretty toy,
Come, buy this fine whistle for your little boy.
Come, maidens, &c.

"Here's garters for hose, and cotton for shoes,
And there's a gilt bodkin, which none would refuse:
This bodkin let John give to sweet Mistriss Jane,
And then of unkindness he shall not complain.
Come, maidens, &c.

"Come buy this fine coife, this dressing, or hood,
And let not your money come like drops of blood:
The Pedlar may well of his fortune complain
If he brings all his ware to the market in vaine.
Then, maidens, &c.

"Here's band strings for men, and there you have lace,
Bone-lace to adorn the fair virgin's sweet face:
Whatever you like, if you will but pay,
As soon as you please you may take it away.
Then, maidens, &c.

"The world is so hard that we find little trade,
Although we have all things to please every maid:
Come, pretty fair maids, then make no delay,
But give me your hansel, and pack me away.
Come, maidens, &c.

"Here's all things that's fine, and all things that's rare,
All modish and neat, all new London ware:
Variety here you plainly may see,
Then give me your money, and we will agree.
Come, maidens, &c.

"We travel all day through dirt and through mire,
To fetch you fine laces and what you desire;
No pains do we spare to bring you choice ware,
As gloves and perfumes, and sweet powder for hair.
Then, maidens, &c.

"We have choice of songs, and merry books, too,
All pleasant and witty, delightful and new,
Which every young swain may whistle at plough,
And every fair milk-maid may sing at her cow.
Then, maidens, &c.

"Since trading's so dead we must needs complain,
And, therefore, pray let us have some little gain:
If you will be free, we will you supply
With what you do want; therefore, pray come and buy.
The world is so hard, that although we take pains,
When we look in our purses we find little gains.

"Printed for J. BACK, at the Black-boy, on London Bridge."

In "Merry Drollery Complete, or, a Collection of Jovial Poems, Merry Songs, Witty Drolleries, Intermixed with Pleasant Catches, London, Printed for *William Miller*, at the *Gilded Acorn*, in *St. Paul's* Church-yard, 1661," the *Catch* which follows will be found. The Rev. J. Woodfall Ebsworth, M.A., Cantab, who has carefully edited and reprinted [1875] "Both Parts"; says in his *Appendix of Notes*:—"Hare-skin and Rabbit-skin collectors, have always been queer characters. This catch is by JOHN FLETCHER, in his 'Beggar's Bush,' act iii, sc. 1., where it is sung by 'Clause' his boy. Clause, the vagabond beggar, was a popular favourite, reproduced in 'Drolls.' We see him represented in the frontispiece of *The Wits*, by Kirkman and Cox."

A CATCH.

"Bring forth your Cunny skins, fair maids, to me,
And hold them fair that I may see
Gray, black, and blue; for your smaller skins—
I'll give you Glasses, Laces, Pins:
And for your whole Cunny
I'll give ready money.

"Come, gentle *Jone*, do thou begin
With thy black, black, black Cunny skin,
And *Mary* then, and *Kate* will follow
With their silver'd hair'd skins, and their yellow;
Your white Cunny skin I will not lay by,
Though it be fat, it is not fair to the Eye.

"Your gray it is warm, but for my money
Give me the bonny, bonny black Coney;
Come away, fair maids, your skins will decay,
Come take money, maids, put your ware away;
I have fine Bracelets, Rings,
And I have silver Pins
Coney skins, Coney skins,
Maids, have you any Coney skins."

In the same Collection there is a vigorous song exposing the cheats of mendicants. The hero of which declares:—"*I am a Rogue, and a stout one.*" And that among the many cheats, counterfeits, deceits and dodges he has to resort to, at times he may be seen:—

"In *Pauls* Church-yard, by a pillar,
Sometimes you see me stand, Sir,
With a writ that shows what cares, what woes
I have passed by Sea and Land, Sir,
Then I do cry, &c.

"Come buy, come buy a Horn-book,
Who buys my Pins and Needles:
Such things do I in the City cry
Oftimes to 'scape the Beadles,
Then I do cry, &c."

For the counterpart of this Rogue and Vagabond, the reader is referred to Vol. 1, No. 42-3 of the Roxburghe Ballads—(British Museum.) Where there is one entitled:—

THE CUNNING NORTHERN BEGGAR.

Who all the by-standers doth earnestly pray
To bestow a penny upon him to-day.

TO THE TUNE OF *Tom of Bedlam*.

I am a lusty beggar,
And live by others giving!
I scorn to work,
But by the highway lurk,
And beg to get my living:
I'll i'the wind and weather,
And wear all ragged garments;
Yet, though I'm bare,
I'm free from care,—
A fig for high preferments!

Therefore I'll cry, &c.

* * * * * * *

My flesh I can so temper
That it shall seem to fester,
And look all o'er
Like a raw sore,
Whereon I stick a plaister.
With blood I daub my face then,
To feign the falling sickness,
That in every place
They pity my case,
As if it came through weakness.

Therefore I'll cry, &c.

* * * * * * *

No tricks at all shall escape me,
But I will by my maunding,
Get some relief
To ease my grief
When by the highway standing:

'Tis better be a Beggar,
And ask of kind good fellows,
And honestly have
What we do crave,
Than steal and go to the gallows.

Therefore I'll cry, " Good your worship, good sir,
Bestow one poor denier, sir,
Which, when I've got,
At the Pipe and Pot
I soon will it cashier, sir."

FINIS.

Printed at London for F. Coules.

The following ballad was published in "Playford's Select Ayres," 1659, p. 95; with music by Dr. John Wilson, and Musical Companion, 1673. It is in the Percy Folio MS., iii., 308-11. Also in "Windsor Drollery," 2; and "Le Prince d'Amour," 1660, p. 177. It is attributed to Shakespeare, but with only manuscript evidence.

"THE SONG OF THE PEDLARS.

"From the fair Lavinian shore,
I your markets come to store,
Muse not though so far I dwell
And my wares come here to sell:
Such is the insatiate thirst after gold,
Then come to my pack
While I cry, what d'ye lack,
What d'ye buy? for here it is to be sold.

"Courteous Sir, I've wares for you,
Garters red and stockings blue,
Dainty gaudes for Sunday gear,
Beads and laces for your dear,
First let me have but a touch of your gold
Then come—Not a swain,
Half so neat,
On the plain
Shall we meet
So comely to behold.

"Madam, come, here you may find
Rings with posies to your mind,
Silken bands for true-love-knot,
And complexion I have got.
First let me have but a touch of your gold,
Then come—To your face,
I'll restore
Every grace
Though you're more
Than three score and ten years old.

"Gentles all, now fare you well,
I must trudge my wares to sell;
Lads so blythe and Dames so young,
Drop a guerdon for my song.
Just let me have but a touch of your gold,
I'll come with my pack
Again to cry,
What d'ye lack,
What d'ye buy?
For here it is to be sold."

Mr. John Payne Collier, in his "*A Book of Roxburghe Ballads*," London, 1847, reproduces a capital ditty; "ryhte merrie and very excellent in its way," relating to the popular pursuits and the customs of London and the Londoners in the early part of the seventeenth century. It is printed *verbatim* from a broad-side, signed W. Turner, and called :—

"The Common Cries of London Town,
Some go up street and some go down.

With Turner's Dish of Stuff, or a Gallymaufery
To the tune of *Wotton Towns End.** Printed for F. C [oles,] T. V [ere,] and W. G [ilbertson.] 1662."

The only known copy is dated 1662, but contains internal evidence, in the following stanza (which occurs in the opening of The Second Part,) that it was written in the reign of James I.

"That's the fat foole of the Curtin:
And the lean fool of the Bull:
Since *Shancke* did leave to sing his rimes,
He is counted but a gull.

"The players on the Bankside,
The round Globe and the Swan,
Will teach you idle tricks of love,
But the Bull will play the man."

Shancke.—John Shancke the comic actor here mentioned was celebrated for singing rhymes, and what were technically "jigs"

* *The Tune of Wotton Towns End*, is the same as "Peg a' Ramsey," mentioned by Shakespeare in Twelfth Night, and is at least as old as 1589. It is also in "Robin Good-Fellow: His Mad Pranks, And Merry Jests, Full of Honest Mirth, &c., 1628."

on the stage. In this respect, as a low comedian he had been the legitimate successor of Tarlton, Kempe, Phillips, and Singer. He was on the stage from 1603 to 1635, when he died. Then, John Taylor the *Water Poet*, no mean authority, informs us that the Swan Theatre, on the Bankside, in the Liberty of Paris Gardens, had been abandoned by the players in 1613. The Curtain Theatre in Holywell street—or Halliwell street, as it was usually spelt at that time—Shoreditch Fields* had also fallen into disuse before the reign of Charles I. The Globe on the Bankside, and the [Red] Bull Theatre at the upper end of St. John's street, Clerkenwell were employed until after the restoration. The allusion to the Waterman carrying "bonny lasses over to the plays," is also a curious note of time. With these matters before us, we may safely conclude that "Turner's Dish of Stuff" is but a reprint of an earlier production. As we find it, so we lay it before our readers: thus :—

---

* The Curtain Road, now notorious for cheap and shoddy furniture, still marks the site of the Curtain Theatre; at the same date there was another playhouse in the parish of St. Leonard, Shoreditch, distinguished as "The Theatre," where the Chamberlain's Company had settled. John Stow, in his Survey of London, 1598, speaking of the priory of St. John Baptist, says: "And neere thereunto are builded two publique houses for acting of shews of comedies, tragedies, and histories, for recreation. Whereof is one called the "Courtein," the other "The Theatre;" both standing on the South West side toward the field." In both these James Burbadge may have been interested; his long residence in the parish may fairly lead to the conclusion, that he was a sharer in at least one of them. Richard Tarlton, the famous actor of clown's parts, was a near neighbour of James Burbadge, and a shareholder and performer at the Curtain. Thomas Pope, a performer of rustic clowns, by his will dated July, 1603, left—"All my part, right, title, and interest which I have in the playhouse, called the Curtein, situated and being in Halliwell, in the parish of St. Leonard's in Shoreditch, in the County of Middlesex." At what date one or the other of these early Suburban playhouses ceased to be occupied, we have little or no satisfactory evidence.

"THE COMMON CRIES OF LONDON TOWN:
SOME GO UP STREET, SOME GO DOWN.

With Turner's Dish of Stuff, or a Gallymaufery.

To the tune of Wotton Towns End."

"My masters all, attend you,
if mirth you love to heare,
And I will tell you what they cry
in London all the yeare.
Ile please you if I can,
I will not be too long:
I pray you all attend awhile,
and listen to my song.

"The fish-wife first begins,
Anye muscles lilly white!
Herrings, sprats or plaice,
or cockles for delight.
Anye welflet oysters!
Then she doth change her note:
She had need to have her tongue be greas'd,
for the rattles in the throat.

"For why, they are but Kentish,
to tell you out of doubt.
Her measure is too little;
goe, beat the bottom out.
Half a peck for two pence?
I doubt it is a bodge.
Thus all the City over
the people they do dodge.

"The wench that cries the kitchin stuff,
I marvel what she ayle,
She sings her note so merry,
but she hath a draggle tayle:
An empty car came running,
and hit her on the bum;
Down she threw her greasie tub,
and away straight she did run

"But she did give her blessing
to some, but not to all,
To bear a load to Tyburne,
and there to let it fall:
The miller and his golden thumb,
and his dirty neck,
If he grind but two bushels,
he must needs steal a peck.

"The weaver and the taylor,
cozens they be sure,
They cannot work but they must steal,
to keep their hands inure;
For it is a common proverb
thorowout the town,
The taylor he must cut three sleeves
to every woman's gown.

"Mark but the waterman
attending for his fare,
Of hot and cold, of wet and dry,
he alwaies takes his share:
He carrieth bonny lasses
over to the playes,
And here and there he gets a bit,
and that his stomach staies.

"There was a singing boy
who did not ride to Rumford;
When I go to my own school
I will take him in a comfort;
But what I leave behind
shall be no private gain;
But all is one when I am gone:
let him take it for his pain.

"Old shoes for new brooms!
the broom-man he doth sing,
For hats or caps or buskins,
or any old pouch ring.
Buy a mat, a bed-mat!
a hassock or a presse,
A cover for a close stool,
a bigger or a lesse.

"Ripe, cherry ripe!
the coster-monger cries;
Pippins fine or pears!
another after hies,
With basket on his head
his living to advance,
And in his purse a pair of dice
for to play at mumchance.

"Hot pippin pies!
to sell unto my friends,
Or pudding pies in pans,
well stuft with candle's ends.
Will you buy any milk?
I heard a wench that cries:
With a pale of fresh cheese and cream,
another after hies.

"Oh! the wench went neatly;
me thought it did me good,
To see her cherry cheeks
so dimpled ore with blood:
Her waistcoat washed white
as any lilly floure;
Would I had time to talk with her
the space of half an hour.

"Buy black! saith the blaking man,
the best that ere was seen;
Tis good for poore citizens
to make their shoes to shine.
Oh! tis a rare commodity,
it must not be forgot;
It will make them to glister galantly,
and quickly make them rot.

"The world is full of thread-bare poets
that live upon their pen,
But they will write too eloquent,
they are such witty men.
But the tinker with his budget,
the beggar with his wallet,
And Turners turned a gallant man
at making of a ballet."

THE SECOND PART.

To the same Tune.

"That's the fat foole of the Curtin,
and the lean fool of the Bull:
Since Shancke did leave to sing his rimes,
he is counted but a gull.
The players on the Bankside,
the round Globe and the Swan,
Will teach you idle tricks of love,
but the Bull will play the man.

"But what do I stand tattling
of such idle toyes?
I had better go to Smith-Field
to play among the boyes:
But you cheating and deceiving lads,
with your base artillery,
I would wish you to shun Newgate,
and withall the pillory.

" And some there be in patcht gownes,
I know not what they be,
That pinch the country-man
with nimming of a fee;
For where they get a booty,
they'le make him pay so dear,
They'le entertain more in a day,
then he shall in a year.

" Which makes them trim up houses
made of brick and stone,
And poor men go a begging,
when house and land is gone.
Some there be with both hands
will swear they will not dally,
Till they have turn'd all upside down,
as many use to sally.

" You pedlers, give good measure,
when as your wares you sell:
Tho' your yard be short, your thumb will slip
your tricks I know full well.
And you that sell your wares by weight,
and live upon the trade,
Some beams be false, some waits too light;
such tricks there have been plaid.

" But small coals, or great coals!
I have them on my back:
The goose lies in the bottom;
you may hear the duck cry quack.
Thus Grim the black collier,
whose living is so loose,
As he doth walk the commons ore,
sometimes he steals a goose.

" Thou usurer with thy money bags
that livest so at ease,
By gaping after gold thou dost
thy mighty God displease ;
And for thy greedy usury,
and thy great extortion,
Except thou dost repent thy sins,
Hell fire will be thy portion.

" For first I came to Houns-Ditch,
then round about I creep,
Where cruelty was crowned chief
and pity fast asleep :
Where usury gets profit,
and brokers bear the bell.
Oh, fie upon this deadly sin !
it sinks the soul to hell.

" The man that sweeps the chimnyes
with the bush of thorns,
And on his neck a trusse of poles
tipped all with horns,
With care he is not cumbered,
he liveth not in dread?
For though he wear them on his pole,
some wear them on their head.

" The landlord with his racking rents
turns poor men out of dore ;
Their children go a begging
where they have spent their store.
I hope none is offended
with that which is endited
If any be, let him go home
and take a pen and write it.

" Buy a trap, a mouse trap,
    a torment for fleas !
The hangman works but half the day ;
    he lives too much at ease.
Come let us leave this boyes play
    and idle prittle prat,
And let us go to nine holes,
    to spurn-point, or to cat.

" Oh ! you nimble fingered lads
    that live upon your wits,
Take heed of Tyburn ague,
    for they be dangerous fits ;
For many a proper man,
    for to supply his lack.
Doth leap a leap at Tyburn,
    which makes his neck to crack.

" And to him that writ this song
    I give this simple lot :
Let every one be ready
    to give him half a pot.
And thus I do conclude,
    wishing both health and peace
To those that are laid in their bed,
    and cannot sleep for fleas.

W. TURNER "

The "tink, terry tink" of the Tinker's "Cry" is preserved in a Miscellany of the year 1667, called "*Catch that Catch Can; or, the Musical Champion.*"

"THE TINKER.

"Have you any work for a tinker, mistriss?
Old brass, old pots, or kettles?
I'll mend them all with a tink, terry tink,
And never hurt your mettles.
First let me have but a touch of your ale,
'Twill steel me against cold weather,
Or tinkers frees,
Or vintners lees,
Or tobacco chuse you whether.
But of your ale,
Your nappy ale,
I would I had a ferkin,
For I am old
And very cold
And never wear a jerkin."

The tinker's "Cry" forms the opening lines ol "Clout the Cauldron," one of the best of our old Scottish songs :—

"'Hae ye ony pots or pans,
Or any broken chanlers,'
I am a tinker to my trade,
And newly come from Flanders."

But the song is so well known to all who take an interest in our northern minstrelsy, and is to be found, moreover, in every good collection of Scottish Songs, that it is enough to refer to it.

Honest John Bunyan was a travelling tinker originally. Reader! just for a moment fancy the inspired author—poet we may call him—of "*The Pilgrim's Progress*," crying the "cry" of his trade through the streets of Bedford, thus—"*Mistress, have you any work for the tinker? pots, pans, kettles I mend, old brass, lead or old copper I buy. Anything in my way to-day, maids?*" While at the same time, through his brain was floating visions of Vanity Fair, the Holy War, the Slough of Despond, the Valley of the Shadow of Death, the Barren Fig Tree, the Water of Life, &c. beneath the long head of hair, shaggy and dirty, too, as a tinker's generally is.

HOT CODLINGS:—*A Catch.*

This will be found in "*Windsor Drollery*," and, with music for three voices, by Thomas Holmes, in John Hilton's "*Catch that Catch Can;*" and also Walsh's "*Catch Club.*" Part II., p. 25.

"Have you observ'd the wench in the street,
She's scarce any hose or shoes to her feet;
And when she cries, she sings,
'I have hot Codlings, hot Codlings.'

"Or have you ever seen or heard,
The mortal with his Lyon tauny beard!
He lives as merrily as heart can wish,
And still he cries, 'Buy a brush, buy a brush.'

"Since these are merry, why should we take care?
Musicians, like Camelions, must live by the Aire;
Then let's be blithe and bonny, no good meeting baulk,
What though we have no money, we shall find Chalk."

The best known collection of cries is "The Cryes of the City of London. Drawne after the Life. P. Tempest, *Excudit*," a small folio volume, which when published, in 1688, consisted of only fifty plates, as the following advertisement, extracted from the *London Gazette* of May 28-31, 1688, sufficiently proves :—

"There is now published the Cryes and Habits of London, lately drawn after the Life in great variety of Actions. Curiously Engraven upon 50 Copper plates, fit for the Ingenious and Lovers of Art. Printed and Sold by P. Tempest, over-against Somerset House, in the Strand."

Samuel Pepys, the eccentric diarist, who died 1703, left to Magdalene College, Cambridge, an invaluable collection of ballads, manuscript naval memoirs, ancient English poetry, three volumes of "Penny Merriments," and a numerous assemblage of etchings and engravings. Among the latter are a number of Tempest's Cries in the first state. These are still preserved in the Pepysian Library in the same College.

In 1711 another edition of Tempest's Cries was published, containing seventy-four plates, several of which can scarcely be called cries. They are popular "London Characters" rather than "criers." As the book, however, is extremely rare, and consequently costly, and as a history of the old London Cries would be very imperfect without a particular account of Tempest's volume being made, with a few words about Mauron, who designed, and Pearce Tempest, who engraved these cries, that which follows will not, we trust, be altogether out of place. Of Mauron, we can find no better account than the notice in Walpole.

"Marcellus Mauron—sometimes spelt Lauron, was born at the Hague in 1643, and learnt to paint of his father, with whom he came when young into England. Here he was placed with one La Zoon, a portrait-painter, and then with Flesshier, but owed his chief improvement to his own application. He lived several years in Yorkshire, and when he returned again to London he had very much improved himself in his art. He drew correctly, studied nature diligently, copied closely, and so surpassed all his contemporaries in drapery, that Sir Godfrey Kneller employed him to clothe his portraits. He likewise excelled in imitating the different styles of eminent masters, executed conversation pieces of considerable merit. Several prints were made from his works, and several plates he etched and scraped himself. A book on fencing, and the procession at the coronation of William and Mary, were designed by him. He lived in Bow-street, Covent-garden, on the west side, about three doors up, and at the back of Sir Godfrey Kneller's house in the Piazza; there he died of consumption March 11th, 1702."

Of Pearce Tempest, the engraver, the particulars collected by Vertue were so extremely slight that Horace Walpole merely enumerates him among those of whom nothing is known. It may be told of him, however, that he lived in the Strand, over-against Somerset House, and dying in 1717, was buried on the 14th of April, in the church-yard of St. Paul, Covent-garden.

The six woodcuts following are reduced copies of the engraved figures that appear in Marcellus Mauron *cum* Tempest's "The Cryes of the City of London;" first we have :—

FINE WRITING INK!

This engraving pretty well describes the occupation of the figure represented. He carries a barrel on his back—pens in his right hand, with a pint measure and funnel at his side. But since Mauron's time the cry of "*Fine Writing Ink*" has ceased to be heard in the streets of the metropolis, so we no longer hear:—

> "My ink is good—as black as jet
> 'Tis used by Princes—and the state,
> If once you venture it to try,
> Of this I'm sure—none else you'll buy."

BUY AN IRON FORK, OR A SHOVEL?

The demand for such an iron fork, or such a shovel as the old woman carries is now discontinued.

TROOP, EVERY ONE, ONE!

The man blowing a trumpet, "Troop, every one, one!" was a street seller of hobby-horses—toys for children of three hundred years ago.

> "Call'st thou my love, hobby-horse; the hobby-horse is but a colt."
> *Love's Labour Lost,* Act iii., sc. 1.

He carried them, as represented in the engraving, in a partitioned frame, on his shoulder, and to each horse's head was a small flag with two bells attached. It was a pretty plaything for a "little master," and helped him to imitate the galloping of the real and larger hobby-horse in the pageants and mummeries that passed along the streets, or pranced in the shows at fairs and on the stage. Now-a-days we give a boy the first stick at hand to thrust between his legs as a Bucephalus—the shadow of a shadow—or the good natured grandpapa wishing to give my "young master" something of the semblance of the generous animal—for the horse is no less popular with boys than formerly, takes his charge to the nearest toyshop and buys him a painted stick on which is a sawn-out representation of a horse's head, which with the addition of a whip will enable him to:—

> "Ride a cock-horse to Banbury-cross,
> To see what Tommy can buy;
> A penny white loaf, a penny white cake,
> And a twopenny apple-pie."

Buy a Fine Singing Bird!

The *cries* of singing birds are extinct; we have only bird-*sellers.* The above engraving, therefore represents a by-gone character.

STRAWBERRIES RIPE, AND CHERRIES IN THE RISE.

In the earlier days, the above was at once a musical and a poetical cry. It must have come over the ear, telling of sunny gardens not a sparrow's flight from the City, such as that of the Bishop of Ely in Holborn, and of plenteous orchards which could spare their boughs as well as their fruit :—

> " *D. of Glou.*—My lord of Ely, when I was last in Holborn,
> I saw good strawberries in your garden there :
> I do beseech you send for some of them.
> *B. of Ely.*—Marry, and I will, my lord, with all my heart."
>
> *Richard III.*, act iii., sc. 4.

FINE ORANGES AND LEMONS.

The "orange-women" of Ben Jonson we have figured to the life. The familiar mention of the orange-sellers in the "Silent Woman," and this very early representation of one of them, show how general the use of this fruit had become in England at the beginning of the seventeenth century. It is stated, though the story is somewhat apocryphal, that the first oranges were imported by Sir Walter Raleigh. It is probable that about his time they first became an article of general commerce. We now consume about three hundred and fifty millions of oranges every year.

The class of bold young women—"Orange Wenches," that Nell Gwynne made famous is sufficiently alluded to in a passage in the *Spectator*, No. 141:

"But, indeed, by such representations, a poet sacrifices the best part of his audience to the worst; and, as one would think, neglects the boxes to write to the *orange-wenches*."

Rowe and other writers go far to prove that the "Orange Wenches" who frequented theatres had

"Other Fish to fry, and other Fruit to sell,"

beside supplying refreshment to the young gallants of the day.

In Douglas Jerrold's comedy of "*Nell Gwynne*," which was first represented at the Theatre Royal, Haymarket, 9th of January, 1833, with the following cast of characters :—

King Charles the Second	MR. JONES.
Sir Charles Berkeley	MR. FORRESTER.
Charles Hart, Major Mohun, Managers of the King's Theatre, Drury lane, 1667 ..	MR. DURUSET.
Betterton, Manager of the Duke's Theatre, Lincoln's-inn	MR. DIDDEAR.
Joe Haynes	MR. MEADOWS.
Counsellor Crowsfoot	Mr. BLANCHARD.
Stockfish	MR. F. MATTHEWS.
Boy	MASTER MACDONALD
Nell Gwynne	MISS TAYLOR.
Orange Moll	MRS. KEELEY.
Mrs. Snowdrop	MRS. DALY.

There is the following scene and song :—

Enter NELL GWYNNE, *as orange girl, with orange basket. She carries a mask.*

Nell. (*Sings.*) "*Buy oranges!*" Ladies and cavaliers, vouchsafe to look at my basket! Maidens, ripen my fruit with your glances; buy my oranges, as bright as hope and as sweet as courtship.—Though they look as hard as gold, they'll melt in the mouth like a lover's promise.—Their juice is syrup, and their coats as thin as a poet's. Buy, gentlemen; or I'll vow that, being jealous, you hate yellow even in an orange.

Betterton. (*Aside.*) It is—I'd swear to her face—the very girl!

Charles. (*Coming down with Nelly.*) And have your oranges really all these virtues?

Nell. (*Aside.*) So, my gallant mercer. All, and a thousand more;—there's nothing good that may not be said of the orange. It sets special examples to elder brothers, misers, and young travellers.

Charles. Aye? What example to elder brothers?

Nell. This; though full of age, it dwells quietly on the same branch with bud and blossom.

Charles. What does it teach misers?

Nell. That golden coats should cover melting hearts.

Charles. And, lastly, what may the young traveller learn of your orange?

Nell. This much; that he is shipped when green, that he may ripen on the voyage.

Charles. Prettily lectured.

Betterton. (*Aside.*) The king seems dazzled with the wench.—I must secure her for the Duke's.

Nell. But, gentlemen, fair gentlemen, will no one lighten my basket? Buy my oranges!

Song.—NELL GWYNNE.

Buy oranges!—No better sold,—
New brought in Spanish ships;
As yellow bright as minted gold,
As sweet as ladies' lips.
Come, maidens, buy; nor judge my fruit
From beauty's bait—the skin;
Nor think, like fops, with gaudy suit,
They're dull and crude within.
Buy oranges!

Buy oranges!—Buy courtiers, pray,
And as ye drain their juice,
Then, cast the poor outside away,
A thing that's served its use;

Why, courtier, pause; this truth translate,
Imprinted in the rind;
However gay the courtier's state,
'Tis yet of orange kind.
Buy oranges!

Buy oranges!--Coquetting fair,—
As sweet reproach come buy;
And, as the fruit ye slice and share,
Remember with a sigh—
A heart divided needs must cast
The faith which is its soul;
If, maidens, ye would have it last,
Give none—if not the whole.
Buy oranges!

(The by-standers all applaud.)

The orange-woman who carried the golden fruit through every street and alley, with the musical cry of:—" *Fine Oranges and Lemons*," lasted for a century or two. Then the orange-woman became, as everything else became, a more prosaic person as she approached our own times. She was a barrow-woman at the end of the last century: and Porson has thus described her:—

"As I walked through the Strand, so cheerful and gay,
I met a young girl a-wheeling a barrow;
'Fine fruit, sir,' says she, 'and a bill of the play.'"

The transformation was the same with the strawberry and cherry-women.

From the "Collection of Ancient Songs and Ballads, written on various subjects, and printed between the years MDLX. and MDCC." in the British Museum, and now known as the ROXBURGHE BALLADS, we take the ballad of :—

THE CRIES OF LONDON.

Tune—*The Merry Christ-church Bells.*

Hark ! how the cries in every street
Make lanes and allies ring :
With their goods and ware, both nice and rare,
All in a pleasant lofty strain ;
Come buy my gudgeons fine and new.
Old cloaths to change for earthen ware,
Come taste and try before you buy,
Here's dainty poplin pears.
Diddle, diddle, diddle dumplins, ho !
With walnuts nice and brown.
Let none despise the merry, merry cries
Of famous London town.

Any old cloaths, suits, or coats.
Come buy my singing birds.
Oranges or lemons. Newcastle salmon.
Come buy my ropes of onions, ho !
Come buy my sand, fine silver sand.
Two bunches a penny, turnips, ho !
I'll change you pins for coney-skins.
Maids, do you want any milk below ?
Here's an express from Admiral Hawke,
The Admiral of renown.
Let none despise the merry, merry cries
Of famous London town.

Maids, have you any kitchen stuff?
Will you buy fine artichoaks?
Come buy my brooms to sweep your rooms.
Will you buy my white-heart cabbages, ho!
Come buy my nuts, my fine small nuts,
Two cans a penny, crack and try.
Here's cherries round, and very sound.
Maids, shall I sweep your chimnies high?
Tinkle, tinkle, tinkle, goes the tinker's pan,
With a merry cheerful sound.
Let none despise the merry, merry cries
Of famous London town.

Here's fine herrings, eight a groat.
Hot codlins, pies and tarts.
New mackerel I have to sell.
Come buy my Wellfleet oysters, ho!
Come buy my whitings fine and new.
Wives, shall I mend your husbands' horns?
I'll grind your knives to please your wives,
And very nicely cut your corns.
Maids, have you any hair to sell.
Either flaxen, black, or brown?
Let none despise the merry, merry cries
Of famous London town.

Work for a cooper, maids give ear,
I'll hoop your tubs and pails.
Come Nell and Sue, and buy my blue.
Maids, have you any chairs to mend?
Here's hot spiced-gingerbread of the best,
Come taste and try before you buy.
Here's elder-buds to purge your bloods.
But black your shoes is all the cry.
Here's hot rice milk, and barley broth.
Plumb-pudding a groat a pound.
Let none depise the merry, merry cries
Of famous London town.

Here's fine rosemary, sage, and thyme.
Come buy my ground ivy.
Here's fatherfew, gilliflowers and rue.
Come buy my knotted marjorum, ho!
Come buy my mint, my fine green mint.
Here's fine lavender for your cloaths.
Here's parsley and winter-savory.
And heart's-ease which all do choose.
Here's balm and hissop, and cinquefoil,
All fine herbs, it is well known.
Let none despise the merry, merry cries
Of famous London town.

Here's pennyroyal and marygolds.
Come buy my nettle-tops.
Here's water-cresses and scurvy-grass.
Come buy my sage of virtue, ho!
Come buy my wormwood and mugwort.
Here's all fine herbs of every sort.
Here's southernwood, that's very good,
Dandelion and houseleek.
Here's dragon's-tongue and wood-sorrel.
With bear's-foot and horehound,
Let none despise the merry, merry cries
Of famous London town.

Here's green coleworts and brocoli.
Come buy my radishes.
Here's fine savoys, and ripe hautboys.
Come buy my young green hastings, ho!
Come buy my beans, right Windsor beans.
Two pence a bunch young carrots, ho!
Here's fine nosegays, ripe strawberries.
With ready picked salad, also.
Here's collyflowers and asparagus.
New prunes two-pence a pound.
Let none despise the merry, merry cries
Of famous London town.

Here's cucumbers, spinnage, and French beans.
Come buy my nice sallery.
Here's parsnips and fine leeks.
Come buy my potatoes, ho!
Come buy my plumbs, and fine ripe plumbs.
A groat a pound, ripe filberts, ho!
Here's corn-poppies and mulberries.
Gooseberries and currants also.
Fine nectarines, peaches, and apricots.
New rice two-pence a pound.
Let none despise the merry, merry cries
Of famous London town.

Buy a rabbit, wild duck, or fat goose.
Come buy a choice fat fowl.
Plovers, teal, or widgeons, come buy my pigeons.
Maids, do you want any small coal?
Come buy my shrimps, my fine new shrimps,
Two pots a penny, taste and try.
Here's fine saloop, both hot and good.
But Yorkshire muffins is the cry.
Here's trotters, calf's feet, and fine tripes.
Barrel figs, three-pence a pound.
Let none despise the merry, merry cries
Of famous London town.

Here's new-laid eggs for ten a groat.
Come buy water'd cod.
Here's plaice and dabs, lobsters and crabs.
Come buy my maids, and flounders, ho!
Come buy my pike, my fine live pike.
Two-pence a hundred cockles, ho!
Shads, eels, and sprats. Lights for your cats.
With haddocks, perch, and tench also.
Here's carp and tench, mullets and smelts.
Butter sixpence a pound.
Let none despise the merry, merry cries
Of famous London town.

Printed and sold at the Printing-office in *Bow-church-yard, London.*

"Holloway cheese-cakes" was once one of the London cries; they were sold by a man on horseback; and in "*Jack Drum's Entertainment*," a Comedy, 1601, in a random song, the festive character of this district is denoted :—

"Skip it and trip it nimbly, nimbly,
Tickle it, tickle it, lustily,
Strike up the tabor for the wenches favour,
Tickle it, tickle it, lustily.
Let us be seene on Hygate-Greene,
To dance for the honour of Holloway.
Since we are come hither, let's spare for no leather,
To dance for the honour of Holloway."

Drunken Barnaby, at the "Mother Red Cap," at Holloway, found very bad company :—

Veni Holloway, pileum rubrum,
In cohortem muliebrem,
Me adonidem *vocant omnes*
Meretricis Babylonis;
Tangunt, tingunt, molliunt, mulcent,
At egentem, foris pulsant.

Addison, the essayist and poet, 1672-1719, contributed a capital paper to the *Spectator*, on the subject of London Cries, which we deem so much to the purpose, that it is here reproduced *in extenso*.

THE SPECTATOR.

No. 251. TUESDAY, DECEMBER 18.

———*Linguæ centum sunt, oraque centum,*
———*Ferrea vox*——— VIRG., En. 6., v. 625.

———A hundred mouths, a hundred tongues,
And throats of brass, inspir'd with iron lungs. DRYDEN.

THERE is nothing which more astonishes a foreigner, and frightens a country 'squire, than the *cries of London*. My good friend Sir *Roger* often declares that he cannot get them out of his head, or go to sleep for them, the first week that he is in town. On the contrary, *Will Honeycombe* calls them the *Ramage de la ville*, and prefers them to the sound of larks, and nightingales, with all the music of the fields and woods. I have lately received a letter from some very odd fellow upon this subject, which I shall leave with my reader, without saying anything further of it.

SIR,

I AM a man out of all business, and would willingly turn my head to anything for an honest livelihood. I have invented several projects for raising many millions of money without burdening the subject, but I cannot get the parliament to listen to me, who look upon me forsooth as a crack, and a projector ; so that despairing to enrich either myself or my country by this public-spiritedness, I would make some proposals to you relating to a design which I have very much at heart, and which may procure me a handsome subsistence, if you will be pleased to recommend it to the cities of London and Westminster.

The post I would aim at, is to be comptroller-general of the London cries, which are at present under no manner of rules or discipline. I think I am pretty well qualified for this place, as being a man of very strong lungs, of great insight into all the branches of our British trades and manufactures, and of a competent skill in music.

The cries of London may be divided into vocal and instrumental. A freeman of London has the privilege of disturbing a whole street for an hour together with the twankling of a brass kettle or a frying-pan. The watchman's thump at midnight startles us in our beds, as much as the breaking in of a thief. The sow-gelder's horn has indeed something musical in it, but this is seldom heard within the liberties. I would therefore propose that no instrument of this nature should be made use of, which I have not tuned and licensed, after having carefully examined in what manner it may affect the ears of her majesty's liege subjects.

Vocal cries are of a much larger extent, and indeed so full of incongruities and barbarisms, that we appear a distracted city to foreigners, who do not comprehend the meaning of such enormous outcries. Milk is generally sold in a note above *Ela*, and it sounds so exceedingly shrill, that it often sets our teeth on edge. The chimney-sweeper is confined to no certain pitch; he sometimes utters himself in the deepest bass, and sometimes in the sharpest treble; sometimes in the highest, and sometimes in the lowest note of the gamut. The same observation might be made on the retailers of small coal, not to mention broken glasses or brick-dust. In these therefore, and the like cases, it should be my care to sweeten and mellow the voices of these itinerant tradesmen, before they make their appearance in our streets, as also to accommodate their cries to their respective wares; and to take care in paritcular, that those may not make the most noise who have the least to sell, which is very observable in the venders of card matches, to whom I cannot but apply that old proverb of *Much cry, but little wool.*

Some of these last mentioned musicians are so very loud in the sale of these trifling manufactures, that an honest splenetic gentleman of my acquaintance bargained with one of them never to come into the street where he lived; but what was the effect of this contract? Why, the whole tribe of card-match-makers which frequent that quarter, passed by his door the very next day, in hopes of being bought off after the same manner.

It is another great imperfection in our London-cries, that there is no just time nor measure observed in them. Our news should indeed be published in a very quick time, because it is a commodity that will not keep cold. It should not, however, be cried with the same precipitation as fire; yet this is generally the case: a bloody battle arms the town from one end to another in an instant. Every motion of the French is published in so great a hurry, that one would think the enemy were at our gates. This likewise I would take upon me to regulate in such a manner, that there should be some distinction made between the spreading of a victory, a march, or an encampment, a Dutch, a Portugal, or a Spanish mail. Nor must I omit, under this head, those excessive alarms with which several boisterous rustics infest our streets in turnip-season; and which are more inexcusable, because these are wares which are in no danger of cooling upon their hands.

There are others who affect a very slow time, and are, in my opinion, much more tunable than the former; the cooper in particular swells his last note in a hollow voice, that is not without its harmony; nor can I forbear being inspired with a most agreeable melancholy, when I hear that sad and solemn air with which the public are very often asked, If they have any chairs to mend? Your own memory may suggest to you many other lamentable ditties of the same nature, in which music is wonderfully languishing and melodious.

I am always pleased with that particular time of the year which is proper for the pickling of dill and cucumbers; but alas! this cry, like the song of the nightingale, is not heard above two months. It would therefore be worth while to consider, whether the same air might not in some cases be adapted to other words.

It might likewise deserve our most serious consideration, how far, in a well-regulated city, those humourists are to be tolerated, who, not content with the traditional cries of their forefathers, have invented particular songs and tunes of their own: such as was not many years since, the pastry-man, commonly known by the name of the Colly-Molly-Puff; and such as is at this day the vender of powder and wash-ball, who, if I am rightly informed, goes under the name of *Powder-Watt.*

Colly-Molly-Puff.

I must not here omit one particular absurdity which runs through this whole vociferous generation, and which renders their cries very often not only incommodious, but altogether useless to the public; I mean that idle accomplishment which they all of them aim at, of crying so as not to be understood. Whether or no they have learned this from several of our affected singers, I will not take upon me to say; but most certain it is, that people know the wares they deal in rather by their tunes than by their words: insomuch that I have sometimes seen a country boy run out to buy apples of a bellows-mender, and ginger-bread from a grinder of knives and scissors. Nay, so strangely infatuated are some very eminent artists of this particular grace in a cry, that none but their acquaintance are able to guess at their profession; for who else can know, *that work if I had it*, should be the signification of a corn-cutter.

Forasmuch, therefore, as persons of this rank are seldom men of genius or capacity, I think it would be very proper, that some man of good sense and sound judgment should preside over these public cries, who should permit none to lift up their voices in our streets, that have not tunable throats, and are not only able to overcome the noise of the crowd, and the rattling of coaches, but also to vend their respective merchandises in apt phrases, and in the most distinct and agreeable sounds. I do therefore humbly recommend myself as a person rightly qualified for this post; and if I meet with fitting encouragement, shall communicate some other projects which I have by me, that may no less conduce to the emolument of the public.

I am,

Sir, &c.

RALPH CROTCHET.

A curious parallel might be carried out between the itinerant occupations which the progress of society has entirely superseded, and those which even the most advanced civilization is compelled to retain. We here only hastily glance at a few of these differences.

Of the street trades which are past and forgotten, the small-coal-man was one of the most remarkable. He tells the tale of a city with few fires; for who could now imagine a man earning a living by bawling "*Small Coals*" from door to door, without any supply but that in the sack which he carries on his shoulders? His cry had, however, a rival in that of "*Any Wood to cleave.*"

* * * * * * * * * *

But here we must pause awhile to make a passing remark—even if it be no more than a mere wayside nod to the memory of Thomas Britton, the celebrated "Musical Small Coal Man,"—1654-1714.—to whom Britain is greatly indebted for the introduction and cultivation of concerted music, and whose influence has been indirectly felt in musical circles throughout the world:—

> "Of Thomas Britton every boy
> And Britain ought to know;
> To Thomas Britton, 'Small Coal Man.'
> All Britain thanks doth owe."*

This singular man had a small coal shop at the corner of a passage in Aylesbury-street, Clerkenwell-green, and his concert-room! which was over that, could only be reached by stairs from the outside of the house. The facetious Ned Ward, confirms this statement, thus:—

> "Upon Thursdays repair
> To my palace, and there
> Hobble up stair by stair;
> But I pray ye take care—
> That you break not your shins by a stumble."

* Stoke's Rapid Plan of Teaching Music.

THOMAS BRITTON,
The Musical Small Coal Man.

Britton was buried in the church-yard of Clerkenwell, being attended to the grave by a great concourse of people, especially by those who had been used to frequent his concerts.

To resume our argument, we may ask what chance would an aged man now have with his flattering solicitation of "*Pretty Pins, pretty Women?*" and the musical distich:—

> "Three-rows-a-penny, pins,
> Short whites, and mid-de-lings!"

Every stationer's or general-shop can now supply all the "*Fine Writing-ink*," wanted either by clerks or authors. There is a grocer's shop, or co-operative store at every turn; and who therefore needs him who cried aloud "*Lilly white Vinegar, threepence a quart?*" When everybody, old and young, wore wigs—when the price for a common one was a guinea, and a journeyman had a new one every year; when it was an article in every city apprentice's indenture that his master should find him in "One good and sufficent wig, yearly, and every year, for, and during, and unto the expiration of the full end and term of his apprenticeship"—then, a wig-seller made his stand in the street, or called from door to door, and talked of a "*Fine Tie, or a fine Bob-wig sir?*" Formerly, women cried "*Four pair for a shilling, Holland Socks*," also "*Long Thread Laces, long and strong*," "*Scotch or Russian Cloth*," "*Buy any Wafers or Wax*." "*London's Gazette, here?*" The history of cries is a history of social changes. Many of the *working* trades, as well as the vendors of things that can be bought in every shop, are now nearly banished from our thoroughfares. "*Old Chairs to mend*," or "*A brass Pot or an iron Pot to mend?*" still salutes us in some retired suburb; and we still see the knife-grinder's wheel; but who vociferates "*Any work for John Cooper?*" The trades are gone to those who pay scot and lot. What should we think of prison discipline, now-a-days, if the voice of lamentation was heard in every street, "*Some Bread and Meat for the poor*

Prisoners; for the Lord's sake, pity the Poor?" John Howard put down this cry. Or what should we say of the vigilance of excise-officers if the cry of "*Aqua Vitæ*" met our ears? The Chiropodist has now his guinea, a country villa, and railway season ticket; in the old days he stood at corners, with knife and scissors in hand, crying "*Corns to pick.*" There are some occupations of the streets, however, which remain essentially the same, though the form be somewhat varied. The sellers of food are of course among these. "*Hot Peascod,*" and "*Hot Sheep's-feet,*" are not popular delicacies, as in the time of Lydgate. "*Hot Wardens,*" and "*Hot Codlings,*" are not the cries which invite us to taste of stewed pears and baked apples. But we have still apples hissing over a charcoal fire; also roasted chesnuts, and potatoes steaming in a shining apparatus, with savoury salt-butter to put between the "fruit" when cut; the London pieman still holds his ground in spite of the many penny pie-shops now established. Rice-milk is yet sold out in halfpennyworths. But furmety, barley broth, greasy sausages—"bags of mystery," redolent of onions and marjoram—crisp brown flounders, and saloop are no longer in request.

The cry of "*Water-cresses*" used to be heard from some barefoot nymph of the brook, who at sunrise had dipped her foot into the bubbling runnel, to carry the green luxury to the citizens' breakfast-tables. Water-cresses are now cultivated, like cabbages, in market-gardens. The cry of "*Rosemary and Briar*" once resounded through the thoroughfares; and every alley smelt "like Bucklersbury in simple time," when the whole street was a mart for odoriferous herbs. Cries like these are rare enough now; yet we do hear them occasionally, when crossing some bye-street, and have then smelt an unwonted fragrance in the air; and as someone has truly said that scents call up the most vivid associations, we have had visions of a fair garden afar off, and the sports of childhood, and the song of the lark that :—

> "At my window bade good morrow
> Through the sweet briar."

Then comes a pale-looking woman with little bunches in her hand, who, with a feeble voice, cries "*Buy my sweet Briar, any Rosemary?*" There are still, however, plenty of saucy wenches—of doubtful morality—in the more crowded and fashionable thoroughfares, who present the passengers with moss-roses, and violets. Gay tells us :—

> "Successive cries the seasons' change declare,
> And mark the monthly progress of the year.
> Hark! how the streets with treble voices ring,
> To sell the bounteous product of the spring."

We no longer hear the cries which had some association of harmonious sounds with fragrant flowers. The din of "noiseful gain" exterminated them.

THE WATER CARRIER.

"Any fresh and fair Spring Water here?"

This was formerly a very popular London cry, but has now become extinct, although it was long kept in vogue by reason of the old prejudices of old fashioned people, whose sympathy was with the complaints of the water-bearer, who daily vociferated in and about the environs of London, "Any fresh and fair spring water here! none of your pipe sludge?"—though their own old tubs were often not particularly nice and clean to look at, and the water was likely to receive various impurities in being carried along the streets in all weathers.—"Ah dear?" cried his customers, "Ah dear! Well, what'll the world come to!—they won't let poor people live at all by-and-bye—Ah dear! here they are breaking up all the roads and footpaths again, and we shall be all under water some day or another with all their fine new fandangle goings on, but I'll stick to the poor old lame and nearly blind water-carrier, as my old father did before me, as long as he has a pailful and I've a penny, and when we haven't we must go to the workhouse together."

This was the talk and reasoning of many honest people of that day, who preferred taxing themselves, to the daily payment of a penny and very often twopence to the water-carrier, in preference to having "*Company's water*" at a fixed or *pro-rata* sum per annum.

THE FIRST VIEW OF THE NEW RIVER—FROM LONDON.

This is seen immediately on coming within view of Sadler's Wells, a place of dramatic entertainment; after manifold windings and tunnellings from its source the New River passes beneath the arch in the engraving, and forms a basin within the large walled enclosure, from whence diverging main pipes convey the water to all parts of London. At the back of the boy angling on the wall is a public-house, with tea-gardens and skittle-ground, and known as *Sir Hugh Myddleton's Head*, also as *Deacon's Music Hall*, which has been immortalized by Hogarth in his print of EVENING. But how changed the scene from what he represented it! To this stream, as the water nearest London favourable to sport, anglers of inferior note *used* to resort:—

> "Here 'gentle anglers,' and their rods withal,
> Essaying, do the finny tribe enthral.
> Here boys their penny lines and bloodworms throw,
> And scare, and catch, the 'silly fish' below."

We have said above, anglers *used* to resort, and we have said so advisedly, as that portion of the river is now arched over to the end of Colebrooke Row.

The New River, Islington, its vicinity, and our own favourite author—Charles Lamb, are, as it were, so inseparably bound together, that we hope to be excused for occupying a little of our reader's time with *Elia*—His Friends—His Haunts—His Walks, and Talk(s), particularly about the neighbourhood of:—

> "———Islington!
> Thy green pleasant pastures, thy streamlet so clear,
> Old classic village! to *Elia* were dear—
> Rare child of humanity! oft have we stray'd
> On Sir Hugh's pleasant banks in the cool of the shade.
>
> "Joy to thy spirit, aquatic Sir Hugh!
> To the end of old time shall thy River be New!
> Thy Head, ancient Parr, * too, shall not be forgotten;
> Nor thine, Virgin (?) Queen, tho' thy timbers are rotten."
>
> George Daniel's "*The Islington Garland.*"

* The Old Parr's Head, in Upper Street, Islington.

Into the old parlour of the ancient "Sir Hugh Myddleton's Head"—*Elia*, would often introduce his own, for there he would be. sure to find, from its proximity to Sadler's Wells Theatre, some play-going old crony with whom he could exchange a convival "crack," and hear the celebrated Joe Grimaldi call for his tumbler of rum-punch; challenging Boniface to bring it to a *rummer!* Many a gleeful hour has been spent in this once rural hostelrie. But:—"All, all are gone, the old familiar faces."

COLEBROOKE COTTAGE.

——"to Colebrooke-row, within half a stone's throw of a cottage; endeared to me, in later years by its being the abode of 'as much virtue as can live.'" Hone, in his *Every-day Book*, Oct. 10, 1827.

Colebrooke Row was built in 1708. Here Charles Lamb, resided with his sister Mary, from 1823 to 1826; during which period—viz, on Tuesday, the 29th March, 1825, he closed his thirty-three years' clerkship at the East India House. Lamb very graphically describes the event in a letter to Bernard Barton, dated September 2, 1823, thus:—

"When you come Londonward, you will find me no longer in Covent Garden; I have a cottage in Colebrooke Row, Islington—a cottage, for it is detached—a white house, with six good rooms in it. The New River (rather elderly by this time) runs (if a moderate walking-pace can be so termed) close to the foot of the house; and behind is a spacious garden, with vines (I assure you), pears, strawberries, parsnips, leeks, carrots, cabbages, to delight the heart of old Alcinous. You enter without passage into a cheerful dining-room, all studded over and rough with old books; and above is a lightsome drawing-room, three windows, full of choice prints. I feel like a great lord, never having had a house before."

And again, in the November following, in a letter to Robert Southey, he informs the bard, who had promised him a call, that he is "at Colebrooke Cottage, left hand coming from Sadler's Wells." It was here that that amiable bookworm, George Dyer, editor of the Delphin Classics, walked quietly into the New River from Charles Lamb's door, but was soon recovered, thanks to the kind care of Miss Lamb.

The late Mr. George Daniel, of Canonbury Square, Islington, who formerly possessed the "ELIZABETHAN GARLAND," which consists of Seventy Ballads, printed between the years 1559 and 1597; a pleasing chatty writer and great snapper-up of unconsidered literary trifles, was an old friend and jolly companion of Charles Lamb's and frequently accompanied him in his favourite walks on the banks of the New River, and to the ancient hostelries in and round-about "Merrie Islington." At the

THE OLD QUEEN'S HEAD.

Old Queen's Head, they, in company with many retired citizens, and thirsty wayfarers, met, on at least one occasion, with Theodore Hook, indulged in reminiscences of bygone days, merrily puffed their long pipes of the true "Churchwarden" or *yard of clay* type, and quaffed nut-brown ale, out of the festivious tankard presented by a choice spirit!—one Master Cranch,—to a former host; and in the old oak parlour, too, where, according to tradition, the gallant Sir Walter Raleigh received, "full souse" in his face, the humming contents of a jolly Black Jack* from an affrighted clown, who, seeing clouds of tobacco-smoke curling from the knight's nose and mouth, thought he was all on fire! fire!! fire!!!.

* BLACK JACK. A huge leather drinking vessel. A Frenchman speaking of it says, "The English drink out of their boots."—*Heywood.*

CANONBURY TOWER.

"Here stands the tall relic, old Canonbury Tow'r,
Where Auburn's sweet bard won the muse to his bow'r,
The Vandal that pulls thy grey tenements down,
When falls the last stone, may that stone crack his crown!"
G. Daniel's "*The Islington Garland.*"

Lamb took special delight in watching the setting sun from the top of old Canonbury Tower, until the cold night air warned him to retire. He was intimate with Goodman Symes, the then tenant-keeper of the Tower, and bailiff of the Manor, and a brother antiquary in a small way; who took pleasure in entertaining him in the antique panelled chamber where Goldsmith wrote his *Traveller*, and supped frugally on buttermilk; and in pointing to a small portrait of Shakespeare, in a curiously carved gilt frame, which Lamb would look at longingly. He was never weary of toiling up and down the winding and narrow stairs of this suburban pile, and peeping into its quaint corners and cupboards, as if he expected to discover there some hitherto hidden clue to its mysterious origin.

"What village can boast like fair Islington town
Such time-honour'd worthies, such ancient renown?
Here jolly Queen Bess, after flirting with Leicester,
'Undumpish'd,' herself, with Dick Tarlton her Jester.

"Here gallant gay Essex, and burly Lord Burleigh
Sat late at their revels, and came to them early;
Here honest Sir John took his ease at his inn—
Bardolph's proboscis, and Jack's double chin.

From Islington, Charles Lamb moved to Enfield Chase Side, there he lived from 1827 to 1833, shut out almost entirely from the world, and his favourite London in particular.

CHARLES LAMB'S HOUSE, ENFIELD.

Lamb, in a merry mood, writing to Novello, in 1827, says:—

"We expect you four (as many as the table will hold without squeezing) at Mrs. Westwood's *Table d'Hôte* on Thursday. You will find the *White House* shut up, and us moved under the wing of the *Phœnix*, which gives us friendly refuge. Beds for guests, marry we have none, but cleanly accommodings [*sic.*] at the *Crown and Horse-shoes*.

"Yours harmonically,

"C. L.

"Vincentio (what, ho!) Novello, a Squire.
66, Great Queen Street, Lincoln's-Inn Fields."

THE CROWN AND HORSE SHOES INN, ENFIELD CHASE SIDE.

The above represents one of the humble and wayside "Pubs" of the neighbourhood in which Charles Lamb is said to have tested the friendship of "fine" friends, by proposing to them a drink of unsophisticated porter from bright pewter pots. So did he treat Wordsworth, and that "Child of Nature" actress, Miss Frances Maria Kelly, who without hesitation entered the tavern, with :—

> "The whitewash'd wall, the nicely sanded floor,
> The varnish'd clock that click'd behind the door,
> The chest contriv'd a double debt to pay,—
> A bed by night, a chest of drawers by day."

About the Midsummer of 1833, Charles Lamb and his sister removed to Bay-cottage, Church-street, Edmonton, kept by

HOUSE AT EDMONTON WHERE CHARLES LAMB DIED.

Mr. Walden, whose wife acted as a professional nurse. There, in that poor melancholy looking tenement, the delightful humourist found the home in which he breathed his last on Saturday, the 27th December, 1834. He was buried in:—

EDMONTON CHURCH.

> "Oh, Mirth and Innocence! Oh, Milk and Water!
> Ye happy mixtures of more happy days!."
>
> Byron's, *Beppo.* St. 80.

Time and circumstances have effectually disposed of the water-carrier, his occupation is gone, it is impossible London can ever again see a man bent beneath the weight of a yoke and two enormous pails, vociferating "*Any fresh and fair Spring Water here?*" But the cry of "Milk," or the rattle of the milk-pail will never cease to be heard in our streets. There can be no reservoirs of milk, no pipes through which it flows into the houses. The more extensive the great capital becomes, the more active must be the individual exertion to carry about this article of food. The old cry was "*Any Milk here?*" and it was sometimes mingled with the sound of "*Fresh Cheese and Cream;*" and it then passed into "*Milk, maids below;*" and it was then shortened into "*Milk below;*" and was finally corrupted into "*Mio,*" which some wag interpreted into *mi-eau—demi-eau*—half water. But it must still be cried, whatever be the cry. The supply of milk to the metropolis is perhaps one of the most beautiful combinations of industry we have. The days have long since passed when Finsbury had its pleasant groves, and Clerkenwell was a village, and there were green pastures in Holborn, when St. Pancras boasted only a little church standing in meadows, and St. Martin's was literally in the fields. Slowly but surely does the baked clay of Mr. Jerry, "the speculative builder" stride over the clover and the buttercup; and yet every family in London may be supplied with milk by eight o'clock every morning at their own doors. Where do the cows abide? They are congregated in wondrous herds in the suburbs; and though in spring-time they go out to pasture in the fields which lie under the Hampstead and Highgate hills, or in the vales of Dulwich and Sydenham, and there crop the tender blade,—

> "When proud pied April, dress'd in all his trim,
> Has put a spirit of youth in everything."

yet for the rest of the year the coarse grass is carted to their stalls, or they devour what the breweries and distilleries cannot extract from the grain harvest. Long before "the unfolding star wakes up the shepherd" are the London cows milked; and the great wholesale vendors of the commodity, who have it consigned to them daily from more distant parts to the various railway stations in the metropolis, bear it in carts to every part of the town, and distribute it to the hundreds of shopkeepers and itinerants, who are anxiously waiting to receive it for re-distribution amongst their own customers. It is evident that a perishable commodity which everyone requires at a given hour, must be so distributed. The distribution has lost its romance. Misson, in his "Travels" published at the beginning of the last century, tells of May-games of the London milkmaids thus :—"On the first of May, and the five or six days following, all the pretty young country girls that serve the town with milk, dress themselves up very neatly, and borrow abundance of Silver-Plate, whereof they make a pyramid, which they adorn with ribbons and flowers, and carry upon their heads, instead of their common milk pails. In this equipage, accompanied with some of their fellow milk-maids, and a bagpipe or fiddle, they go from door to door, dancing before the houses of their customers, in the midst of boys and girls that follow them in troops, and everybody gives them something." Alas ! the May-games and pretty young country girls have both departed, and a milk-woman has become a very unpoetical personage. There are few indeed of milkwomen who remain. So it is with most of the occupations that associate London with the country.

KATE SMITH,
The Merry Milkmaid.

"'Where are you going' my pretty maid?'
'I'm going a milking, sir,' she said.'"

Thirty years ago there appeared in the "Quarterly Review" a remarkable article on the Commissariat of London, from the pen of Dr. Andrew Wynter. In it we were told for how many miles the beasts brought annually to the metropolis would stretch, if ranged ten abreast in a seemingly interminable column. In order to convey some notion of the stupendous quantities of ale, beer, and porter consumed, Dr. Wynter fixed upon Hyde Park as his exhibition ground, and piled together all the barrels containing the malt liquor drunk by what, in 1854, was a population of two million and a half souls. He came to the conclusion that these barrels would form a thousand columns not far short of a mile in perpendicular height. And among other statistics, Dr. Wynter calculated that there were at that time about twenty thousand cows in the metropolitan and suburban dairies, some of which establishments contained five hundred cows apiece. He also noticed that, the London and suburban dairies could not alone supply the population of the metropolis, seeing that twenty thousand cows, giving on an average twelve quarts each per diem, would not yield more than two hundred and forty thousand quarts. If we suppose this quantity increased by the

iron-tailed cow to three hundred thousand quarts, the allowance to each of the two millions and a half of human beings then living within the Bills of Mortality would be about a quarter of a pint per head. The "Quarterly" Reviewer, therefore, assumed that, to meet the existing demands of the tea-table, the nursery, and the kitchen, half as much again as three hundred thousand quarts was consumed annually in London. For this excess he looked to the country to supplement the efforts of the metropolis and of its suburbs as suppliers of milk, and noticed that the precious white liquid was brought daily to London from farms lying as far away as eighty miles from the metropolitan railway stations to which it was consigned.

Nothing can be more instructive and entertaining than to turn back in 1884 to facts, figures, calculations, estimates, and inferences which fitted the London of 1854. Instead of two millions and a half, the population resident at this moment within the metropolitan and city police districts amounts at least to four millions and three-quarters. The area already covered by the mighty town, which adds another big town to its entirety each successive year, is about four hundred and fifty thousand square acres, and there are more than seven hundred thousand houses to be provided for, of which it may be presumed that few can do without at least a pint of milk per diem. Assuming, however, that each member of this enormous population consumed no more than a quarter of a pint of milk—that is to say, a small tumblerful—per diem, we come to the astounding conclusion that nearly six hundred thousand quarts are wanted every day, nearly four million two hundred thousand quarts every week, and nearly two hundred and seventeen million quarts every year, to meet the demands of London. Few of us are able to fathom the meaning of two hundred million quarts of liquid until we are told what an immense reservoir, ten feet deep, it would take to hold such an amount. More intelligible are the calculations which tell us that, assuming a cow to yield ten—not twelve—quarts of milk daily, it would require nearly sixty thousand milch cows to maintain this supply from year's end to year's end. If these patient and valuable milkers are estimated as being worth no more than twenty-pounds apiece, they would represent in their aggregate a capital of little less than one million four hundred thousand pounds. Pure milk of a reliable character, costs fivepence per quart, and therefore, on the above basis, there is spent on milk, in the metropolis and its circumjacent districts, twelve thousand four hundred pounds per day, nearly eighty-seven thousand pounds per week, and considerably more than four and a half million pounds per annum. There are States which have made a considerable noise in the world, whose total revenue does not reach what London spends annually in milk alone. As for the distribution of this inconceivable amount of liquid, which is delivered every morning and afternoon in small quantities all over the enormous area of bricks-and-mortar to which we have referred, it would utterly baffle the most marvellous organiser and administrator that ever existed upon earth, to extemporise human machinery for carrying on so minute and yet so gigantic a trade. Nevertheless, how smoothly and imperceptibly, not only in this one small detail, but throughout the whole of its vast and endless complications and ramifications, does the commissariat of London work! We are told, for instance, that to distribute every sixteen gallons of milk one person is necessary, and that, without counting managers, clerks, shopmen and shopwomen, nearly five thousand human beings, assisted by more than fifteen hundred horses and mules, are needed to furnish London with milk every twenty-four hours. More than a quarter of a million pounds go yearly in wages to milkmen and milkwomen with whom we are all so familiar, and who will doubtless, acquire additional importance in the eyes of those who reflect that these humble servitors are but, in Pope's words, "parts of that stupendous whole" without whose useful, patient, and unintermitted labours the faultless machinery of the grandest camp of men that ever yet existed would instantly stand still.

Then it must not be forgotten that the milk trade exacts constant and unintermitted work from its employés—work from which neither Sundays nor holidays bring any relief—and demanding very early rising in the morning, to say nothing of the greatest personal cleanliness, and of an immense array of cans, varying from those capable of holding many gallons down to those which contain no more than half-a-pint—the milk-pail and its daily history might well attract notice from writers not inferior in grasp and imagination to Defoe or Dickens. In 1854 Dr. Wynter calculated that, as regards distribution, the commissariat of London was carried on by an army of one hundred thousand persons. In thirty years the population has all but doubled, and the machinery of distribution has been so improved that its working at present approaches very nearly to perfection. This perfection is due solely to freedom of trade and to universal competition, which so nicely adjust all the varying conditions of life, that, in serving themselves, they accomplish more than all the Governments on earth could effect by the most ingenious system of centralisation that human wit could devise.

Attic Poet:—"There is a pleasure in poetic pains which only Poets know."

In our neighbourhood, which, as the lodging-house-keepers advertise in *The Kingsland and Shacklewell Slopbasin*, and *The Dalston Dusthole*, is situate close to "Bus, Tram, and Rail," we have a milkman who is given to Poetry! and he circulates his "verses" pretty freely in the areas and letter-boxes about once a month.—

Glorious News! Glorious News!

How F. Wilson Meets his Customers' Views.

My readers may credit the words of my muse.
When telling how Wilson meets Customers' Views;
Wilson studies a straightforward system of trade,
Whereby to elicit encouraging aid.

The pure farm-house Milk he daily brings out,
Is such as we have no reason to doubt;
Encouraged in business his course he pursues,
And fails not in meeting his Customers' Views.

You'll not have occasion to doubt what I say,
When testing his Pure Milk day after day;
For cheapness and quality you'll find him in trade,
As you did when he first asked the public for aid.

His farm-house Milk and Eggs, which thoroughly please,
Are positive proofs of assertions like these;
'Tis certain that better can ne'er be supplied,
He trusts that in this you'll all coincide.

The highest of interest his Milk doth possess,
Thus boldly we state, for we cannot state less;
F. Wilson supplies what all purchasers choose,
And thus he is meeting his Customers' Views.

Terms Cash.

Customers can have their Milk left in cans any time after 5 a.m.

Note the address ☞ * * *

All complaints to be addressed to Mr. F. Wilson.

TIDDY DIDDY DOLL—LOLL, LOLL, LOLL.

This celebrated vendor of gingerbread, from his eccentricity of character, and extensive dealing in his particular way, was always hailed as the King of itinerant tradesmen. He was a constant attendant in the crowd at all metropolitan fairs, mob meetings, Lord Mayor's shows, public executions, and all other holiday and festive gatherings! In his person he was tall, well made, and his features handsome. He affected to dress like a person of rank; white and gold lace suit of clothes, lace ruffled shirt, laced hat and feather, white stockings, with the addition of a white apron. Among his harangues to gain customers, take the following piece as a fair sample of the whole :—

"Mary, Mary, where are you *now*, Mary? I live, when at home, at the second house in Litttle diddy-ball-street, two steps under ground, with a wiscum, riscum, and a why-not. Walk in, ladies and gentlemen; my shop is on the second-floor backwards, with a brass knocker on the door, and steel steps before it. Here is your nice gingerbread, it will melt in your mouth like a red-hot brickbat, and rumble in your inside like Punch and his wheelbarrow." He always finished his address by singing this fag end of some popular ballad :—

"Ti-tid-ty, ti-tid-ty. Ti-tid-ty—tiddy-loll.
Ti-tid-ty, ti-tid-ty. Ti-tid-ty—tiddy-doll."

Hence arose his nickname "*Tiddy-Doll.*" In Hogarth's print of the "IDLE 'PRENTICE EXECUTED AT TYBURN." Tiddy-Doll is seen holding up a gingerbread cake with his left hand, his right hand within his coat, to imply that he is speaking the truth from his heart, while describing the superiority of his wares over those of any other vendor in the fair! while he still anxiously inquires :—

"Mary, Mary, where are you *now*, Mary?"

His proper name was Ford, and so well known was he that, on his once being missed for a week from his usual stand in the Haymarket, on the occasion of a visit which he paid to a country fair, a "Catch penny" account of his alleged murder was printed, and sold in the streets by thousands.

Allusions to Tiddy-Doll, and sayings derived from him, have reached to our own time, thus, we still say to an over-dressed person— "You are as tawdry as Diddy-doll," "You are quite Tiddy-doll, you look as fine as Tiddy-doll," he or she is said to be "All Tiddy-doll," &c.

The class of men formerly well known to the citizens of London as News-criers, or Hornmen, must now be spoken of in the past sense, as the further use of the horn was prohibited long ago by the magistracy, subject to a penalty of ten shillings for the first offence, and twenty shillings on the conviction of repeating so heinous a crime.

"GREAT NEWS, BLOODY BATTLE, GREAT VICTORY!
EXTRAORDINARY GAZETTE!
SECOND EDITION!"

were the usual loud bellowing of fellows with stentorian lungs, accompanied by a loud blast of a long tin-horn, which announced to the delighted populace of London the martial achievements of a Marlborough, Howe, Hood, Nelson, or Wellington. A copy of the "Gazette" or newspaper they "cried" was usually affixed under the hatband, in front, and their demand was generally one shilling.

At least one of these news criers has been immortalized. In a volume of "Miscellaneous Poems," edited by Elijah Fenton, and printed by Bernard Lintot, without date, but anterior to 1720, there are the lines that follow, to one old Bennet, who seems to have made a great noise in the world of London during the early part of last century :—

"ON THE DEATH OF OLD BENNET,
THE
NEWS CRYER

"One evening, when the sun was just gone down,
And I was walking thro' the noisy town,
A sudden silence through each street was spread,
As if the soul of London had been fled.
Much I enquired the cause, but could not hear,
Till fame, so frightened, that she did not dare
To raise her voice, thus whisper'd in my ear:—
Bennet, the prince of hawkers, is no more,
Bennet, my *Herald* on the British shore,
Bennet, by whom, I own myself outdone,
Tho' I a hundred mouths, he had but one,
He, when the list'ning town he would amuse,
Made *Echo* tremble with his '*Bloody news* !'
No more shall *Echo*, now his voice return,
Echo for ever must in silence mourn,—
Lament, ye heroes, who frequent the wars,
The great proclaimer of your dreadful scars.
Thus wept the conqueror who the world o'ercame,
Homer was waiting to enlarge his fame,
Homer, the first of hawkers that is known,
Great News from Troy, cried up and down the town,
None like him has there been for ages past,
Till our stentorian Bennet came at last,
Homer and Bennet were in this agreed,
Homer was blind, and Bennet could not read!"

In our own days there has been legislation for the benefit of tender ears; and there are now penalties, with police constables to enforce them, against "All persons blowing any horn or using any other noisy instrument, for the purpose of calling persons together, or of announcing any show or entertainment, or for the purpose of hawking, selling, distributing, or collecting any article, or of obtaining money or alms." These are the words of the Police Act of 1839; and they are stringent enough to have nearly banished from our streets all those uncommon noises which did something to relieve the monotony of the one endless roar of the tread of feet and the rush of wheels.

Mr. Henry Mayhew, in his admirable work of "London Labour and London Poor," writing in 1851, under the head "Of the Sellers of Second Editions," says:—

"I believe that there is not now in existence—unless it be in a workhouse and unknown to his fellows, or engaged in some other avocation, and lost sight of by them—any one who sold 'Second Editions' of the *Courier* evening paper at the time of the Duke of York's Walcheren expedition, at the period of the battle of the Nile, during the continuance of the Peninsular war, or even at the battle of Waterloo. There were a few old men—some of whom had been soldiers or sailors, and others who have simulated it—surviving within these five or six years and some later, who 'worked Waterloo,' but they were swept off, I was told, by the cholera."

CLEAN YOUR HONOUR'S SHOES.

"Temper the foot within this vase of oil,
And let the little tripod aid thy toil;
On this methinks I see the walking crew,
At thy request, support the miry shoe;
The foot grows black that was with dirt embrown'd,
And in thy pocket jingling halfpence sound."

Gay's "Trivia."

"About thirty years before the cry of 'Clean your boots, sir!' became familiar to the ears of the present generation of Londoners," Mr. Charles Knight informs us that :—"In one of the many courts on the north side of Fleet-street, might be seen, somewhere about the year 1820, 'The last of the London shoe-blacks.' One would think that he deemed himself dedicated to his profession by Nature, for he was a Negro. At the earliest dawn he crept forth from his neighbouring lodging, and planted his tripod on the quiet pavement, where he patiently stood till noon was past. He was a short, large-headed son of Africa, subject, as it would appear, to considerable variations of spirits, alternating between depression and excitement, as the gains of the day presented to him the chance of having a few pence to recreate himself beyond what he should carry home to his wife and children. For he had a wife and children, this last representative of a falling trade; and two or three little woolly-headed *décrotteurs* nestled around him when he was idle, or assisted in taking off the roughest of the dirt when he had more than one client. He watched, with a melancholy eye, the gradual improvement of the streets; for during some twenty or thirty years he had beheld all the world combining to ruin him. He saw the foot pavements widening; the large flag-stones carefully laid down; the loose and broken piece, which discharged a slushy shower on the unwary foot, and known to him and London chairmen as a '*Beau-trap*'* instantly removed: he saw the kennels diligently cleansed, and the drains widened: he saw experiment upon experiment made in the repair of the carriage-way, and the holes, which were to him as the 'old familiar faces' which he loved, filled up with a haste that appeared quite unnecessary, if not insulting. One solitary country shopkeeper, who had come to London once a year during a long life, clung to our sable friend; for he was the only one of the fraternity that he could find remaining, in his walk from Charing-cross to Cheapside."

* BEAU-TRAP:—A loose stone in the pavement under which the water lodges in rainy weather, which when trodden on squirts it up to the great damage of light-coloured clothes and clean stockings. First invented by Sedan-chairmen, whose practice it was to loosen a flat-stone so that in wet weather those that choose to save their money by walking, might, by treading on the "trap" dirt their shoes and stockings.

Hone, in "*The Table Book*," 1827, under an article on the Old London cries has :—" A Shoeblack ; A boy, with a small basket beside him, brushes a shoe on a stone, and addresses himself to a wigged beau, who carries his cocked hat under his left arm, with a crooked-headed walking stick in his left hand, as was the fashion among the dandies of old times. I recollect shoeblacks formerly at the corner of almost every street, especially in great thoroughfares. There were several every morning on the steps of St. Andrew's church, Holborn, till late in the forenoon. But the greatest exhibition of these artists was on the site of Finsbury-square, when it was an open field, and a depository for the stones used in paving and street-masonry. There, a whole army of shoeblacks intercepted the citizens and their clerks on their way from Islington and Hoxton to the counting-houses and shops in the city, with 'Shoeblack, your honour !' Black your shoes, sir !'"

Each of them had a large, old tin-kettle, containing his apparatus, viz :—a capacious pipkin, or other large earthen-pot, containing the blacking, which was made of ivory-black, the coarsest moist sugar, and pure water with a little vinegar—a knife, two or three brushes, and an old wig. The old wig was an indispensable requisite to a shoeblack ; it whisked away the dust, or thoroughly wiped off the wet dirt, which his knife and brushes could not entirely detach ; a rag tied to the end of a stick smeared his viscid blacking on the shoe, and if the blacking was "real japan," it shone. The old experienced shoe-wearers preferred an oleaginous, lustreless blacking. A more liquid blacking, which took a polish from the brush, was of later use and invention. Nobody at that time wore boots except on horseback ; and everybody wore breeches and stockings :

pantaloons, or trousers, were unheard of. The old shoeblacks operated on the shoes while they were on the feet, and so dexterously as not to soil the fine white cotton stocking, which was at that time the extreme of fashion, or to smear the buckles, which were universally worn. Latterly, you were accommodated with an old pair of shoes to stand in, and the yesterday's paper to read, while your shoes were cleaning and polishing, and your buckles were whitened and brushed. When shoestrings first came into vogue, the Prince of Wales (Geo. IV.) appeared with them in his shoes, when immediately a deputation from the buckle-makers of Birmingham presented a petition to his Royal Highness to resume the wearing of buckles, which was good-naturedly complied with. Yet, in a short time, shoestrings entirely superseded buckles. The first incursion on the shoe-blacks was by the makers of "Patent Cake Blacking" on sticks formed with a handle, like a small battledoor; they suffered a more fearful invasion from the makers of liquid blacking in bottles. Soon afterwards, when "Day and Martin" manufactured the *ne plus ultra* of blacking, private shoeblacking became general, public shoeblacks rapidly disappeared, and in [1827] they became extinct. The last shoeblack that I remember in London sat under the covered entrance of Red Lion-court, Fleet-street within the last six years. This unfortunate, "The Last of the London Shoeblacks"—was probably the "short, large headed son of Africa" alluded to by Charles Knight, under the heading of "Clean your honour's shoes," in his "History of London."

In 1851, some gentlemen connected with the Ragged Schools determined to revive the brotherhood of boot cleaners for the convenience of the foreign visitors to the Exhibition, and commenced the experiment by sending out five boys in the now well-known red uniform. The scheme succeeded beyond expection; the boys were patronized by natives as well as aliens, and the Shoeblack Society and its brigade were regularly organized. During the exhibition season, about twenty-five boys were constantly employed, and cleaned no less than 100,000 pairs of boots. The receipts of the brigade during its first year amounted to £656. Since that time, thanks to the combination of discipline and liberality, the Shoeblack Society has gone on and prospered, and proved the Parent of other Societies. Every district in London now has its corps of shoeblacks, in every variety of uniform, and while the number of boys has increased from tens to hundreds, their earnings have increased from hundreds to thousands. Numbers of London waifs and strays have been rescued from idleness and crime. The Ragged School Union, and Shoeblack Brigades, therefore hold a prominent place among the indirectly preventive agencies for the suppression of crime: for since ignorance is generally the parent of vice, any means of securing the benefits of education to those who are hopelessly deprived of it, must operate in favour of the well-being of society.

"'Tis education forms the common mind;
Just as the twig is bent, the tree's inclined."

THE HEARTH-STONE MERCHANT.

"Hearth-stones! Do you want any hearth-stones? Now, my maids, here's your right sort—reg'lar good'uns, and no mistake—vorth two o'your shop harticles, and at half the price. Now my pretty von, lay out a *tanner*, and charge your missus a *bob*—and no cheating neither! the cook has always a right to make her market penny and to assist a poor cove like me in the bargain.

"They're good uns, you vill find—
  Choose any, marm, as you prefer:
You look so handsome and so kind,
  I'm sure you'll be a customer.
Three halfpence, marm, for this here pair—
  I only vish as you vould try 'em;
I'm sure you'll say the price is fair—
  Come marm, a penny if you'll buy 'em."

THE FLYING STATIONER, OTHERWISE PATTERER.

"Here's tidings sad, for owld and young,
Of von who liv'd for years by macing;
And vos this werry morning hung,
The Debtor's Door at Newgate facing.

"Here's his confession upon hoath,
The vords he spoke ven he vos dying,
His birth and eddycation both—
The whole pertic'lers—vell vorth the buying.

"Here's an account of robberies sad,
In vich he alus vos a hactor;
You must to read the life be glad—
Of such a famous malefactor!

How to the mob he spinn'd a yarn,
And varn'd them from a course unproper,
You may, vith all his history, larn—
For the small valley of a copper!"

"Now my kind-hearted, haffectionated and wery ready-money Christian-hearted, pious and hinfidel customers, here you have the last speech and dying vords, life, character, and behaviour of the hunfortunate malefactor that vas hexecuted this morning hopposit the Debtor's door in the Hold Bailey! together with a full confession of the hoffence vherevith he vos found guilty before a hupright Judge and a wery himpartial Jury! Here you have likewise a copy of a most affecting letter, written by the criminal in the condemned cell the night afore hexecution to his hinnocent vife and hunoffending babbies, vith a copy of werses consarning the same—all for the small charge of von halfpenny. Yes, my friends, von halfpenny buys the werses as follows—von arter the 'tother:—

"Come, all you blessed Christians dear,
That's a-tender, kind, and free,
While I a story do relate
Of a dreadful tragedy,
Which happened in London town,
As you shall all be told;
But when you hear the horrid deed
'Twill make your blood run cold.—
For the small charge of a ha'penny!

"'Twas in the merry month of May,
When my true love I did meet;
She look'd all like an angel bright,
So beautiful and sweet.
I told her I loved her much,
And she could not say nay;
'Twas then I stung her tender heart,
And led her all astray.—
Only a ha'penny!"

JAMES—or as he was popularly called, "*Jemmy*," or, "*Old Jemmy*" Catnach, *(Kat-nak,)* late of the Seven Dials, London, printer and publisher of ballads, battledores, lotteries, primers, &c., and whose name is ever associated with the literature of the streets, was the son of John Catnach, a printer, of Alnwick, an ancient borough, market town, and parish of Northumberland, where he was born on August 18th, 1792.

At the time Jemmy Catnach commenced business in Seven Dials it took all the prudence and tact which he could command to maintain his position, as at that time "Johnny" Pitts,* of the Toy and Marble Warehouse, No. 6, Great St. Andrew-street, was the acknowledged and established printer of street literature for the "Dials" district; therefore, as may be easily imagined, a powerful rivalry and vindictive jealousy soon arose between these "two of a trade"—most especially on the part of "Old Mother" Pitts, who is described as being a coarse and vulgar-minded personage, and as having originally followed the trade of a bumboat woman at Portsmouth: she "wowed wengeance" against the young fellow in the court for daring to set up in their business, and also spoke of him as a young "Catsnatch," "Catblock," "Cut-throat;" many other opprobrious terms being also freely given to the new comer. Pitts' staff of "bards" were duly cautioned of the consequences which would inevitably follow should they dare to write a line for Catnach—the new *cove* in the court. The injunction was for a time obeyed, but the "Seven Bards of the Seven Dials" soon found it not

* Pitts, a modern publisher of love garlands, merriments, penny ballads, &c.

"Who, ere he went to heaven,
Domiciled in Dials Seven!"

George Daniel's, "*Democritus in London*."

only convenient, but also more profitable to sell copies oı their effusions to both sides at the same time, and by keeping their council they avoided detection, as each printer accused the other of buying an early sold copy, and then reprinting it off with the utmost speed, and which was in reality often the case, as "Both Houses" had emissaries on the constant look-out for any new production suitable for street-sale. Now, although this style of "double dealing" and competition tended much to lessen the cost price to the "middle-man," or vendor, the public in this case did not get any of the reduction, as a penny broadside was still a penny, and a quarter-sheet still a halfpenny to them, the "street-patterer" obtaining the whole of the reduction as extra profit.

The feud existing between these rival publishers, who have been somewhat aptly designated as the Colburn and Bentley of the "paper" trade, never abated, but, on the contrary, in creased in acrimony of temper until at last not being content to vilify each other by words alone, they resorted to printing off virulent lampoons, in which Catnach never failed to let the world know that "Old Mother Pitts" had been formerly a bumboat woman, while the Pitts' party announced that—

> "All the boys and girls around,
> Who go out prigging rags and phials,
> Know Jemmy *Catsnatch* ! ! ! well,
> Who lives in a back slum in the Dials.
> He hangs out in Monmouth Court,
> And wears a pair of blue-black breeches,
> Where all the 'Polly Cox's crew' do resort
> To chop their swag for badly printed Dying Speeches."

A mournful and affecting

COPY OF VERSES

on the death of

ANN WILLIAMS,

Who was barbarously and cruelly murdered by her sweetheart, W. JONES, near Wirksworth, in Derbyshire, July, 1823.

William Jones, a young man aged 20, has been fully committed to Derby gaol for the murder of his sweetheart, under circumstances of unheard of barbarity. The poor victim was a servant girl, whom under pretence of marriage he seduced. On her proving with child the villain formed the horrid design of murdering her, and carried his diabolical plan into execution on Monday evening last. The following verses are written upon the occasion, giving a complete detail of this shocking affair ;—

Come all false hearted young men
 And listen to my song,
'Tis of a cruel murder,
 That lately has been done
On the body of a maiden fair
 The truth I will unfold,
The bare relation of this deed
 Will make your blood run cold.
Near Wirksworth town in Derbyshire,
 Ann Williams she did dwell,
In service she long time had lived,
 Till this to her befel.
Her cheeks were like the blushing rose
 All in the month of May,
Which made this wicked young man
 Thus unto her did say :
Nancy, my charming creature,
 You have my heart ensnared,
My love is such I am resolved
 To wed you I declare.
Thus by his false deluding tongue
 Poor Nancy was beguil'd,
And soon to her misfortune,
 By him she proved with child.
Some days ago this damsel fair
 Did write to him with speed,
Such tenderness she did express
 Would make a heart to bleed.
She said, my dearest William,
 I am with child by thee ;
Therefore, my dear, pray let me know
 When you will marry me.
The following day at evening,
 This young man did repair,
Unto the town of Wirksworth,
 To meet his Nancy there.
Saying, Nancy dear, come let us walk,
 Among the flowery fields,
And then the secrets of my heart
 To you I will reveal.
O then this wicked young man
 A knife he did provide,
And all unknown to his true love
 Concealed it by his side.
When to the fatal spot they came,
 These words to her did say :
All on this very night I will
 Your precious life betray.
On bended knees she then did fall,
 In sorrow and despair,
Aloud for mercy she did call,
 Her cries did rend the air ;
With clasped hands and uplift eyes
 She cried, Oh spare my life,
I never more will ask you
 To make me your wedded wife.
O then this wicked young man said,
 No mercy will I show ;
He took the knife all from his side,
 And pierced her body through.
But still she smiling said to him,
 While trembling with fear,
Ah! William, William, spare my life ;
 Think on your baby dear.
Twice more then with the bloody knife
 He ran her body through,
Her throat was cut from ear to ear,
 Most dreadful for to view ;
Her hands and arms and beauteous face
 He cut and mangled sore,
While down upon her milk white breast
 The crimson blood did pour.
He took the shawl from off her neck,
 And round her body tied,
With pebble stones he did it fill,
 Thinking the crime to hide.
O then into the silver stream
 He plunged her straightway,
But with her precious blood was stained,
 Which soon did him betray.
O then this young man taken was,
 And into prison sent,
In ratling chains he is confin'd,
 His crime for to lament,
Until the Assizes do come on
 When trembling he must stand,
Reflecting on the deed he's done ;
 Waiting the dread command.
Now all you thoughtless young men
 A timely warning take ;
Likewise ye fair young maidens,
 For this poor damsel's sake.
And Oh beware of flattering tongues,
 For they'll your ruin prove ;
So may you crown your future day,
 In comfort, joy, and love.

Printed at J. Pitts, Wholesale Toy and Marble Warehouse, 6, Great St. Andrew Street, Seven Dials.

There can be little doubt that Catnach, the great publisher of the Seven Dials, next to children's books, had his mind mostly centred upon the chronicling of doubtful scandals, fabulous duels between ladies of fashion, "cooked" assassinations, and sudden deaths of eminent individuals, apochryphal elopements, real or catch-penny accounts of murders, impossible robberies, delusive suicides, dark deeds and public executions, to which was usually attached the all-important and necessary "Sorrowful Lamentations," or "Copy of Affectionate Verses," which, according to the established custom, the criminal composed in the condemned cell the night before his execution, after this manner:—

> "All you that have got feeling hearts, I pray you now attend
> To these few lines so sad and true, a solemn silence lend;
> It is of a cruel murder, to you I will unfold——
> The bare recital of the tale must make your blood run cold."

Or take another and stereotyped example, which from time to time has served equally well for the verses *written by* the culprit—Brown, Jones, Robinson, or Smith:

> "Those deeds I mournfully repent,
> But now it is too late,
> The day is past, the die is cast,
> And fixed is my fate.

Occasionally the Last Sorrowful Lamentations contained a "Love Letter"—the criminal being unable, in some instances, to read or write, being no obstacle to the composition—written according to the street patterer's statement: "from the depths of the condemned cell, with the condemned pen, ink, and paper."

This mode of procedure in "gallows" literature, and this style of composition having prevailed for from sixty to seventy years.

Then they would say: "Here you have also an exact likeness of the murderer, taken at the bar of the Old Bailey by an eminent artist!" when all the time it was an old woodcut that had been used for every criminal for many years.

"There's nothing beats a stunning good murder after all," said a "running patterer" to Mr. Henry Mayhew, the author of "London Labour and London Poor." It is only fair to assume that Mr. James Catnach shared in the sentiment, for it is said that he made over £500 by the publication of:—

"The Full, True and Particular Account of the Murder of Mr. Weare by John Thurtell and his Companions, which took place on the 24th of October, 1823, in Gill's Hill-lane, near Elstree, in Hertfordshire:—Only One Penny." There were eight formes set up, for old Jemmy had no notion of stereotyping in those days, and pressmen had to re-cover their own sheep-skins. But by working night and day for a week they managed to get off about 250,000 copies with the four presses, each working two formes at a time.

As the trial progressed, and the case became more fully developed, the public mind became almost insatiable. Every night and morning large bundles were despatched to the principal towns in the three kingdoms.

One of the many street-ballads on the subject informed the British public that:—

> "Thurtell, Hunt, and Probert, too, for trial must now prepare,
> For that horrid murder of Mr. William Weare."

THURTELL MURDERING MR. WEARE.

In connection with the murder of Mr. Weare by Thurtell and Co., Sir Walter Scott, collected the printed trials with great assiduity, and took care always to have to hand the contemporary ballads and prints bound up with them. He admired particularly this verse of Theodore Hook's* broadside :—

"They cut his throat from ear to ear,
His brains they battered in ;
His name was Mr. William Weare,
He dwelt in Lyon's Inn."

* Lockhart's "Life of Sir Walter Scott."

THE CONFESSION AND EXECUTION OF JOHN THURTELL AT HERTFORD GAOL,

On Friday, the 9th of January, 1824.

THE EXECUTION.

Hertford, half-past twelve o'clock.

This morning, at ten minutes before twelve, a bustle among the javelin-men stationed within the boarded enclosure on which the drop was erected, announced to the multitude without that the preparations for the execution were nearly concluded. The javelin-men proceeded to arrange themselves in the order usually observed upon these melancholy but necessary occurrences. They had scarcely finished their arrangements, when the opening of the gate of the prison gave an additional impulse to public anxiety

When the clock was on the stroke of twelve, Mr Nicholson, the Under-Sheriff, and the executioner ascended the platform, followed on to it by Thurtell, who mounted the stairs with a slow but steady step. The principal turnkey of the gaol came next, and was followed by Mr Wilson and two officers. On the approach of the prisoner being intimated by those persons who, being in an elevated situation, obtained the first view of him, all the immense multitude present took off their hats.

Thurtell immediately placed himself under the fatal beam, and at that moment the chimes of a neighbouring clock began to strike twelve. The executioner then came forward with the rope, which he threw across it. Thurtell first lifted his eyes up to the drop, gazed at it for a few moments, and then took a calm but hurried survey of the multitude around him. He next fixed his eyes on a young gentleman in the crowd, whom he had frequently seen as a spectator at the commencement of the proceedings against him. Seeing that the individual was affected by the circumstance, he removed them to another quarter, and in so doing recognised an individual well known in the sporting circles, to whom he made a slight bow.

The prisoner was attired in a dark brown great coat, with a black velvet collar, white corduroy breeches, drab gaiters and shoes. His hands were confined with handcuffs, instead of being tied with cord, as is usually the case on such occasions, and, at his own request, his arms were not pinioned. He wore a pair of black kid gloves, and the wrists of his shirt were visible below the cuffs of his coat. As on the last day of his trial, he wore a white cravat. The irons, which were very heavy, and consisted of a succession of chain links, were still on his legs, and were held up in the middle by a Belcher handkerchief tied round his waist.

The executioner commenced his mournful duties by taking from the unhappy prisoner his cravat and collar. To obviate all difficulty in this stage of the proceedings, Thurtell flung back his head and neck, and so gave the executioner an opportunity of immediately divesting him of that part of his dress. After tying the rope round Thurtell's neck, the executioner drew a white cotton cap over his countenance, which did not, however, conceal the contour of his face, or deprive him entirely of the view of surrounding objects.

At that moment the clock sounded the last stroke of twelve. During the whole of this appalling ceremony, there was not the slightest symptom of emotion discernible in his features; his demeanour was perfectly calm and tranquil, and he behaved like a man acquainted with the dreadful ordeal he was about to pass, but not unprepared to meet it. Though his fortitude was thus conspicuous, it was evident from his appearance that in the interval between his conviction and his execution he must have suffered much. He looked careworn; his countenance had assumed a cadaverous hue, and there was a haggardness and lankness about his cheeks and mouth, which could not fail to attract the notice of every spectator.

The executioner next proceeded to adjust the noose by which Thurtell was to be attached to the scaffold. After he had fastened it in such a manner as to satisfy his own mind, Thurtell looked up at it, and examined it with great attention. He then desired the executioner to let him have fall enough. The rope at this moment seemed as if it would only give a fall of two or three feet. The executioner assured him that the fall was quite sufficient. The principal turnkey then went up to Thurtell, shook hands with him, and turned away in tears. Mr Wilson, the governor of the gaol, next approached him. Thurtell said to him, "Do you think, Mr Wilson, I have got enough fall?" Mr Wilson replied, "I think you have, Sir. Yes, quite enough." Mr Wilson then took hold of his hand, shook it, and said, "Good bye, Mr Thurtell, may God Almighty bless you." Thurtell instantly replied, "God bless *you*, Mr Wilson, God bless *you*." Mr Wilson next asked him whether he considered that the laws of his country had been dealt to him justly and fairly, upon which he said, "I admit that justice has been done me—I am perfectly satisfied."

A few seconds then elapsed, during which every person seemed to be engaged in examining narrowly Thurtell's deportment. His features, as well as they could be discerned, appeared to remain unmoved, and his hands, which were extremely prominent, continued perfectly steady, and were not affected by the slightest tremulous motion.

Exactly at two minutes past twelve the Under-Sheriff, with his wand, gave the dreadful signal—the drop suddenly and silently fell—and

JOHN THURTELL WAS LAUNCHED INTO ETERNITY.

Printed at J. Pitts, Wholesale Toy and Marble Warehouse, 6, Great St. Andrew Street, Seven Dials.

ATROCIOUS MURDER OF A YOUNG WOMAN IN SUFFOLK.

SINGULAR DISCOVERY OF THE BODY FROM A DREAM.

THE RED BARN.

THE SCENE OF THE MURDER, AND WHERE THE BODY OF MARIA MARTEN WAS FOUND CONCEALED.

Four years after the Thurtell and Weare affair, namely, in the month of April, 1828, another "sensational" murder was discovered—that of Maria Marten, by William Corder, in the Red Barn, at Polstead, in the county of Suffolk. The circumstances that led to the discovery of this most atrocious murder were of an extraordinary and romantic nature, and manifest an almost special interposition of Providence in marking out the offender. As the mother of the girl had on three several nights dreamt that her daughter was murdered and buried in Corder's Red Barn, and as this proved to be the case, an additional "charm" was given to the circumstance. Hence the "Catnach Press" was again set working both day and night to meet the great demand for the "Full Particulars." In due course came the gratifying announcement of the apprehension of the murderer! and the sale continued unabatingly, in both town and country, every "Flying Stationer" making great profits by the sale.

LIKENESS OF WILLIAM CORDER.

The trial of Corder took place at Bury St. Edmonds, on the 7th of August, 1828, before the Lord Chief Baron (Anderson), The prisoner pleaded "*Not Guilty*," and the trial proceeded. On being called on for his defence, Corder read a manuscript paper. He declared that he deeply deplored the death of the unfortunate deceased, and he urged the jury to dismiss from their minds all that prejudice which must necessarily have been excited against him by the public press, &c. Having concluded his address, the Lord Chief Baron summed up, and a verdict of "*Guilty*" was returned. The Last Dying Speech and confession had an enormous sale—estimated at 1,166,000, a *fac-simile* copy of which, with the "Lamentable Verses," said to have been written by Old Jemmy Catnach, will be found on the opposite page.

CONFESSION AND EXECUTION OF WILLIAM CORDER, THE MURDERER OF MARIA MARTEN.

Since the tragical affair between Thurtell and Weare, no event has occurred connected with the criminal annals of our country which has excited so much interest as the trial of Corder, who was justly convicted of the murder of Maria Marten on Friday last.

THE CONFESSION.

"Bury Gaol, August 10th, 1828.—Condemned cell.
"Sunday evening, half-past Eleven.

"I acknowledge being guilty of the death of poor Maria Marten, by shooting her with a pistol. The particulars are as follows:—When we left her father's house, we began quarrelling about the burial of the child: she apprehended the place wherein it was deposited would be found out. The quarrel continued about three quarters of an hour upon this sad and about other subjects. A scuffle ensued, and during the scuffle, and at the time I think that she had hold of me, I took the pistol from the side pocket of my velveteen jacket and fired. She fell, and died in an instant. I never saw her even struggle. I was overwhelmed with agitation and dismay:—the body fell near the front doors on the floor of the barn. A vast quantity of blood issued from the wound, and ran on to the floor and through the crevices. Having determined to bury the body in the barn (about two hours after she was dead. I went and borrowed a spade of Mrs Stow, but before I went there I dragged the body from the barn into the chaff-house, and locked the barn. I returned again to the barn, and began to dig a hole, but the spade being a bad one, and the earth firm and hard, I was obliged to go home for a pickaxe and a better spade, with which I dug the hole, and then buried the body. I think I dragged the body by the handkerchief that was tied round her neck. It was dark when I finished covering up the body. I went the next day, and washed the blood from off the barn-floor. I declare to Almighty God I had no sharp instrument about me, and no other wound but the one made by the pistol was inflicted by me. I have been guilty of great idleness, and at times led a dissolute life, but I hope through the mercy of God to be forgiven. WILLIAM CORDER."

Witness to the signing by the said William Corder,
JOHN ORRIDGE.

Condemned cell, Eleven o'clock, Monday morning, August 11th, 1828.

The above confession was read over carefully to the prisoner in our presence, who stated most solemnly it was true, and that he had nothing to add to or retract from it.—W. STOCKING, chaplain; TIMOTHY R. HOLMES, Under-Sheriff.

THE EXECUTION.

At ten minutes before twelve o'clock the prisoner was brought from his cell and pinioned by the hangman, who was brought from London for the purpose. He appeared resigned, but was so weak as to be unable to stand without support; when his cravat was removed he groaned heavily, and appeared to be labouring under great mental agony. When his wrists and arms were made fast, he was led round twards the scaffold, and as he passed the different yards in which the prisoners were confined, he shook hands with them, and speaking to two of them by name, he said, "Good bye, God bless you." They appeared considerably affected by the wretched appearance which he made, and "God bless you!" "May God receive your soul!" were frequently uttered as he passed along. The chaplain walked before the prisoner, reading the usual Burial Service, and the Governor and Officers walking immediately after him. The prisoner was supported to the steps which led to the scaffold; he looked somewhat wildly around, and a constable was obliged to support him while the hangman was adjusting the fatal cord. There was a barrier to keep off the crowd, amounting to upwards of 7,000 persons, who at this time had stationed themselves in the adjoining fields, on the hedges, the tops of houses, and at every point from which a view of the execution could be best obtained. The prisoner, a few moments before the drop fell, groaned heavily, and would have fallen, had not a second constable caught hold of him. Everything having been made ready, the signal was given, the fatal drop fell, and the unfortunate man was launched into eternity. Just before he was turned off, he said in a feeble tone, "I am justly sentenced, and may God forgive me"

The Murder of Maria Marten.

BY W. CORDER.

COME all you thoughtless young men, a warning take by me,
And think upon my unhappy fate to be hanged upon a tree;
My name is William Corder, to you I do declare,
I courted Maria Marten, most beautiful and fair.

I promised I would marry her upon a certain day,
Instead of that, I was resolved to take her life away.
I went into her father's house the 18th day of May,
Saying, my dear Maria, we will fix the wedding day.

If you will meet me at the Red-barn, as sure as I have life,
I will take you to Ipswich town, and there make you my wife;
I then went home and fetched my gun, my pickaxe and my spade,
I went into the Red-barn, and there I dug her grave.

With heart so light, she thought no harm, to meet him she did go
He murdered her all in the barn, and laid her body low;
After the horrible deed was done, she lay weltering in her gore,
Her bleeding mangled body he buried beneath the Red-barn floor.

Now all things being silent, her spirit could not rest,
She appeared unto her mother, who suckled her at her breast,
For many a long month or more, her mind being sore oppress'd,
Neither night or day she could not take any rest.

Her mother's mind being so disturbed, she dreamt three nights o'er,
Her daughter she lay murdered beneath the Red-barn floor;
She sent the father to the barn, when he the ground did thrust,
And there he found his daughter mingling with the dust.

My trial is hard, I could not stand, most woeful was the sight,
When her jaw-bone was brought to prove, which pierced my heart quite;
Her aged father standing by, likewise his loving wife,
And in her grief her hair she tore, she scarcely could keep life.

Adieu, adieu, my loving friends, my glass is almost run,
On Monday next will be my last, when I am to be hang'd,
So you, young men, who do pass by, with pity look on me,
For murdering Maria Marten, I was hang'd upon the tree.

Printed by J. Catnach, 2 and 3, Monmouth Court.—Cards, &c., Printed Cheap.

LIFE, TRIAL, CONFESSION, & EXECUTION

OF

JAMES GREENACRE,

FOR THE

EDGEWARE ROAD MURDER.

On the 22nd of April, James Greenacre was found guilty of the wilful murder of Hannah Brown, and Sarah Gale with being accessary after the fact. A long and connected chain of evidence was produced, which showed, that the sack in which the body was found was the property of Mr. Ward; that it was usually deposited in a part of the premises which led to the workshop, and could without observation have been carried away by him; that the said sack contained several fragments of shavings of mahogany, such as were made in the course of business by Ward; and that it contained some pieces of linen cloth, which had been patched with nankeen; that this linen cloth matched exactly with a frock which was found on Greenacre's premises, and which belonged to the female prisoner. Feltham, a police-officer, deposed, that on the 26th of March he apprehended the prisoners at the lodgings of Greenacre; that on searching the trowsers pockets of that person, he took therefrom a pawnbroker's duplicate for two silk gowns, and from the fingers of the female prisoner two rings, and also a similar duplicate for two veils, and an old-fashioned silver watch, which she was endeavouring to conceal; and it was further proved that these articles were pledged by the prisoners, and that they had been the property of the deceased woman.—Two surgeons were examined, whose evidence was most important, and whose depositions were of the greatest consequence in throwing a clear light on the manner in which the female, Hannah Brown, met with her death. Mr. Birtwhistle deposed, that he had carefully examined the head; that the right eye had been knocked out by a blow inflicted while the person was living; there was also a cut on the cheek, and the jaw was fractured, these two last wounds were, in his opinion, produced after death; there was also a bruise on the head, which had occurred after death; the head had been separated by cutting, and the *bone sawed nearly through*, and then broken off; there were the marks of a saw, which fitted with a saw which was found in Greenacre's box. Mr. Girdwood, a surgeon, very minutely and skilfully described the appearances presented on the head, and showed incontestibly, that the head had been severed from the body *while the person was yet alive;* that this was proved by the retraction, or drawing back, of the muscles at the parts where they were separated by the knife, and further, by the blood-vessels being empty; the body was drained of blood. This part of the evidence produced a thrill of horror throughout the court, but Greenacre remained quite unmoved.

After a most impressive and impartial summing up by the learned Judge, the jury retired, and, after the absence of a quarter of an hour, returned into court, and pronounced a verdict of "Guilty" against both the prisoners.

The prisoners heard the verdict without evincing the least emotion, or the slightest change of countenance. After an awful silence of a few minutes, the Lord Chief Justice said they might retire, as they would be remanded until the end of the session.

They were then conducted from the bar, and on going down the steps, the unfortunate female prisoner kissed Greenacre with every mark of tenderness and affection.

The crowd outside the court on this day was even greater than on either of the preceding; and when the result of the trial was made known in the street, a sudden and general shout succeeded, and continued huzzas were heard for several minutes.

THE EXECUTION.

At half past seven the sheriff arrived in his carriage, and in a short time the press-yard was thronged with gentlemen who had been admitted by tickets. The unhappy convict was now led from his cell. When he arrived in the press-yard, his whole appearance pourtrayed the utmost misery and spirit-broken dejection; his countenance haggard, and his whole frame agitated; all that self-possesion and fortitude which he displayed in the early part of his imprisonment, had utterly forsaken him, and had left him a victim of hopelessness and despair. He requested the executioner to give him as little pain as possible in the process of pinioning his arms and wrists; he uttered not a word in allusion to his crime; neither did he make any dying request, except that his spectacles might be given to Sarah Gale; he exhibited no sign of hope; he showed no symptom of reconciliation with his offended God! When the venerable ordinary preceded him in the solemn procession through the vaulted passage to the fatal drop, he was so overcome and unmanned, that he could not support himself without the aid of the assistant executioner. At the moment he ascended the faithless floor, from which he was to be launched into eternity, the most terrific yells, groans, and cheers were vociferated by the immense multitude surrounding the place of execution. Greenacre bowed to the sheriff, and begged he might not be allowed to remain long in the concourse; and almost immediately the fatal bolt was withdrawn, and, without a struggle, he became a lifeless corse.—Thus ended the days of Greenacre, a man endowed with more than ordinary talents, respectably connected, and desirably placed in society; but a want of probity, an absolute dearth of principle, led him on from one crime to another, until at length he perpetrated the sanguinary deed which brought his career to an awful and disgraceful period, and which has enrolled his name among the most notorious of those who have expiated their crime on the gallows.

On hearing the death-bell toll, Gale became dreadfully agitated; and when she heard the brutal shouts of the crowd of spectators, she fainted, and remained in a state of alternate mental agony and insensibility throughout the whole day.

After having been suspended the usual time, his body was cut down, and buried in a hole dug in one of the passages of the prison, near the spot where Thistlewood and his associates were deposited.

J. Catnach, Printer, 2 and 3, Monmouth Court.

The following is a fac-simile of the "Execution Paper," from the press of Paul and Co.,—successors of Catnach.

TRIAL, SENTENCE, CONFESSION, & EXECUTION

OF

F. B. COURVOISIER,

FOR THE

Murder of Lord Wm. Russell.

THE VERDICT.

OLD BAILEY, SATURDAY EVENING,
June 20*th*, 1840.

After the jury had been absent for an hour and twenty minutes, they returned into court, and the prisoner was again placed at the bar

The names of the jury were then called over, and the clerk of the court said—"How say you, gentlemen, have you agreed on your verdict? Do you find the prisoner Guilty or Not Guilty of the felony of murder with which he stands charged?"

The foreman of the jury, in a low voice, said—"We find him GUILTY!"

The Clerk of the Court then said· François Benjamin Courvoisier, you have been found Guilty of the wilful murder of William Russell, Esq., commonly called Lord William Russell; what have you to say why the court should not give you sentence to die according to law?

The prisoner made no reply. The usual proclamation for silence was then made.

SENTENCE.

The LORD CHIEF JUSTICE TINDAL, having put on the black cap, said: François Benjamin Courvoisier, you have been found guilty by an intelligent, patient, and impartial jury of the crime of wilful murder. That crime has been established against you, not indeed by the testimony of eye-witnesses as to the fact, but by a chain of circumstances no less unerring, which have left no doubt of your guilt in the minds of the jury, and all those who heard the trial. It is ordained by divine authority that the murderer shall not escape justice, and this ordination has been exemplified in your case, in the course of this trial, by the disclosure of evidence which has brought the facts to bear against you in a conclusive manner. The murder, although committed in the dark and silent hour of night, has nevertheless been brought clearly to light by Divine interposition. The precise motive which induced you to commit this guilty act can only be known to your own conscience; but it now only remains for me to recommend you most earnestly to employ the short time you have to live in prayer and repentance, and in endeavouring to make your peace with that Almighty Being whose law you have broken, and before whom you must shortly appear. The Learned Judge then passed sentence on the prisoner in the usual form.

The court was very much crowded to the last.

THE CONFESSION OF THE CONVICT.

After the Learned Judge had passed sentence on the convict, he was removed from the bar, and immediately made a full confession of his guilt.

THE EXECUTION.

At eight o'clock this morning, Courvoisier ascended the steps leading to the gallows, and advanced, without looking round him, to the centre of the platform, followed by the executioner and the ordinary of the prison, the Rev. Mr Carver. On his appearance a few yells of execration escaped from a portion of the crowd; but the general body of the people, great as must have been their abhorrence of his atrocious crime, remained silent spectators of the scene which was passing before their eyes. The prisoner's manner was marked by an extraordinary appearance of firmness. His step was steady and collected, and his movements free from the slightest agitation or indecision. His countenance indeed was pale, and bore the trace of much dejection, but it was at the same time calm and unmoved. While the executioner was placing him on the drop he slightly moved his hands (which were tied in front of him, and strongly clasped one within the other) up and down two or three times; and this was the only visible symptom of any emotion or mental anguish which the wretched man endured. His face was then covered with the cap, fitting so closely as not to conceal the outlines of his countenance, the noose was then adjusted. During this operation he lifted up his head and raised his hands to his breast, as if in the action of fervent prayer. In a moment the fatal bolt was withdrawn, the drop fell, and in this attitude the murderer perished. He died without any violent struggle In two minutes after he had fallen his legs were twice slightly convulsed, but no further motion was observable, excepting that his raised arms, gradually losing their vitality, sank down from their own lifeless weight.

After hanging one hour, the body was cut down and removed within the prison.

AFFECTING COPY OF VERSES.

Attention give, both old and young,
  Of high and low degree,
Think while this mournful tale is sung,
  Of my sad misery.
I've slain a master good and kind,
  To me has been a friend,
For which I must my life resign,
  My time is near an end.

Oh hark! what means that dreadful sound?
  It sinks deep in my soul;
It is the bell that sounds my knell,
  How solemn is the toll.
See thousands are assembled
  Around the fatal place,
To gaze on my approaching,
  And witness my disgrace.

There many sympathising hearts,
  Who feel another's woe,
Even now appears in sorrow,
  For my sad overthrow.
Think of the aged man I slew,
  Then pity's at an end,
I robb'd him of property and life,
  And the poor man of a friend.

Let pilfering passions not intrude,
  For to lead you astray,
From step to step it will delude,
  And bring you to dismay.
Think of the wretched Courvoisier,
  Who thus dies on a tree,
A death of shame, I've nought to blame,
  But my own dishonesty.

Mercy on earth I'll not implore,
  To crave it would be vain,
My hands are dyed with human gore,
  None can wash off the stain,
But the merits of a Saviour,
  Whose mercy alone I crave;
Good Christians pray, as thus I die,
  I may his pardon have.

PAUL & Co., Printers, 2, 3, Monmouth, Court, Seven Dials.

But the gallows was not always a fruit-bearing tree, and a "stunning good murder" did not happen every day. Nevertheless the street patterer must live, and lest the increase of public virtue should condemn him to starvation, the "Seven Dials Press," stepped forward to his aid, and considerately supplied him with a species of street-literature well known to the trade as "Cocks," and which are defined in "Hotton's Slang Dictionary" thus:—

COCKS, fictitious narratives, in verse or prose, of murders, fires and terrible accidents, sold in the streets as true accounts. The man who hawks them, a patterer, often changes the scene of the awful event to suit the taste of the neighbourhood he is trying to delude. Possibly a corruption of *cook*—a cooked statement, or may be "the story of a cock and bull" may have had something to do with the term. Improvements in newspapers, especially in those published in the evening, and increased scepticism on the part of the public have destroyed this branch of a once-flourishing business.

The late Mr. Albert Smith, the humourist and novelist, has very happily hit off this style of thing in "The Man in the Moon," one of the many rivals to "Punch," and edited by that very promising son of genius, the late Angus B. Reach, 1832-56. It is entitled—

A COPY OF VERSES

Found among the Papers of Mr. Catnach, the spirited Publisher of Seven Dials; originally intended to have been "printed and published at the Toy and Marble Warehouse, 2 and 3, Monmouth Court, Seven Dials."

DEDICATED TO THE AUTHOR OF "LUCRETIA."

I.

The Hero claims the attention of virtuous persons, and leads them to anticipate a painful disclosure.

Draw hither now good people all
And let my story warn,
For I will tell to you a tale,
What will wrend them breasts of yourn.

II.

He nxmes the place and hour of the disgraceful penalty he is about to undergo.

I am condemn'd all for to die
  A death of scorn and horror;
In front of Horsemonger-lane Gaol,
  At eight o'clock to-morrer.

III.

He hints at his atrocity; and the ebullition produced by the mere recollection of it.

The crime of which I was found guilty,
  Oh! it was shocking vile;
The very thoughts of the cruel deed
  Now makes my blood to bile.

IV.

He speaks of the happy hours of Childhood, never more to return.

In Somersetshire I was born'd,
  And my little sister dear
Didn't think then that my sad end
  Would be like unto this here.

V.

The revelation of his name and profession; and subsequent avowal of his guilt.

James Guffin is my hated name,
  And a footman I'm by trade;
And I do confess that I did slay
  My poor fellow-servant maid.

VI.

He acknowledges the justice of his sentence.

And well I do deseve, I own,
  My fate which is so bitter:
For 'twas most wicked for to kill
  So innicent a critter.

VII.

And pictures what might have taken place but for the interference of Destiny.

Her maiden name was Sarey Leigh,
  And was to have been Guffin;
For we was to have been marri-ed,
  But Fate brought that to nuffin.

VIII.

He is particular as to the date of the occurrence.

All on a Wednesday afternoon,
On the ninth of Janivary,
Eighteen hundred and forty-four,
Oh! I did kill my Sarey.

IX.

Ana narrates the means employed, and the circumstances which led him to destroy his betrothed.

With arsenic her I did destroy,
How could I be so vicious!
But of my young master I was jealous,
And so was my old Missus.

X.

He is led away by bad passions.

I thought Sarey Leigh warn't true to me,
So all pity then despising,
Sure I was tempted by the Devil
To give to her some p'ison.

XI.

His bosom is torn by conflicting resolutions; but he is at last decided.

Long—long I brooded on the deed,
'Til one morning of a sudden,
I did determine for to put
It in a beef-steak puddin.

XII.

The victim falls into the snare.

Of the fatal pudding she did partake,
Most fearful for to see,
And an hour arter was to it a martyr,
Launch'd into eternity.

XIII.

He feels that his perception comes too late.

Ah! had I then but viewed things in
The light that I now does 'em,
I never should have know'd the grief
As burns in this here buzum.

XIV.

He commits his secret to the earth.

So when I seed what I had done,
In hopes of justice retarding,
I took and buried poor Sarey Leigh
Out in the kitching garding.

XV.

But the earth refuses to keep it.

But it did haunt me, so I felt
As of a load deliver'd,
When three weeks after the fatal deed,
The body was diskiver'd.

XVI.

Remorse and self examination.

O! why did I form of Sarey Leigh
Such cruel unjust opinions,
When my young master did her find
Beneath the bed of inions.

XVII.

His countrymen form a just estimate of his delinquency.

Afore twelve jurymen I was tried,
And condemned the perpetrator
Of this here awful Tragedy,
As shocks one's human natur.

XVIII.

He conjures up a painful image.

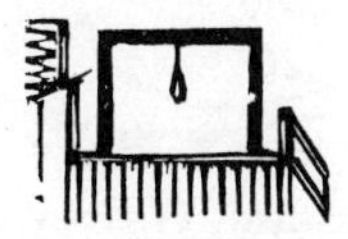

But the bell is tolling for my end ;
How shocking for to see
A footman gay, in the prime of life,
Die on the fatal tree.

XIX.

His last words convey a moral lesson.

THE MORAL ! ! !

Take warning, then, all ye as would
Not die like malefactors ;
Never the company for to keep
Of them with bad characters.

LITTLE Boys and Girls will find
At CATNACH's something to their mind;
From great variety may choose,
What will instruct them and amuse.
The prettiest plates that you can find,
To please at once the eye and mind.

One class of literature which the late Jemmy Catnach made almost his own, was children's farthing and halfpenny books. Among the great many that he published we select, from our own private collection, the following as a fair sample:—"The Tragical Death of an Apple Pie," "The House that Jack Built," "Jumping Joan," "The Butterflies Ball and Grasshoppers' Feast," "Jerry Diddle and his Fiddle," "Nurse Love-Child's Gift," "The Death and Burial of Cock Robin," "The Cries of London," "Simple Simon," "Jacky Jingle and Suky Shingle," and—"Here you have just prin—ted and pub—lish—ed, and a—dor—ned with eight beau—ti—ful and ele—gantly engraved embellish—ments, and for the low charge of one *farden*—Yes! one *farden* buys."

NURSERY RHYMES.

See-saw, sacradown,
Which is the way to London town?
One foot up, and the other down,
And that is the way to London town.

Hey diddle, the cat and the fiddle,
The cow jumped over the moon,
The little dog laughed to see the sport,
And the dish ran away with the spoon.

Ding, dong bell!
Pussy's in the well.
Who put her in?
Little Johnny Green.
Who pulled her out?
Little Johnny Snout.
What a naughty boy was that,
To drown poor pussy cat,
Who never did him any harm,
And kill'd the mice in his father's barn.

Jack and Jill went up the hill,
To get a pail of water;
Jack fell down and broke his crown,
And Jill came tumbling after.

Cock a doodle do,
The dame has lost her shoe,
And master's lost his fiddle stick
And don't know what to do.

I had a little husband,
No bigger than my thumb,
I put him in a quart pot,
And there I bid him drum.

Who's there? A Grenadier!
What do you want? A pot of beer.
Where's your money? Oh, I forgot,
Then get you gone, you drunken sot.

Hush-a-bye, baby, on the tree top,
When the wind blows the cradle will rock,
When the bough breaks the cradle will fall,
Down comes the baby, cradle and all.

There was an old woman that lived in a shoe,
She had so many children she knew not what to do;
She gave them some broth without any bread,
Then she beat them all well, and sent them to bed.

My mother and your mother
Went over the way;
Said my mother to your mother,
It's chop-a-nose day!

J. Catnach, Printer, 2, Monmouth Court, 7 Dials.

THE CRIES OF LONDON.

Cherries.

Here's round and sound,
Black and white heart cherries,
Two-pence a pound.

Oranges.

Here's oranges nice,
At a very small price,
I sell them all two for a penny.
Ripe, juicy, and sweet,
Just fit for to eat,
So customers buy a good many,

Milk below.

Rain, frost, or snow, or hot or cold,
I travel up and down,
The cream and milk you buy of me
Is best in all the town.
For custards, puddings, or for tea,
There's none like those you buy of me.

Crumpling Codlings.

Come buy my Crumpling Codlings,
Buy all my Crumplings.
Some of them you may eat raw,
Of the rest make dumplings,
Or pies, or puddings, which you please.

Filberts.

Come buy my filberts ripe and brown,
They are the best in all the town,
I sell them for a groat a pound,
And warrant them all good and sound,
You're welcome for to crack and try,
They are so good, I'm sure you'll buy.

Sweep.

Sweep, chimney sweep,
Is the common cry I keep,
If you rightly understand me;
With my brush, broom, and my rake,
Such cleanly work I make,
There's few can go beyond me.

Clothes Pegs, Props, or Lines.

Come, maids, and buy my pegs and props,
Or lines to dry your clothes,
And when they are dry they'll smell as sweet
As any damask rose.
Come buy and save your clothes from dirt,
They'll save you washing many a shirt.

Peas and Beans.

Four pence a peck, green Hastings!
And fine garden beans.
They are all morning gathered,
Come hither, my queens.
Come buy my Windsor beans and peas,
You'll see no more this year like these.

Young Lambs to Sell.

Get ready your money and come
to me,
I sell a young lamb for a penny.
Young lambs to sell! young lambs
to sell!
If I'd as much money as I could
tell,
I never would cry young lambs to
sell.

Here's your toys for girls and
boys,
Only a penny, or a dirty phial or
bottle.

Strawberries.

Rare ripe strawberries and
Hautboys, sixpence a pottle.
Full to the bottom, hautboys.
Strawberries and Cream are charm-
ing and sweet,
Mix them and try how delightful
they eat.

When Good Friday comes,
The old woman runs
With Hot Cross Buns,
One a penny, Buns,
Two a penny, Buns,
All Hot Buns.

LONDON:
Printed by J. Catnach, 2, Monmouth
Court, 7 Dials.

"Songs! Songs! Songs! Beautiful songs! Love songs; Newest songs! Old songs! Popular songs! Songs, *Three Yards a Penny!*" was a "standing dish" at the "Catnach Press," and Catnach was the Leo X. of street publishers. And it is said that he at one time kept a fiddler on the premises, and that he used to sit receiving ballad writers and singers, and judging of the merits of any production which was brought to him, by having it sung then and there to some popular air played by his own fiddler, and so that the ballad-singer should be enabled to start at once, not only with the new song, but also the tune to which it was adapted. His broad-sheets contain all sorts of songs and ballads, for he had a most catholic taste, and introduced the custom of taking from any writer, living or dead, whatever he fancied, and printing it side by side with the productions of his own clients.

Catnach, towards the latter part of his time and in his threefold capacity of publisher, compositor, and poet, was in the habit of taking things very easy, and always appeared to the best advantage when in his printing office, or stationed behind the ricketty counter which for a number of years had done good service in the shop in Monmouth-court. In this uncongenial atmosphere, where the rays of the sun are seldom or never seen, Jemmy was as happy as a prince. "A poor man's home is his castle," so says an old proverb, and no one could have been prouder than he was when despatching to almost every town in the kingdom some specialty in the printing department. He naturally had a bit of a taste for old ballads, music, and song writing; and in this respect he was far in advance of many of his contemporaries. To bring within the reach of all, the standard and popular works of the day, had been the ambition of the elder Catnach; whilst the son was, *nolens volens*, incessant in his endeavours in trying to promulgate and advance, not the beauty, elegance, and harmony which pervades many of our national airs and ballad poety, but very often the worst and vilest of each and every description—in other words, those most suitable for street sale. His stock of songs was very like his customers, diversified. There were all kinds, to suit all classes. Love, sentimental, and comic songs were so interwoven as to form a trio of no ordinary amount of novelty. At ordinary times, when the Awfuls and Sensationals were flat, Jemmy did a large stroke of business in this line.

It is said that when the "Songs—*Three-yards-a-penny*"—first came out and had all the attractions of novelty, some men sold twelve or fourteen dozen on fine days during three or four of the summer months, so clearing between 6s. and 7s. a day, but on the average about 25s. per week profit. The "long songs," however, have been quite superseded by the "Monster" and "Giant Penny Song Books." Still there are a vast number of halfpenny ballad-sheets worked off, and in proportion to their size, far more than the "Monsters" or "Giants." One song book, entitled the "Little Warbler," was published in parts, and had an enormous sale.

There are invariably but two songs printed on the half-penny ballad-sheets—generally a new and popular song with another older ditty, or a comic and sentimental, and "adorned" with two woodcuts. These are selected without any regard to their fitness to the subject, and in most cases have not the slightest reference to the ballad of which they form the head-piece. For instance:—"The Heart that can feel for another" is illustrated by a gaunt and savage-looking lion; "When I was first Breeched," by an engraving of a Highlander *sans culotte;*

"The Poacher" comes under the cut of a youth with a large watering-pot, tending flowers; "Ben Block" is heralded by the rising sun; "The London Oyster Girl," by Sir Walter Raleigh; "The Sailor's Grave," by the figure of Justice; "Alice Grey" comes under the very dilapidated figure of a sailor, or "Jolly Young Waterman;" "Bright Hours are in store for us yet" is *headed* with a *tail-piece* of an urn, on which is inscribed FINIS. (?) "Watercresses," with the portrait of a Silly Billy; "The Wild Boar Hunt," by two wolves chasing a deer; "The Dying Child to its Mother," by an Angel appearing to an old man; "Crazy Jane," by the Royal Arms of England; "Autumn Leaves lie strew'd around," by a ship in full sail; "Cherry Ripe," by Death's Head and Cross Bones; "Jack at the Windlass," falls under a Roadside Inn; while "William Tell" is presented to the British public in form and style of an old woman nursing an infant of a squally nature. Here are a few examples:—

The Smuggler King.

Let me like a Soldier fall.

Fair Phœbe and her Dark-Eyed Sailor.

My Pretty Jane.

The Thorn.

The Saucy Arethusa.

The Gipsy King.

Hearts of Oak.

Harry Bluff.

Death of Nelson.

John Anderson, my Jo.

Old English Gentleman.

The Bleeding Heart.

Wapping Old Stairs.

Poor Bessy was a Sailor's Bride.

Poor Mary Anne.

The Muleteer.

Tom Bowling.

Ye Banks an' Braes.

The Mistletoe Bough.

The Woodpecker.

The Soldier's Tear.

LONG-SONG SELLER.

Besides the chanters, who sing the songs through the streets of every city, town, village, and hamlet in the kingdom—the long-song seller, who shouts their titles on the kerb-stone, and the countless small shop-keepers, who, in swag-shops, toy-shops, sweetstuff-shops, tobacco-shops, and general shops, keep them as part of their stock for the supply of the street boys and the servant girls—there is another important functionary engaged in their distribution, and who is well known to the inhabitants of large towns, this is the pinner-up, who takes his stand against a dead wall or a long range of iron railings, and first festooning it liberally with twine, pins up one or two hundred ballads for public perusal and selection. Time was when this was a thriving trade: and we are old enough to remember the day when a good half-mile of wall fluttered with the minstrelsy of war and love, under the guardianship of a scattered file of pinners-up, along the south side of Oxford-street alone. Thirty years ago the dead walls gave place to shop fronts, and the pinners-up departed to their long homes. As they died out very few succeeded to their honours and emoluments. There is one pinner-up, seemingly the last of his race, who makes his display on the dead wall of the underground railway in Farringdon road.

Catnach, to the day of his retirement from business in 1838, when he purchased the freehold of a disused public-house, which had been known as the Lion Inn, together with the grounds attached at Dancer's-hill, South Mimms, near Barnet, in the county of Middlesex, worked and toiled in the office of the "Seven Dials Press," in which he had moved as the pivot, or directing mind, for upwards of a quarter of a century. He lived and died a bachelor. His only idea of all earthly happiness and mental enjoyment was now to get away in retirement to a convenient distance from his old place of business, so to give him an opportunity occasionally to go up to town and have a chat and a friendly glass with one or two old paper-workers and ballad-writers, and a few others connected with his peculiar trade who had shown any disposition to work when work was to be done. To them he was always willing to give or advance a few pence or shillings, in money or stock, and a glass.

Catnach left the whole of the business to Mrs. Anne Ryle, his sister, charged, nevertheless, to the amount of £1,000, payable at his death to the estate of his niece, Marion Martha Ryle. In the meanwhile Mr. James Paul acted as managing man for Mrs. Ryle. This Mr. Paul—of whom Jemmy was very fond, and rumour saith, had no great dislike to the mother—had grown from a boy to a man in the office of the "Catnach Press." He was, therefore, well acquainted with the customers, by whom he was much respected; and it was by his tact and judgment that the business was kept so well together. At Catnach's death he entered into partnership with Mrs. Ryle, and the business was carried on under the title and style of Paul & Co. In 1845 the partnership was dissolved, Mr. Paul receiving £800 in settlement. He then entered into the public line, taking the Spencer's Arms, at the corner of Monmouth-court. A son that was born to him in 1847, he had christened James Catnach Paul. About this date "The Catnach Press" had a formidable rival in "The Nassau Steam Press," which was originally started in Nassau Street, Soho, and afterwards removed to No. 60, St. Martin's Lane. Mr. Paul was especially engaged to manage the song department at this office. He died in the year 1870, just six weeks after Mrs. Ryle, and lies buried in the next grave but one to Catnach and his sister, in Highgate Cemetery.

After Mr. Paul had left the business it was carried on as A. Ryle & Co., and ultimately became the property of Mr. W. S. Fortey, who still carries on the old business in the same premises. A copy of whose trade announcement runs thus:—

"THE CATNACH PRESS." (Established 1813.)

"William S. Fortey, (late A. Ryle, successor to the late J. Catnach,) Printer, Publisher, and Wholesale Stationer, 2 and 3, Monmouth-court, Seven Dials, London, W.C."

Sir Jeffery Dunstan,

Late Mayor of Garratt, and Itinerant Dealer in Wigs.

Sir Jeffery Dunstan--thrice Mayor of Garratt! was the most popular candidate that ever appeared on the Hustings at that very Free and Independent Borough! His occupation was that of buying old wigs, once an article of trade like that of old clothes. Sir Jeffery usually carried his wig bag over his shoulder, and to avoid the charge of vagrancy, vociferated, as he passed along the street, "Old Wigs," but having a person like Æsop, and a countenance and manner marked by irresistible humour, he never appeared without a train of boys and curious persons, whom he entertained by his sallies of wit, shrewd sayings, and smart repartees; and from whom, without begging, he collected sufficient to help to maintain his dignity of Mayor and Knight.

From the earliest period of Sir Jeffery's life, he was a friend to "good measures," especially those for "spirituous liquors," and he never saw the inside of a pot without going to the bottom of it. This determination of character created difficulties to him; for his freedom was not always regulated by the doctrines of *meum et tuum*, or, of the great Blackstone, "on the rights of persons," and consequences ensued that were occasionally injurious to Sir Jeffery's eyes, face, and nose. The same enlightened Judge's views of "the rights of property," were not comprehended by Sir Jeffery, he had long made free with the porter of manifold pots, and at length he made free with a few of the pots--which the publicans in London seemed to show in the streets as much as to say "Come and steal me." For this he was "questioned" in the high Commission Court of oyer and terminer, and suffered an imprisonment, which, according to his manner of life, and his notions of the liberty of the subject, was "frivolous and vexatious." On his liberation, he returned to an occupation he had long followed, the dealing in "Old Wigs." Some other circumstances, developed in course of the preceding inquiry, seem to favour a supposition that the bag he carried had enabled him to conceal his previous "free trade" in pewter pots. But, be that as it might, it is certain that in his armorial bearings of four wigs, he added a quart pot for a crest.

Sir Jeffery was remarkably dirty in his person, and always had his shirt thrown open, which exposed his breast to public view. This was in him a sort of pride; for he would frequently in an exulting manner say to *inferiors* "I've got a *collar* to my shirt, sir." He had a filthy habit, when he saw a number of girls around him, of spitting in their faces, saying, "There, go about your business."

Sir Jeffery, in the days of his prosperity, took his "Hodges' best," at the "Blind Beggar of Bethnal-green," or the "Horse and Leaping Bar," High-street, Whitechapel, at one or other of these favourite retreats, he got in a regular manner "regularly drunk." Then it was that he sung in his best style various popular "London Cries," mimicking others in their crying, especially one who vended "*Lily, lily, lily, lily white —sand oh! oh!! oh!!!*" this afforded sport to a merry company. Afterwards, should Sir Jeffery receive sufficient metalic support from his friends, he was placed in an arm chair on the table, when he recited to the students of the London Hospital and the Bucks of the East, his mock-election speeches. He was no respecter of persons, and was so severe in his jokes on the corruptions and compromises of power, that he was prosecuted for using what were then called seditious expressions. In consequence of this affair, and some few charges of dishonesty, he lost his popularity, and, at the next general election was ousted by Sir Harry Dimsdale, muffin-seller, a man as much deformed as himself. Sir Jeffery could not long survive his fall, but, in death as in life, he proved a satire on the vices of the proud, for he died, like Alexander the Great, the sailor in Lord Byron's "Don Juan," and many other heroes renowned in history—of suffocation from excessive drinking!.

SIR HARRY DIMSDALE, M.P., FOR GARRATT,
COSMOPOLITE AND MUFFIN-SELLER.

"Those evening bells! those evening bells!
How many a tale their music tells!
Of youth, and home, and that sweet time
When last I heard their soothing chime."

"Muffins, oh! Crumpets, oh," rank among the old cries of London, and at least one of the calling has been made famous, namely, Harry Dimsdale, sometime Mayor of Garratt, who, from the moment he stood as candidate, received mock knighthood, and was ever after known under the appellation of "Sir Harry." This half-witted character was a dealer in tin-ware—together with threads, tapes and bootlaces, during the morning, and a muffin-seller in the afternoon, when he had a little bell, which he held to his ear, and smiling ironically at its tinkling he would cry:—"*Muffins! muffins! ladies come buy me! pretty, handsome, blooming, smiling maids!*"

Mr. J. T. Smith, in his ever-charming work of "A Book for a Rainy Day; or, Recollections of the Events of the Years

1766—1833," writing under date 1787, gives the following graphic sketch of the sayings and doings—taken from life, of "Sir Harry."

"One of the curious scenes I witnessed on a nocturnal visit to the watch house of St. Anne, Soho, afforded me no small amusement. Sir Harry Dinsdale, usually called Dimsdale, a short, feeble little man, was brought in, charged by two colossal guardians of the night with conduct most unruly. 'What have you, Sir Harry, to say to all this?' asked the Dogberry of St. Anne. The knight, who had been roughly handled, commenced like a true orator, in a low tone of voice. 'May it please ye, my magistrate, I am not drunk; it is *languor*. A parcel of the Bloods of the Garden have treated me cruelly, because I would not treat them. This day, sir, I was sent for by Mr. Sheridan, to make a speech upon the table at the Shakespeare Tavern, in *Common* Garden; he wrote the speech for me, and always gives half a guinea; he sends for me to the tavern. You see I didn't go in my Royal robes, I only put 'um on when I stand to be a member.' The constable—'Well, but Sir Harry, why are you brought here?' One of the watchmen then observed, 'That though Sir Harry was but a little *shambling* fellow, he was so *upstroppolus*, and kicked him about at such a rate, that it was as much as he and his comrade could do to bring him along.' As there was no one to support the charge, Sir Harry was advised to go home, which, however, he swore he would not do at midnight without an escort. 'Do you know,' said he, 'there's a parcel of *raps* now on the outside waiting for me.'

"The constable of the night gave orders for him to be protected to the public-house opposite the west end of St. Giles's Church, where he then lodged. Sir Harry, hearing a noise in the street, muttered, 'I shall catch it; I know I shall.' *(Cries without,)* 'See the conquering hero comes.' 'Ay, they always use that tune when I gain my election at Garratt.'

"There are several portraits of this singular little object, by some called 'Honey-juice.' Flaxman, the sculptor, and Mrs. Mathews, of blue-stocking memory, equipped him as a hardware man, and as such I made two etchings of him."

The Muffin Man.

(T. Dibden.)

While you opera-squallers fine verses are singing,
Of heroes, and poets, and such like humguffins;
While the world's running round, like a mill in a sail,
I'll ne'er bother my head with what other folks ail,
But careless and frisky, my bell I keep ringing,
And walk about merrily crying my muffins.

Chorus.

Lily-white muffins, O, rare crumpets smoking,
Hot Yorkshire cakes, hot loaves and charming cakes,
One-a-penny, two-a-penny, Yorkshire cakes.

What matters to me if great folks run a gadding,
For politics, fashions, or such botheration;
Let them drink as they brew, while I merrily bake;
For though I sell muffins, I'm not such a cake—
To let other fools' fancies e'er set me a gadding,
Or burthen my thoughts with the cares of the nation.

Spoken.—What have I to do with politicians? And for your *Parliament cakes.* Why! everybody knows they are *bought* and *sold*, and often *done brown*, and made *crusty* all over the nation. No, no, its enough for me to cry—

Lily-white muffins, &c.

Let soldiers and sailors, contending for glory,
Delight in the rattle of drums and of trumpets;
Undertakers get living by other folks dying,
While actors make money by laughing or crying;
Let lawyers with quizzels and quiddities bore ye,
It's nothing to me, while I'm crying my crumpets.

Spoken.—What do I care for lawyers? A'nt I a baker, and consequently, Master of the Rolls: Droll enough, too, for a Master of the Rolls to be crying—

Lily-white muffins, &c.

THE MUFFIN MAN.

"Muffins, oh! crumpets, oh!
Come buy, come buy of me.
Muffins and crumpets, muffins,
For breakfast or for tea."

The ringing of the muffin-man's bell—attached to which the pleasant associations are not a few—is prohibited by a ponderous Act of Parliament, but the prohibition has been all but inoperative, for the muffin bell still tinkles along the streets, and is rung vigorously in the suburbs, and just at the time when City gents, at winter's eve, are comfortably enveloped in fancy-patterned dressing gowns, prettily-worked smoking-caps, and easy-going and highly-coloured slippers, and saying within themselves or aloud:—

"Now stir the fire, and close the shutters fast,
Let fall the curtains, wheel the sofa round,
And while the bubbling and loud hissing urn
Throws up a steamy column, and the cups,
That cheer but not inebriate, wait on each,
So let us welcome peaceful evening in."

"Hot Cross Buns!" Perhaps no "cry"—though it is only for one day in the year, is more familiar to the ears of a Londoner, than that of "*One-a-penny, two-a penny, hot cross-buns.*" We lie awake early upon Good Friday morning and listen to the London bells:—

> "Oranges and lemons, say the bells of St. Clement's.
> Pancakes and fritters, say the bells of St. Peter's,
> Two sticks and an apple, say the bells of Whitechapel.
> Kettles and pans, say the bells of St. Ann's.
> Pokers and tongs, say the bells of St. John's
> Brickbats and tiles, say the bells of St. Giles'
> Halfpence and farthings, say the bells of St. Martin's.
> Bull's eyes and targets, say the bells of St. Marg'rets."

And all the other London bells having rung—or, rather *toll'd* out their own tale of joy or trouble: then comes—rattling over the stones—W. H. SMITH'S well-known red EXPRESS-CARTS. laden with the early printed newspapers of the coming day, while all night long the carts and waggons come rumbling in from the country to Covent-garden, and not the least pleasant sound—pleasant for its old recollections—is the time-honoured old cry of "Hot Cross-Buns." Century after century passes by, and those who busily drove their carts day after day from Isleworth, Romford, Enfield, Battersea, Blackheath, or Richmond, one hundred years ago, are as still and silent as if they had never been; yet still, Passion week after Passion-week, comes that old cry, nobody knows how old, "Hot Cross Buns, Hot Cross Buns." And as we lie in a half dreamy state we hear and think of the chimes of St. Clement Danes, which may still be heard, as Fallstaff describes, having heard them with Justice Shallow; also, how Pope, as he lay in Holywell-street—now Bookseller's-row; and Addison and Johnson; and, before their time, Waller, at the house of his old friend the merchant of St. Giles's; and the goodly company of poets that lived at the cost of the king, near Whitehall; then of the quaint old gossiping diarist, Samuel Pepys, Secretary of the Admiralty; John Taylor, the *Water-Poet*; even Shakespeare himself, having each in their turn been awakened on the Good Friday morning by the same sound ringing in their ears. For this is a custom which can hardly be traced to a beginning: and all we know about it is, that as far as we can go back, the Good Friday was ushered in by the old Good Friday bun; and that the baker in the towns, and the old good wife in the country, would have thought the day but badly kept, and augured badly for the coming summer's luck, without it.

But between the cakes of Cecrops and the modern Hot Cross Bun there is a wide gulf of 3,400 years; and yet the one may be traced up to the other. There are some, indeed, who would wish to give to the Good Friday Hot Cross Bun a still longer pedigree, and to take it back to the time of the Patriarchs and their consecrated bread; and there are others who would go yet further, and trace it to the earliest age of the world, in a portion of Cain's sacrifice. We may, however, content ourselves with stopping short at the era of the Egyptian Cecrops, founder of Athens, who made his sweet cakes of flour and honey. Such cakes as these, as we learn from the prophet Jeremiah, were offered by the idolatrous Hebrew women to "the Queen of Heaven,"

> "Ashtoreth, whom the Phœnicians called
> Astarte, Queen of Heaven, with cresent horns."

Some can even discern Astarte in our "Easter." The Jews of old had the shew-bread and the wafer of unleavened bread; and the Egyptians, under the Pharaohs, had also their cakes, round, oval, and triangular. The Persians had their sacred cakes of flour and honey; and Herodotus speaks of similar cakes being offered by the Athenians to a sacred serpent in the temple of their citadel. And, not to mention other nations, the circumstance that accompanied the outbreak of the Indian Mutiny, 1857, will make memorable the "chupatties" or sacred cakes of Khrishna.

The cakes that were offered to Luna by the Greeks and Romans were either crescent-shaped, or were marked with the crescent moon; and this stamp must have been very similar to that impressed on the cakes offered by the Hebrew women to the Queen of Heaven. This mark also resembles that representing the horns of the sacred ox which was stamped on the Grecian cakes; and the ox was *bous*, and, in one of its oblique cases, *boun*, so we derive from that word *boun* our familiar "bun." There were not only horn-marked cakes, but horn-marked pieces of money; so that it is very difficult to ascertain the true meaning of that passage in the opening of the "Agamemnon" of Æschylus, where the watchman says that a great *bous* has come, or set foot, upon his tongue. Although it might mean that something as weighty as an ox's hoof had weighed down his tongue, yet it more probably signifies either that he was bribed to silence with a piece of money marked with the ox's horns, or that the partaking of a sacred horn-marked cake had initiated him into a certain secret. Curiously enough, in the *argot* of thieves, at the present day, a crown piece is termed "a bull;" and it may also be noted that *pecunia*, "money," is derived from *pecus*, "cattle;" and "bull" is derived from *bous*, and also "cow" from the same word, through the Sanscrit *gou*, the *b* and *g* being convertible.

Thus, originally, the *boun* or bun was the cake marked with the horns of the sacred ox. The cross mark was first adopted by the Greeks and Romans to facilitate the division of the cake into four equal parts; and two such cross-marked cakes were found in the ruins of Herculaneum. These cakes were adopted by the early Christians in a spirit of symbolism; but, although the cross was marked on the cake in token of the badge of their faith, yet it was also used by the priest for the breaking of the cake, or Eucharistic wafer, into four pieces; and this was so ordered in the Liturgy of St. Chrysostom. The cross-marked buns are now, for popular use, reserved for Good Friday, and, as Lenten cakes, are peculiar to this country. Among the Syrian Christians of Travancore and Cochin, who trace their descent from those who were converted by St. Thomas on his (supposed) visit to India, a peculiar cake is made for "Sorrowful Friday"—as they term Good Friday. The cake is stuffed with sweetmeats in the form of an eye, to represent the evil eye of Judas, coveting the thirty pieces of silver; and the cake is flung at with sticks by the members of the family until the eye is quite put out; they then share the remains of the cake among them.

In the days before the Reformation, *eulogiæ*, or cross-marked consecrated cakes, were made from the dough of the mass-bread, and distributed by the priests to be eaten at home by those who had been prevented by sickness or infirmity from attending the mass. After the Reformation, Protestants would readily retain the custom of eating in their houses a cross marked cake, although no longer connecting it with a sacred rite, but restricting its use to that one day of the year known as "Holy Friday," or "Long Friday"—from the length of the service on that day—but which gradually came to be called, by the Anglican Church, "Good Friday," in remembrance of the good things secured to mankind on that day. The presence upon the breakfast-table of the cross marked bun, flavoured with allspice, in token of the spices that were prepared by the pious women of Galilee, was, therefore, regarded in the light of a remembrancer of the solemnities of the day. The buns were made on the previous evening, Maundy Thursday so called, either from the "maunds," or baskets, in which Easter gifts were distributed, or, more probably, because it was the *Dies mandati*, the day of the command, "That thou doest, do quickly!" as also, "Do this in remembrance of Me!" and that the disciples should love one another and should show humility in the washing of feet.

As Chelsea was long famous for its buns—which are mentioned by Swift to Stella, in 1712—it was not to be wondered at that it should be celebrated for its production of hot cross buns on Good Friday. Early in the present century there were two bun-houses at Chelsea, both claiming to be "Royal" as well as "Original," until, at last, one of the two proclaimed itself to be "The Real Old Original Bun House." These two houses did a roaring trade during the whole of Good Friday, their piazzas being crowded, from six in the morning to six in the evening, by crowds of purchasers, loungers, and gossipers. Good King George the Third would come there with his children; and, of course, the nobility and gentry followed his example. These two bun-houses were swallowed up, in the march of improvement, some forty years ago; but on Good Friday, 1830, 240,000 hot cross buns were sold there.

The cross bun is not without its folk-lore. Country folks attach much virtue to the Good Friday buns; and many are kept for "luck's sake" in cottages from one Good Friday to another. They are not only considered to be preservatives from sickness and disease, but also as safeguards from fire and lightning. They are supposed never to get mouldy, as was noted by "Poor Robin," in his Almanack for 1733, under the head of March:—

> "Good Friday comes this month: the old woman runs
> With one a penny, two a penny hot cross-buns:
> Whose virtue is, if you'll believe what's said,
> They'll not grow mouldy like the common bread."

Furthermore, be it known, then, in the interests of suffering humanity, that if a piece of a Good Friday bun is grated and eaten, it will cure as many diseases as were ever cured by a patent pill; moreover, the animal world is not shut out from sharing in its benefits, for it will cure a calf from "scouring," and mixed in a warm mash, it is the very best remedy for your cow. Thus the bun is good for the *boun;* in fact, it is good both for man and beast.

The sellers of the Good Friday buns are composed of old men and young men, old women and young women, big children and little children, but principally boys, and they are of mixed classes, as, costers' boys, boys habitually and boys occasionally street-sellers, and boys—"some cry now who never cried before," and for that occasion only. One great inducement to embark in the trade is the hope of raising a little money for the Easter holidays following.

The "cry" of the Hot Cross Bun vendor varies at times and in places—as thus:—

> "One-a-penny, two-a-penny, hot cross-buns!
> One-a-penny, two for *tup'ence*, hot cross buns!"

While some of a humorous turn of mind like to introduce a little bit of their own, or the borrowed wit of those who have gone before them, and effect the *one* step which is said to exist from the sublime to the ridiculous, and cry—

> "One-a-penny, poker; two-a-penny, tongs!
> One-a-penny; two-a-penny, hot cross buns.
> One-a-penny, two-a-penny, hot cross-buns!
> If your daughters will not eat them, give them to your sons.
> But if you haven't any of those pretty little elves,
> You cannot then do better than eat them up yourselves;
> One-a-penny, two-a-penny, hot cross buns:
> All, hot, hot, hot, all hot.
> One-a-penny, two-a-penny, hot cross buns!
> Burning hot! smoking hot, r-r-r-roking hot—
> One-a-penny, two-a-penny, hot cross buns."

But the street hot-cross-bun trade is languishing—and languishing, will ultimately die a natural death, as the master bakers and pastrycooks have entered into it more freely, and now send round to their regular customers for orders some few days before each succeeding Good Friday.

A capital writer of NOTES, COMMENT and GOSSIP, who contributes every week to the *City Press*, under the *nom de plume* of "Dogberry," gave—*inter alia*—a few "*Good Words*," the result of his "*Leisure Hours*" in that journal, on the subject of "Good Friday Customs." March 24, 1883, thus:—

"That the buns themselves are as popular as ever they were when the Real Original Bun Houses" existed in Chelsea, was manifest on Thursday evening, though the scene is now changed from the west to the east. Bishopsgate-street was indeed all alive with people of high and low degree crowding in and out of Messrs. Hill & Sons, who, I am told, turned no less than 47 sacks of flour, representing over 13,000 lbs., into the favourite Good Friday cakes. This mass was sweetened by 2,800 lbs. of sugar, moistened with 1,500 quarts of milk, and 'lightened' with 2,200 lbs. of butter. Something like 25,000 paper bags were used in packing the buns, and upwards of 150 pairs of hands were engaged in the making and distribution of the tasty morsels at Bishopsgate and at the West-end branch of Messrs. Hill, at Victoria. The customary business of the firm must have been interrupted considerably by Good Friday, and the forty-seven sacks of flour made into buns represented, I presume, a considerable deduction from the hundred and ninety to two hundred which the firm work up in one form or another every week. But then you can't eat your (Good Friday) cake and have it. There were other bakers and confectioners in the City, too, who appeared to do a thriving trade in buns—notably Messrs. Robertson & Co., in Aldersgate-street. Long live the Good Friday bun!"

DOGBERRY.

HOT CROSS BUNS.

BY MISS ELIZA COOK.

"The clear spring dawn is breaking, and there cometh with the ray,
The stripling boy with 'shining face,' and dame in 'hodden grey:'
Rude melody is breathed by all—young—old—the strong, and weak;
From manhood with its burly tone, and age with treble squeak.
Forth come the little busy 'Jacks' and forth come little 'Jills,'
As thick and quick as working ants about their summer hills;
With baskets of all shapes and makes, of every size and sort;
Away they trudge with eager step, through alley, street, and court.
A spicy freight they bear along, and earnest is their care,
To guard it like a tender thing from morning's nipping air;
And though our rest be broken by their voices shrill and clear,
There's something in the well-known 'cry' we dearly love to hear.
'Tis old, familiar music, when 'the old woman runs'
With 'One-a-penny, two-a-penny, Hot Cross Buns!'
Full many a cake of dainty make has gained a great renown,
We all have lauded 'Gingerbread' and 'Parliament' done brown;
But when did luscious 'Banburies,' or dainty 'Sally Lunns,'
E'er yield such merry chorus theme as 'One-a-penny buns!'
The pomp of palate that may be like old Vitellius fed,
Can never feast as mine did on the sweet and fragrant bread;
When quick impatience could not wait to share the early meal,
But eyed the pile of 'Hot Cross Buns,' and dared to snatch and steal.
Oh, the soul must be uncouth as a Vandal's Goth's, or Hun's.
That loveth not the melody of 'One-a-penny Buns!'"

And so, awaking in the early morning, we hear the streets ringing with the cry, "Hot Cross Buns." And perhaps when all that we have wrought shall be forgotten, when our name shall be as though it had been written on water, and many institutions great and noble shall have perished, this little bun will live on unharmed. Others, as well as ourselves, will, it may be, lie awake upon their beds, and listen to the murmurs going to and fro within the great heart of London, and, thinking on the half-forgotten days of the nineteenth century, wonder perhaps whether, in these olden times, we too heard the sound of "Hot Cross Buns."

The street Pieman with his "cry," of "Pies all hot! hot!! hot!!!—Penny pies, all hot! hot!!—fruit, eel, beef, veal or kidney pies! pies, all hot-hot-hot," is one of the most ancient of street callings, and to London boys of every degree, "Familiar in their mouths as household words." Nor is the itinerant trade in pies—"Eel, beef, veal, kidney or fruit," confined to the great metropolis. All large provincial towns have, from a time going back much farther than even the proverbial "oldest inhabitant" can recollect, had their old and favourite "Penny Pieman," or, "*Old-all-Hot!*" as folks were ever wont to call him. He was generally a merry dog, and mostly to be found where merriment was going on, he scrupled not to force his way through the thickest of the crowd, knowing that the very centre of action was the best market for his wares.

THE PIEMAN;

OR, O LORD! WHAT A PLACE IS A CAMP.

"O Lord! what a place is a camp,
What wonderful doings are there;
The people are all on the tramp,
To me it looks devilish queer:
Here's ladies a swigging of gin,
A crop of macaronies likewise:
And I, with my 'Who'll up and win?
Come, here is your hot mutton pies.'

Here's gallopping this way and that,
With, 'Madam, stand out of the way;'
Here's, 'O fie! sir, what would you be at?—
Come, none of your impudence pray:'
Here's 'Halt—to the right-about-face,'
Here's laughing, and screaming, and cries:
Here's milliners'-men out of place,
And I with my hot mutton pies.

Here's the heath all round like a fair,
Here's butlers, and sutlers, and cooks;
Here's popping away in the air,
And captains with terrible looks:
Here's 'How do you do?'—'Pretty well;
The dust has got into my eyes,'
There's—'Fellow what have you to sell?'
'Why, only some hot mutton pies.'"

History informs us, through the medium of the halfpenny plain and penny coloured chap book, editions issued by the "Catnach Press," that, one :—

"Simple Simon met a Pieman,
Going to the fair ;
Says simple Simon to the Pieman,
'Let me taste your ware.'

Says the Pieman unto Simon,
'First give me a penny ;'
Says Simple Simon to the Pieman,
'I have not got any.'"

But history is silent as to the birth, parentage, or, even place and date of the death of the said Simple Simon, or of this very particular pieman. Halliwell informs us, through one of the "Nursery Rhymes of England," that on one occasion :—

"Punch and Judy
Fought for a pie ;
Punch gave Judy
A sad blow on the eye."

James Lackington—1746-1816—one of the most celebrated of our early cheap booksellers, lived at the "Temple of Muses," Finsbury-place—the shop, into which a coach and six could be driven. This curious mixture of cobbler's wax, piety, vanity, and love of business, has left us in his autobiography, which he published under the title of his "*Memoirs and Confessions*," his experience as a pie-boy ! or seller of pies, thus :—

"At ten years old I cried apple pies in the street. I had noticed a famous pieman, and thought I could do it better myself. My mode of crying pies soon made me a street favourite, and the old pie merchant left off trade. You see, friend, I soon began to make a noise in the world. But one day I threw my master's child out of a wheelbarrow, so I went home again, and was set by my father to learn his trade, continuing with him for several years. My fame as a pieman led to my selling almanacks on the market days at Christmas. This was to my mind, and I sorely vexed the [regular] vendors of 'Moore,' 'Wing,' and 'Poor Robin.' My next move was to be bound apprentice for seven years."

We frequently meet with the pieman in old prints ; and in Hogarth's "March to Finchley," there he stands in the very centre of the crowd, grinning with delight at the adroitness of one robbery, while he is himself the victim of another. We learn from this admirable figure by the greatest painter of English

HOGARTH'S PIEMAN.

life, that the pieman of the last century perambulated the streets in professional costume; and we gather further, from the burly dimensions of his wares that he kept his trade alive by the laudable practice of giving "a good pennyworth for a penny." Justice compels us to observe that his successors of a later generation have not been very conscientious observers of this maxim.

NICE NEW! NICE NEW!

All hot! All Hot Hot! All Hot!

Here they are, two sizes bigger than last week.

At this date there was James Sharpe England, a noted flying pieman, who attended all the metropolitan festive gatherings; he walked about hatless, to sell his savoury wares, with his hair powdered and tied *en queue*, his dress neat, apron spotless, jesting wherever he went, with a mighty voice in recommendation of the puddings and pies, which, for the sake of greater oddity he sometimes carried on a wooden platter.

JAMES SHARPE ENGLAND,
The Flying Pieman.

The London pieman, as he takes his walks abroad, makes a practice of "looking in" at all the taverns on his way. Here his customers are found principally in the tap-room. "Here they are, all 'ot!" the pieman cries, as he walks in; "toss or buy! up and win 'em!" For be it known to all whom it may concern, the pieman is a gambler, both from inclination and principle, and will toss with his customers, either by the dallying shilly-shally process of "best five in nine," or "best two in three," or the desperate dash of "sudden death!" in which latter case the first toss decides the matter, *viz*:—a pie for a penny, or your penny gone for nothing, but he invariably declines the mysterious process of "odd man," not being altogether free from suspicion on the subject of collusion between a couple of hungry, and not over honestly inclined customers.

Of the "stuff" which pie-dealers usually make their wares, much has been sung and said, and in some neighbourhoods the sight of an approaching pieman seems to get about an immediate desire for imitating the harmless cat and its "Mee-yow," or the "Bow-wow-wow!" of the dog. And opprobrious epithets are hurled at the piemen as they parade the streets and alleys, and even kidnapping has been slyly hinted at, for the mother of Tom Cladpole, finding her son so determined to make a "Jurney to Lunnun"—least he should die a fool, tries to frighten the boy out of his fixed intention by informing him in pure Sussex dialect that:—

> "Besides, dey kidnap people dere,
> Ah! ketch um by supprize,
> An send um off where nub'dy knows,
> Or *baak um up in pies*."

It was ever a safe piece of comic business with Old Joey Grimaldi and his favourite pupil and successor, Tom Matthews, together with all other stage clowns following them, that a penny pieman and the bright shining block-tin can should be introduced into every Christmas pantomime. The pataloon is made to be tossing the safe game of—" heads I win, tails you lose " with the stage pieman, while the roguish clown is adroitly managing to swallow the whole of the stock of pies from the can, and which are made by the stage property-man for the occasion out of tissue-paper painted in water-colours. Then follows the wry faces and spasmodic stomach-pinchings of the clown, accompanied with the echoing cries of "*Mee, mee, mow, woo!*" while the pantaloon takes from the pieman's can some seven or eight fine young kittens and the old tabby-cat—also the handy-work of the stage property-man. The whole scene usually finishes by the pantaloon pointedly sympathizing with the now woebegone clown to the tune of "Serve ye right—Greedy! greedy!! greedy!!!" when enter six supernumeraries dressed as large and motherly-looking tabbies with aprons and bibs, and bedizened with white linen night caps of the pattern known in private life to middle-aged married men only. The clown and pantaloon then work together in hunting down, and then handing over the poor pieman to the tender mercies and talons of the stage-cats, who finish up the "business" of the scene by popping the pieman into what looks like a copper of boiling water.

Mr. Samuel Weller,—*otherwise,* Veller, that great modern authority on Ye Manners and Ye Customs, of Ye English in general, and of London Life wery Particular:—for "Mr. Weller's knowldge of London was extensive and peculiar"—has left us his own ideas of the baked "mysteries" of the pieman's ware:—

"Weal pie," said Mr. Weller, soliloquising, as he arranged the eatables on the grass. "Werry good thing is a weal pie, when you know the lady as made it, and is quite sure it an't kittens; and arter all, though, where's the odds, when they're so like weal that the wery piemen themselves don't know the difference?"

"Don't they, Sam?" said Mr. Pickwick.

"Not they, sir," replied Mr. Weller, touching his hat. "I lodged in the same house vith a pieman once, sir, and a wery nice man he was—reg'lar clever chap too—made pies out o' anything, he could. 'What a number o' cats you keep, Mr. Brooks,' says I, when I'd got intimate with him. 'Ah,' says he, 'I do—a good many,' says he. 'You must be wery fond o' cats,' says I. 'Other people is,' say he, a winkin' at me; 'they an't in season till the winter though,' says he. 'Not in season!' says I. 'No,' says he, 'fruits is in, cats is out.' 'Why, what do you mean?' says I. 'Mean?' says he. 'That I'll never be a party to the combination o' the butchers, to keep up the prices o' meat,' says he. 'Mr. Weller,' says he, a squeezing my hand wery hard, and vispering in my ear—'don't mention this here agin—but it's the seasonin' that does it. They're all made o' them noble animals,' says he, a pointin' to a wery nice little tabby kitten, 'and I seasons 'em for beef-steaks, weal, or kidney, 'cordin to demand. And more than that,' says he, 'I can make a weal a beef-steak, or a beef-steak a kidney, or any one on 'em a mutton, at a minute's notice, just as the market changes, and appetites wary!"

"He must have been a very ingenious young man, that, Sam," said Mr. Pickwick, with a slight shudder.

"Just was, sir," replied Mr. Weller, continuing his occupation of emptying the basket, "*and the pies was beautiful.*"

The "gravy" given with the meat-pies is poured out of an oil-can and consists of a little salt and water browned. A hole is made with the little finger in the top of the pie and the "gravy" poured in until the crust rises sufficiently to satisfy the young critical gourmand's taste.

"The London piemen," says, Mr. Henry Mayhew, "May be numbered at about forty in winter, and twice that number in summer." Calculating that there are only fifty plying their trade the year through, and their average earnings at 8s. a week, we find a street expenditure exceeding £1,040, and a street consumption of pies amounting to nearly three quarters of a million yearly.

YOUNG LAMBS TO SELL.

Young lambs to sell! young lambs to sell.
If I'd as much money as I could tell,
I'd not come here with young lambs to sell!
Dolly and Molly, Richard and Nell,
Buy my young lambs, and I'll use you well!

The engraving represents an old "London Crier," one William Liston, from a drawing for which he purposely *stood* in 1826.

This "public character" was born in the City of Glasgow. He became a soldier in the waggon-train commanded by Colonel Hamilton, and served under the Duke of York in Holland, where, on the 6th of October, 1799, he lost his right arm and left leg, and his place in the army. His misfortunes thrust distinction upon him. From having been a private in the ranks, where he would have remained undistinguished, he became one of the popular street-characters of his day.

In Miss Eliza Cook's Poem "Old Cries" she sings in no feeble strain the praises of the old man of her youthful days, who cried—"Merry and free as a marriage bell":—

YOUNG LAMBS TO SELL.

There was a man in olden time,
And a troubador was he;
Whose passing chant and lilting rhyme
Had mighty charms for me.

My eyes grew big with a sparkling stare,
And my heart began to swell,
When I heard his loud song filling the air
About "Young lambs to sell!"

His flocks were white as the falling snow,
With collars of shining gold;
And I chose from the pretty ones "all of a row,"
With a joy that was untold.

Oh, why did the gold become less bright,
Why did the soft fleece lose its white,
And why did the child grow old?

'Twas a blithe, bold song the old man sung;
The words came fast, and the echoes rung,
Merry and free as "a marriage bell;"
And a right, good troubadour was he,
For the hive never swarmed to the chinking key,
As the wee things did when they gathered in glee
To his musical cry—"Young lambs to sell!"

Ah, well-a-day! it hath passed away,
With my holiday pence and my holiday play—
I wonder if I could listen again,
As I listened then, to that old man's strain—
All of a row—"Young lambs to sell."

THE LONDON BARROW-WOMAN.

Round and sound,
Two-pence a pound.
Cherries, rare ripe cherries !

Cherries a ha'penny a stick
Come and pick ! come and pick !
Cherries big as plums ! who comes, who comes.

The late George Cruikshank, whose pencil was ever distinguished by power of decision in every character he sketched, and whose close observation of passing men and manners was unrivalled by any artist of his day, contributed the "London Barrow-woman" to the pages of Hone's *Every-Day Book* in 1826 from his own recollection of her.

BUY A BROOM.

These poor "Buy-a-Broom girls" exactly dress now,
As Hollar etch'd such girls two cent'ries ago;
All formal and stiff, with legs, only at ease—
Yet, pray, judge for yourself; and don't if you please,
* * * * * * * *
But ask for the print, at old print shops—they'll show it,
And look at it, "with your own eyes," and you'll *know* it.

Buy a Broom? was formerly a very popular London-cry, when it was usually rendered thus:—"*Puy a Proom, puy a prooms? a leetle von for ze papy, and a pig vons for ze lady: Puy a Proom.*" Fifty years ago Madame Vestris charmed the town by her singing and displaying her legs as a *Buy-a-Broom Girl.*

Buy a broom, buy a broom,
Large broom, small broom,
No lady should e'er be without one, &c.

But time and fashion has *swept* both the brooms and the girls from our shores.—Madame Vestris lies head-to-head with Charles Mathews in Kensal Green Cemetery. *Tempus omnia revelat.*

THE LADY AS CRIES CATS' MEAT.

Old Maids, your custom I invites,
Fork out, and don't be shabby,
And don't begrudge a bit of lights
Or liver for your Tabby.

Hark! how the Pusses make a rout—
To buy you can't refuse;
So may you never be without
The *music* of their *mews*.

Here's famous meat—all lean, no fat—
No better in Great Britain;
Come, buy a penn'orth for your Cat—
A happ'orth for your Kitten.

Come all my barrow for a bob!
Some charity diskivir;
For faith, it ar'n't an easy job
To *live* by selling *liver*.

Who'll buy? who'll buy of Catsmeat-Nan!
I've bawl'd till I am sick;
But ready money is my plan;
I never gives no tick.

I've got no customers as yet—
In wain is my appeal—
And not to buy a single bit
Is werry ungenteel!

OUR DANDY CATS' AND DOGS' MEAT MAN.

Every morning as true as the clock—the quiet of "Our Village Green" is broken by a peculiar and suggestive cry. We do not hear it yet ourselves, but Pincher, our black and tan terrier dog, and Smut, our black and white cat, have both caught the well known accents, and each with natural characteristic —the one wagging his tail, the other with a stiff perpendicular [dorsel appendage] sidles towards the door, demanding as plainly as possible, to be let out. Yes, it is "Our Dandy Cats' and Dogs' Meat Man," with his "*Ca' me-e-et—dogs' me yet— Ca' or do-args-me-a-yet, me a-t—me-yett!!!*" that fills the morning air, and arouses exactly seven dogs of various kinds, and exactly thirty-one responsive feline voices—there is a cat to every house on "Our Village Green"—and causes thirty-one aspiring cat's-tails to point to the zenith. We do not know how it is, but the Cat's-meat man is the most unerring and punctual of all those peripatetic functionaries who undertake to cater for the public. The baker, the butcher, the grocer, the butterman, the fish-monger, and the coster, occasionally forget your necessities, or omit to call for your orders—the cat's-meat man never!

GUY FAWKES—GUY.

There cannot be a better representation of "Guy Fawkes," as he was borne about the metropolis in effigy in the days "When George the Third was King," than the above sketch by George Cruikshank.

Please to remember the fifth of November,
  Gunpowder treason and plot ;
We know no reason, why gunpowder treason,
  Should ever be forgot !
    Holla boys ! holla boys ! huzza—a—a !
A stick and a stake, for King George's sake,
A stick and a stump, for Guy Fawkes' rump !
    Holla boys ! holla boys ! huzza—a—a !

HENRY LEMOINE,

The Literary and Pedestrian Bookseller and Author,

A well known

Eccentric Character of the City of London.

All Round my Hat I Vears a Green Villow.

All round my hat I vears a green villow,
All round my hat, for a twelvemonth and a day;
If any body axes me the reason vy I vears it,
I tells 'em that my own true love is far far away.
'Twas a going of my rounds, in the streets I first did meet her,
Oh, I thought she vos a hangel just come down from the sky;

Spoken.—She's a nice wegitable countenance; turnup nose, redish cheeks, and carroty hair.

And I never knew a voice more louder or more sweeter,
Vhen she cried, buy my primroses, my primroses come buy.

Spoken.—Here's your fine colliflowers.

All round, &c.

O, my love she was fair, my love she was kind, too,
And cruel vos the cruel judge vot had my love to try :

SPOKEN. –Here's your precious turnups.

For thieving vos a thing she never vos inclined to :
But he sent my love across the seas, far far away.

SPOKEN.—Here's your hard-hearted cabbages.

All round, &c.

For seven long years my love and I is parted,
For seven long years my love is bound to stay.

SPOKEN.—It's a precious long time 'fore I does any trade to-day.

Bad luck to that chap vot'd ever be false-hearted,
Oh, I'll love my love for ever, tho' she's far far away.

SPOKEN.—Here's your nice heads of salary !

All round, &c.

There is some young men so preciously deceitful,
A coaxing of the young gals they vish to lead astray.

SPOKEN.—Here's your Valnuts ; crack'em and try'em, a shilling a hundred !

As soon as they deceives'em, so cruelly they leaves 'em,
And they never sighs nor sorrows ven they're far far away !—

SPOKEN.—Do you vant any hingons to-day, marm ?

All round, &c.

Oh, I bought my love a ring on the werry day she started,
Vich I gave her as a token all to remember me :

SPOKEN.—Bless her h-eyes,

And vhen she does come back, oh, ve'll never more be parted
But ve'll marry and be happy—oh, for ever and a day.

SPOKEN.—Here's your fine spring redishes.

All round, &c.

THE NEW LONDON CRIES.

Tune—"The Night Coach."

Dear me! what a squalling and a bawling,
  What noise, and what bustle in London pervades;
People of all sorts shouting and calling,
  London's a mart, sure, for men of all trades.
The *chummy* so black, sir, with bag on his back, sir,
  Commences the noise with the cry of "sweep, sweep!"
Then Dusty and Crusty with voices so lusty,
  Fish-men and green-men, their nusiances keep.

Dear me, &c.

Fine water cresses, two bunches a penny,
Fine new milk, two-pence ha'p'ny a quart !
Come buy my fine matches—as long as I've any,
Carrots and turnips, the finest e'er bought.
Dainty fresh salmon ! *without* any *gammon*,
Hare skins or rabbit skins ! hare skins, cook I buy !
'Taters all sound, sir, two-pence six pounds, sir,
Coals ten-pence a bushel, buy them and try.
Dear me, &c.

Here's songs three yards for a penny !
Comic songs, love songs, and funny songs, too ;
Billy Barlow,—Little Mike,—Paddy Denny!
The Bailiffs are coming—The Hero of Waterloo.
Eels four-pence a pound—pen knives here ground,
Scissors ground sharp, a penny a pair !
Tin kettles to mend, sir, your fenders here send, sir,
For six-pence a piece, I will paint 'em with care.
Dear me, &c.

Come buy my *old man*, a penny a root,
The whole true account of the murder last night !
Fine Seville oranges, ne'er was such fruit,
Just printed and published, the last famous fight.
Arrived here this morning—strange news from Greece,
A victory gain'd o'er the great Turkish fleet ;
Chairs to mend—hair brooms, a shilling a piece !
Cap box, bonnet box—cats' and dogs' meat.
Dear me, &c.

Here's *inguns* a penny a rope,
Pots and pans—old clothes, clo' for sale !
A dread storm near the Cape of Good Hope.
Greens two pence a bunch twenty pence a new pail.
Sprats, a penny a plateful—I should feel werry grateful,
Kind friends for a ha'p'ny for my babe's sakes ;
Shrimps, penny a pot—baked 'taters all hot !
Muffins and crumpets, or fine Yorkshire cakes.
Dear me, &c.

"Had I a *Garden*, a *Field* and a *Gate*,
I would not care for the Duke of Bedford's estate;
That is, I would not care for the Duke of Bedford's estate,
If I had *Covent Garden*, *Smithfield*, and *Billingsgate*."

Billingsgate has from time immemorial had much to do with "The Cries of London," and although a rough and unromantic place at the present day, has an ancient legend of its own, that associates it with royal names and venerable folk. Geoffrey of Monmouth deposeth that about 400 years before Christ's nativity, Belin, a king of the Britons, built this gate and gave it its name, and that when he was dead the royal body was burnt, and the ashes set over the gate in a vessel of brass, upon a high pinnacle of stone. The London historian, John Stow, more prosaic, on the other hand, is quite satisfied that one Biling once owned the wharf, and troubles himself no further.

Byllngsgate Dock is mentioned as an important quay in "Brompton's Chronicle" (Edward III.), under the date 976, when King Ethelred, being then at Wantage, in Berkshire, made laws for regulating the customs on ships at Byllngsgate, then the only wharf in London. 1. Small vessels were to pay one halfpenny. 2. Larger ones, with sails, one penny. 3. Keeles, or hulks, still larger, fourpence. 4. Ships laden with wood, one log shall be given for toll. 5. *Boats with fish*, according to size, a halfpenny. 6. Men of Rouen, who came with wine or peas, and men of Flanders and Liege, were to pay toll before they began to sell, but the Emperor's men (Germans of the Steel Yard) paid an annual toll. 7. Bread was tolled three times a week, cattle were paid for in kind, and butter and cheese were paid more for before Christmas than after.

Hence we gather that at a very early period Billingsgate was not merely a fish-market, but for the sale of general commodities Paying toll in kind is a curious fiscal regulation; though, doubtless, when barter was the ordinary mode of transacting business, taxes must have been collected in the form of an instalment of the goods brought to market.

Our ancestors four hundred years ago had, in proportion to the population of London, much more abundant and much cheaper fish than we have now. According to the "Noble Boke off Cookry," a reprint of which, from the rare manuscript in the Holkham Collection, has just been edited by Mrs. Alexander Napier, Londoners in the reign of Henry VII. could regale on "baked porpois," "turbert," "pik in braissille," "mortins of ffishe," "eles in bruet," "fresh lamprey bak," "breme," in "sauce" and in "brasse," "soal in brasse," "sturgion boiled," "haddock in cevy," "codling haddock," "congur," "halobut," "gurnard or rocket boiled," "plaice or flounders boiled," "whelks boiled," "perche boiled," "freeke makrell," "bace molet," "musculles," in "shelles" and in "brothe," "tench in cevy," and "lossenge for ffishe daies." For the rich there were "potages of oysters," "blang mang" and "rape" of "ffishe," to say nothing of "lampry in galantyn" and "lampry bak." Our forefathers ate more varieties of fish, cooked it better, and paid much less for it than we do, with all our railways and steamboats, our Fisheries' Inspectors, our Fisheries Exhibion and new Fish Markets with their liberal rules and regulations. To be sure, those same forefathers of ours not only enacted certain very stringent laws against "forestalling" and "regrating," but were likewise accustomed to enforce them, and to make short work upon occasion of the forestallers and regraters of fish, as of other commodities.

In Donald Lupton's "London and the Covntrey Carbonadoed and Quartred into seuerall Characters. London, Printed by Nicholas Okes, 1632," the nymphs of the locality are thus described :—

FISHERWOMEN :—These crying, wandering, and travelling creatures carry their shops on their heads, and their storehouse is ordinarily Byllyngsgate, or Ye Brydge-foot ; and their habitation Turnagain Lane. They set up every morning their trade afresh. They are easily furnished ; get something and spend it jovially and merrily. Five shillings, a basket, and a good cry, are a large stock for them. They are the merriest when all their ware is gone. In the morning they delight to have their shop full ; at evening they desire to have it empty. Their shop is but little, some two yards compass, yet it holds all sort of fish, or herbs, or roots, and such like ware. Nay, it is not destitute often of nuts, oranges, and lemons. They are free in all places, and pay nothing for rent, but only find repairs to it. If they drink their whole stock, it is but pawning a petticoate in Long Lane, or themselves in Turnbull Street, to set up again. They change daily ; for she that was for fish this day, may be to-morrow for fruit, next day for herbs, another for roots ; so that you must hear them cry before you know what they are furnished withal. When they have done their Fair, they meet in mirth, singing, dancing, and end not till either their money, or wit, or credit be clean spent out. Well, when on any evening they are not merry in a drinking house, it is thought they have had bad return, or else have paid some old score, or else they are bankrupt : they are creatures soon up and soon down.

The above quaint account of the ancient Billingsgate ladies answers exactly to the costermonger's wives of the present day, who are just as careless and improvident ; they are merry over their rope of onions, and laugh over a basketful of stale sprats. In their dealings and disputes they are as noisy as ever, and rather apt to put decency and good manners to the blush. Billingsgate eloquence has long been proverbial for coarse language, so that low abuse is often termed, "*That's talking Billingsgate!*"

THE CRIER OF POOR JOHN.

"It is well thou art not a fish, for then thou would'st have been *Poor John*."—*Romeo and Juliet.*

or, that, "*You are no better than a Billingsgate fish-fag*"—*i.e.*, You are as rude and ill-mannered as the women of Billingsgate fish-market (Saxon, *bellan*, "to bawl," and *gate*, "quay," meaning the noisy quay). The French say "Maubert," instead of Billingsgate, as "*Your compliments are like those of the Place Maubert*"—*i.e.*, No compliments at all, but vulgar dirt-flinging. The "Place Maubert," has long been noted for its market.

The introduction of steamboats has much altered the aspect of Billingsgate. Formerly, passengers embarked here for Gravesend and other places down the river, and a great many sailors mingled with the salesmen and fishermen. The boats sailed only when the tide served, and the necessity of being ready at the strangest hours rendered many taverns necessary for the accommodation of travellers. The market formerly opened two hours earlier than at present, and the result was demoralising and exhausting. Drink led to ribald language and fighting, but the refreshment now taken is chiefly tea or coffee, and the general language and behaviour has improved. The fish-fags of Ned Ward's time have disappeared, and the business is done smarter and quicker. As late as 1842 coaches would sometimes arrive at Billingsgate from Dover or Brighton, and so affect the market. The old circle from which dealers in their carts attended the market, included Windsor, St. Alban's, Hertford, Romford, and other places within twenty-five miles. Railways have now enlarged the area of purchasers to an indefinite degree.

To see this market in its busiest time, says Mr. Mayhew, "the visitor should be there about seven o'clock on a Friday morning." The market opens at four, but for the first two or three hours it is attended solely by the regular fishmongers and "bummarees," who have the pick of the best there. As soon as these are gone the costermonger's sale begins. Many of the costers that usually deal in vegetables buy a little fish on the Friday. It is the fast day of the Irish, and the mechanics' wives run short of money at the end of the week, and so make up their dinners with fish: for this reason the attendance of costers' barrows at Billingsgate on a Friday morning is always very great. As soon as you reach the Monument you see a line of them, with one or two tall fishmongers' carts breaking the uniformity, and the din of the cries and commotion of the distant market begin to break on the ear like the buzzing of a hornet's nest. The whole neighbourhood is covered with hand-barrows, some laden with baskets, others with sacks. The air is filled with a kind of sea-weedy odour, reminding one of the sea-shore; and on entering the market, the smell of whelks, red herrings, sprats, and a hundred other sorts of fish, is almost overpowering. The wooden barn-looking square* where the fish is sold is, soon after six o'clock, crowded with shiny cord jackets and greasy caps. Exerybody comes to Billingsgate in his worst clothes; and no one knows the length of time a coat can be worn until they have been to a fish sale. Through the bright opening at the end are seen the tangled rigging of the oyster boats, and the red-worsted caps of the sailors. Over the hum of voices is heard the shouts of the salesmen, who, with their white aprons, peering above the heads of the mob, stand on their tables roaring out their prices. All are bawling together—salesmen and hucksters of provisions, capes, hardware, and newspapers—till the place is a perfect Babel of competition.

"Ha-a-andsome cod! best in the market! All alive! alive! alive, oh!"—"Ye-o-o! ye-o-o! Here's your fine Yarmouth bloaters! Who's the buyer?"—"Here you are, governor; splendid whiting! some of the right sort!"—"Turbot! turbot! All alive, turbot!"—"Glass of nice pepper-

* The whole market has been rebuilt during these last few years, & Darkhouse-lane abolished.—C. H.

mint, this cold morning? Halfpenny a glass!"—"Here you are, at your own price! Fine soles, oh!"—"Oy! oy! oy! Now's your time! Fine grizzling sprats! all large, and no small!"—"Hullo! hullo, here! Beautiful lobsters! good and cheap. Fine cock crabs, all alive, oh!"—"Five brill and one turbot—have that lot for a pound! Come and look at 'em, governor; you won't see a better lot in the market!"—"Here! this way; this way, for splendid skate! Skate, oh! skate, oh!"—"Had-had-had-had-haddock! All fresh and good!" "Currant and meat puddings! a ha'penny each!—"Now, you mussel-buyers, come along! come along! come along! Now's your time for fine fat mussels!"—"Here's food for the belly, and clothes for the back; but I sell food for the mind!" shouts the newsvendor.—"Here's smelt, oh!"—"Here ye are, fine Finney haddick!"—"Hot soup! nice pea-soup! a-all hot! hot!"—"Ahoy! ahoy, here! Live plaice! all alive, oh!"—"Now or never! Whelk! whelk! whelk!" "Who'll buy brill, oh! brill, oh?"—"Capes! waterproof capes! Sure to keep the wet out! A shilling apiece!"—"Eels, oh! eels, oh! Alive, oh! alive oh!"—"Fine flounders, a shilling a lot! Who'll have this prime lot of flounders?"—"Shrimps! shrimps! fine shrimps!"—"Wink! wink! wink!"—"Hi! hi-i! here you are; just eight eels left—only eight!"—"O ho! O ho! this way—this way—this way! Fish alive! alive! alive, oh."

Billingsgate; or, the School of Rhetoric.

Near London Bridge once stood a gate,
  Belinus gave it name,
Whence the green Nereids oysters bring,
  A place of public fame.

Here eloquence has fixed her seat,
  The nymphs here learn by heart
In mode and figure still to speak,
  By modern rules of art.

To each fair oratress this school
  Its rhetoric strong affords;
They double and redouble tropes,
  With finger, fish, and words.

Both nerve and strength and flow of speech,
  With beauties ever new,
Adorn the language of these nymphs,
  Who give it all their due.

O, happy seat of happy nymphs!
  For many ages known,
To thee each rostrum's forc'd to yield—
  Each forum in the town.

Let other academies boast
  What titles else they please;
Thou shalt be call'd "the gate of tongues,"
  Of tongues that never cease.

The sale of hot green peas in the streets of London is of great antiquity, that is to say, if the cry of "*Hot peascods! one began to cry*," recorded by Lydgate in his *London Lackpenny*, may be taken as having intimated the sale of the same article under the modern cry of "*Hot green peas! all hot, all hot! Here's your peas, hot, hot, hot!*" In many parts of the country it is, or was, customary to have a "*scalding of peas*," as a sort of rustic festivity, at which green peas scalded or slightly boiled with their pods on are the main dish. Being set on the table in the midst of the party, each person dips his peapod in a common cup of melted butter, seasoned with salt and pepper, and extracts the peas by the agency of his teeth. At times one bean, shell and all is put into the steaming mass, whoever gets this bean is to be first married.

The sellers of green peas "hot, all hot!" have no stands but carry them in a tin pot or pan which is wrapped round with a thick cloth, to retain the heat. The peas are served out with a ladle, and eaten by the customers out of basins provided with spoons by the vendor. Salt and pepper are supplied *at discretion*, but the *fresh!* butter to grease 'em (*avec votre permission.*)

The hot green peas are sold out in halfpennyworths and pennyworths, some vendors, in addition to the usual seasoning supplied, add *a suck of bacon*. The "suck of bacon" is obtained by the street Arabs from a piece of that article, securely fastened by a string, to obtain a "relish" for the peas, or as is usually said "to flavour 'em;" sometimes these young gamins manage to bite the string and then *bolt* not only the bacon, but away from the vendors. The popular saying "a plate of veal cut with a *hammy* knife" is but a refined rendering of the pea and suck-'o-bacon, street luxury trick.

Pea soup is also sold in the streets of London, but not to the extent it was twenty years ago, when the chilled labourer and others having only a halfpenny to spend would indulge in a basin of—"*All hot!*"

THE FLOWER-POT MAN.

Here comes the old man with his flowers to sell,
  Along the streets merrily going ;
Full many a year I've remember'd him well,
  With, "Flowers, a-growing, a-blowing."

Geraniums in dresses of scarlet and green ;
  Thick aloes, that blossom so rarely ;
The long creeping cereus with prickles so keen ,
  Or primroses modest and early.

The myrtle dark green, and the jessamine pale,
  Sweet scented and gracefully flowing,
This flower-man carries and offers for sale,
  "All flourishing, growing, and blowing."

With the coming in of spring there is a large sale of Palm; on the Saturday preceding and on Palm Sunday; also of May, the fragrant flower of the hawthorn, and lilac in flower. But perhaps the pleasantest of all cries in early spring is that of "*Flowers—All a-growing—all a-blowing*," heard for the first time in the season. Their beauty and fragrance gladden the senses; and the first and unexpected sight of them may prompt hopes of the coming year, such as seem proper to the spring.

"Come, gentle spring! ethereal mildness! come."

The sale of English and Foreign nuts in London is enormous, the annual export from Tarragona alone is estimated at 10,000 tons. Of the various kinds, we may mention the "Spanish," the "Barcelona," the "Brazil," the "Coker-nut," the "Chesnut," and "Though last, not least, in love"—The "Walnut!"

"As jealous as Ford, that search'd a hollow wall-nut for his wife's lemon."—*Merry Wives of Windsor*.

The walnut-tree has long existed in England, and it is estimated that upwards of 50,000 bushels of walnuts are disposed of in the wholesale markets of the London district annually. Who is not pleased to hear every Autumn the familiar cry of:—

"Crack 'em and try 'em, before you buy 'em,
Eight a-penny –All new walnuts.
Crack 'em and try 'em, before you buy 'em,
A shilling a-hundred—All new-walnuts.

The history of the happy and social walnut involves some curious misconceptions. Take its name to begin with. Why walnut? What has this splendid, wide-spreading tree to do with walls, except such as are used as stepping-stones for the boys to climb up into the branches and steal the fruit? Nothing whatever! for, if we are to believe the learned in such matters, this fine old English tree, as it is sometimes called, is not an English tree at all, but a distinct and emphatic foreigner, and hence the derivation. The walnut is a native of Persia, and has been so named to distinguish the naturalised European from its companions, the hazel, the filbert, and the chesnut. In "the authorities" we are told that "gual" or "wall" means "strange" or "exotic," the same root being found in Welsh and kindred tongues; hence walnut. It is true, at any rate, that in France they retain the distinctive name "Noix Persique." There is another mistaken theory connected with the tree which bears a fruit so dear to society at large, for someone has been hazardous enough to assert that:—

> "A woman, a spaniel, and a walnut tree,
> The more you beat them the better they be."

And this ribald rhyme—which is of Latin origin, is now an established English proverb, or proverbial phrase, but variously construed. See Nash's "*Have with you to Saffron-Walden; or, Gabriel Harvey's Hunt is up*," 1596.—Reprinted by J. P. Collier, 1870. Moor, in his "*Suffolk Words*," pp. 465, furnishes another version, which is rather an epigram than a proverb:—

> "Three things by beating better prove;
> A Nut, an Ass, a Woman;
> The cudgel from their back remove,
> And they'll be good for no man."

> "Nux, asinus, mulier simili sunt lege ligata.
> Hæc tria nil recté faciunt si verbera cessant.
> Adducitur a cognato, est temen novum."—MARTIAL.

"*Sam* . . . . Why he's married, beates his wife, and has two or three children by her: for you must note, that any woman beares the more when she is beaten."—*A Yorkshire Tragedy*: "Not so New, as Lamentable and true—1608," edition 1619.—Signature, *A. Verso.*

> "*Flamineo.*—Why do you kick her, say?
> Do you think that she's like a walnut tree?
> Must she be cudgell'd ere she bear good fruit?"

—Webster's "*White Devil*," 1612. iv.4. (Works, edited by W. C. Hazlitt, II. 105.)

Now all these statements are at once unkind and erroneous all round. We know what is declared of the "man who, save in the way of kindness, lays his hand upon a woman," to say nothing of the punishment awaiting him at the adjacent police court.* As to dogs, those who respect the calves of their legs had best beware of the danger of applying this recipe to any but low-spirited animals. In the case of the walnut-tree, the recommendation is again distinctly false, and the results misdescribed. Possibly there are walnut-trees, as there are women, dogs, and horses, who seem none the worse for the stick; but, as a general rule, kindly treatment, for vegetable and animal alike, is the best, and, in the long run, the wisest.

In "*The Miller's Daughter*," one of the most homely and charming poems ever penned by the Poet Laureate, occurs a quatrain, spoken by an old gentleman addressing his faithful spouse:—

"So sweet it seems with thee to talk,
And once again to woo thee mine;
'Tis like an after-dinner talk
Across the walnuts and the wine."

* In the glee, "Merrily rang the Bells of St. Michael's Tower," we are told that Richard Penlake had a shrew for a wife, and though she had a tongue that was longer, yet—

"Richard Penlake a crabstick would take
And show her that he was the stronger,"

The Christmas Holly.

"The Holly! the Holly! oh, twine it with bay—
 Come give the Holly a song;
For it helps to drive stern Winter away,
 With his garments so sombre and long.
It peeps through the trees with its berries so red,
 And its leaves of burnished green,
When the flowers and fruits have long been dead,
 And not even the daisy is seen.
Then sing to the Holly, the Christmas Holly,
 That hangs over the peasant and king:
While we laugh and carouse 'neath its glittering boughs,
 To the Christmas Holly we'll sing."

Eliza Cook.

In London a large sale is carried on in "Christmasing," or in the sale of holly, ivy, laurel, evergreens, bay, and mistletoe, for Christmas sports and decorations, by the family greengrocer and the costermongers. The latter of whom make the streets ring with their stentorian cry of:—

Holly! Holly!! Holly, oh!!! Christmas Holly, oh!

Old Cries.

By Miss Eliza Cook.

Oh! dearly do I love "Old Cries"
 That touch my heart and bid me look
On "Bough-pots" plucked 'neath summer skies,
 And "Watercresses" from the brook.
It may be vain, it may be weak,
To list when common voices speak;
But rivers with their broad, deep course,
Pour from a mean and unmarked source:
And so my warmest tide of soul
From strange, unheeded spring will roll.

"Old Cries," "Old Cries"—there is not one
But hath a mystic tissue spun
  Around it, flinging on the ear
  A magic mantle rich and dear,
From "Hautboys," pottled in the sun,
  To the loud wish that cometh when
The tune of midnight waits is done
  With "A merry Christmas, gentlemen,
And a Happy New Year—Past one-
  O'clock, and a frosty morning!"

And there was a "cry" in the days gone by,
That ever came when my pillow was nigh;
When, tired and spent I was passively led
By a mother's hand, to my own sweet bed—
My lids grew heavy, and my glance was dim,
As I yawned in the midst of a cradle hymn—
When the watchman's echo lulled me quite,
With "Past ten o'clock, and a starlight night!"

Well I remember the hideous dream,
When I struggled in terror, and strove to scream,
As I took a wild leap o'er the precipice steep,
And convulsively flung off the incubus sleep.
How I loved to behold the moonshine cold
Illume each well-known curtain-fold;
And how I was soothed by the watchman's warning,
Of "Past three o'clock, and a moonlight morning!"

Oh, there was music in this "old cry,"
Whose deep, rough tones will never die:
No rare serenade will put to flight
The chant that proclaimed a "stormy night."

The "watchmen of the city" are gone,
The church-bell speaketh, but speaketh alone;
We hear no voice at the wintry dawning,
With "Past five o'clock, and a cloudy morning!"
Ah, well-a-day! it hath passed away,
  But I sadly miss the cry
That told in the night when the stars were bright,
  Or the rain-cloud veiled the sky.
Watchmen, Watchmen, ye are among
The bygone things that will haunt me long.

"Three bunches a penny, Primroses!"
Oh, dear is the greeting of Spring;
When she offers her dew-spangled posies;
The fairest Creation can bring.

"Three bunches a penny, Primroses!"
The echo resounds in the mart;
And the simple "cry" often uncloses
The worldly bars grating man's heart.

We reflect, we contrive, and we reckon
How best we can gather up wealth;
We go where bright finger-posts beckon,
Till we wander from Nature and Health.

But the "old cry," shall burst on our scheming,
The song of "Primroses" shall flow,
And "Three bunches a penny" set dreaming
Of all that we loved long ago.

It brings visions of meadow and mountain,
Of valley, and streamlet, and hill,
When Life's ocean but played in a fountain—
Ah, would that it sparkled so still!

It conjures back shadowless hours,
When we threaded the dark, forest ways;
When our own hand went seeking the flowers,
And our own lips were shouting their praise.

The perfume and tint of the blossom;
Are as fresh in vale, dingle, and glen;
But say, is the pulse of our bosom
As warm and as bounding as then?

"Three bunches a penny,—Primroses!"
"Three bunches a penny,—come, buy!"
A blessing on all the sweet posies,
And good-will to the poor ones who cry.

"Lavender, sweet Lavender!"
With "Cherry Ripe!" is coming;
While the droning beetles whirr,
And merry bees are humming.

"Lavender, sweet Lavender!"
  Oh, pleasant is the crying;
While the rose-leaves scarcely stir,
  And downy moths are flying,

Oh, dearly do I love "Old Cries,"
  Your "Lilies all a-blowing!"
Your blossoms blue, still wet with dew,
  "Sweet Violets all a-growing!"

Oh, happy were the days, methinks,
  In truth the best of any;
When "Periwinkles, winkle, winks!"
  Allured my last, lone penny.

Oh, what had I to do with cares
  That bring the frown and furrow,
When "Walnuts" and "Fine mellow Pears"
  Beat Catalani thorough.

Full dearly do I love "Old Cries,"
  And always turn to hear them;
And though they cause me some few sighs,
  Those sighs do but endear them.

My heart is like the fair sea-shell,
  There's music ever in it;
Though bleak the shore where it may dwell,
  Some power still lives to win it.

When music fills the shell no more,
  'Twill be all crushed and scattered;
And when this heart's deep tone is o'er,
  'Twill be all cold and shattered.

Oh, vain will be the hope to break
  Its last and dreamless slumbers;
When "Old Cries" come, and fail to wake
  Its deep and fairy numbers!

Dust, O!—Dust, O!—Bring it out to day,
Bring it out to-day, I sha'n't be here to-mor-row!

DUST, O!—DUST, O!.

His noisy bell the dustman rings,
Her dust the housemaid gladly brings:
Ringing he goes from door to door,
Until his cart will hold no more.

THE DUSTMAN.

Bring out your dust, the dustman cries,
  Whilst ringing of his bell:
If the wind blows, pray guard your eyes,
  To keep them clear and well.

I am very glad 'tis not my luck
  To get my bread by carting muck;
I am sure I never could be made
  To work at such a dirty trade.

Hold, my fine spark, not so fast,
  Some proud folks get a fall at last;
And you, young gentleman, I say,
  May be a Dustman, one fine day.

All working folks, who seldom play,
  Yet get their bread in a honest way,
Though not to wealth or honours born,
  Deserve respect instead of scorn.

Such rude contempt they merit less
  Than those who live in idleness;
Who are less useful, I'm afraid,
  Than I, the Dustman, am by trade.

THE BIRDMAN.

Have pity, have pity on poor little birds,
Who only make music, and cannot sing words;
And think, when you listen, we mean by our strain,
O! let us fly home to our woodlands again.

Our dear woody coverts, and thickets so green,
Too close for the school-boy to rustle between;
No foot to alarm us, no sorrow, no rain,
O! let us fly home to our woodlands again.

There perched on the branches that wave to the wind,
No more in this pitiless prison confined,
How gaily we'll tune up our merriest strain,
If once we get home to our woodlands again.

BUY A DOOR-MAT OR A TABLE-MAT.

Stooping o'er the ragged heath,
  Thick with thorns and briers keen,
Or the weedy bank beneath,
  Have I cut my rushes green;
While the broom and spiked thorn
Pearly drops of dew adorn.

Sometimes across the heath I wind,
  Where scarce a human face is seen,
Wandering marshy spots to find,
  Where to cut my rushes green;
Here and there, with weary tread,
Working for a piece of bread.

Then my little child and I
  Plat and weave them, as you see;
Pray my lady, pray do buy,
  You can't have better than of me;
For never, surely were there seen
Prettier mats of rushes green.

I sweep your Chimnies clean, O,
Sweep your Chimney clean, O!

THE CHIMNEY SWEEPER.

With drawling tone, brush under arm,
And bag slung o'er his shoulder:
Behold the sweep the streets alarm,
With Stentor's voice, and louder.

Buy my Diddle Dumplings, hot! hot!
Diddle, diddle, diddle, Dumplings hot!

THE DUMPLING WOMAN.

This woman's in industry wise,
She lives near Butcher-row;
Each night round Temple-bar she plies,
With *Diddle Dumplings, ho!*

Yorkshire Cakes, Who'll buy Yorkshire Cakes,
All piping hot—smoking hot! hot!!

THE YORKSHIRE CAKE MAN.

Fine Yorkshire Cakes; Who'll buy Yorkshire cakes?
They are all piping hot, and nicely made;
His daily walk this fellow takes,
And seems to drive a pretty trade.

Buy my Flowers, sweet Flowers, new-cut Flowers,
New Flowers, sweet Flowers, fresh Flowers, O!

FLOWERS, CUT FLOWERS.

New-cut Flowers this pretty maid doth cry,
  In Spring, Summer and Autumn, gaily ;
Which shows how fast the Seasons fly—
  As we pass to our final home, daily.

Buy green and large Cucumbers, Cucumbers,
Green and large Cucumbers, twelve a penny.

CUCUMBERS.

A penny a dozen, Cucumbers!
Tailors, hallo! hallo!
Now from the shop-board each man runs,
For Cucumbers below.

Buy Rosemary! Buy Sweetbriar!
Rosemary and Sweetbriar, O!

ROSEMARY AND SWEETBRIAR.

Rosemary and briar sweet,
This maiden now doth cry,
Through every square and street,
Come buy it sweet, come buy it dry.

Newcastle Salmon! Dainty fine Salmon!
Dainty fine Salmon! Newcastle Salmon!

NEWCASTLE SALMON.

Newcastle salmon, very good,
Is just come in for summer food;
No one hath better fish than I,
So if you've money come and buy.

Buy my Cranberries! Fine Cranberries!
Buy my Cranberries! Fine Cranberries!

CRANBERRIES.

Buy Cranberries, to line your crust,
In Lincolnshire they're grown;
Come buy, come buy, for sell I must
Three quarts for half-a-crown.

Come buy my Walking-Sticks or Canes!
I've got them for the young or old.

STICKS AND CANES.

How sloven like the school-boy looks,
Who daubs his books at play;
Give him a new one? No, adzooks!
Give him a Cane, I say.

Buy my fine Gooseberries! Fine Gooseberries!
Three-pence a quart! Ripe Gooseberries!

GOOSEBERRIES.

Ripe gooseberries in town you'll buy
As cheap as cheap can be;
Of many sorts you hear the cry;
Pray purchase, sir, of me!

Pears for pies! Come feast your eyes!
Ripe Pears, of every size, who'll buy?

RIPE PEARS.

Pears ripe, pears sound,
  This woman cries all day;
Pears for pies, long or round,
  Come buy them while you may.

One a penny, two a penny, hot Cross Buns!
One a penny, two a penny, hot Cross Buns!

HOT CROSS BUNS.

Think on this sacred festival;
Think why Cross Buns were given;
Then think of Him who dy'd for all,
To give you right to Heaven.

Maids, I mend old Pans or Kettles,
Mend old Pans or Kettles, O!

THE TINKER.

Hark, who is this? the Tinker bold,
To mend or spoil your kettle,
Whose wife I'm certain is a scold,
Made of basest metal.

Buy my Capers! Buy my nice Capers!
Buy my Anchovies! Buy my nice Anchovies!

CAPERS, ANCHOVIES.

How melodious the voice of this man,
The Capers he says are the best;
His Anchovies too, beat 'em who can,
Are constantly found in request.

Mulberries, all ripe and fresh to day!
Only a groat a pottle—full to the bottom!

MULBERRIES.

Mulberries, ripe and fresh to-day,
They warm and purify the blood;
Have them a groat a pottle you may.
They are all fresh! they are all good!

Buy my Cockles! Fine new Cockles!
Cockles fine, and Cockles new!

NEW COCKLES

Cockles fine; and cockles new,
 They are as fine as any.
Cockles! New cockles, O!
 I sell a good lot for a penny, O!

Buy fine Flounders! Fine Dabs! All alive, O!
Fine Dabs! Fine live Flounders, O!

BUY FINE FLOUNDERS! FINE DABS!

There goes a tall fish-woman sounding her cry,
"Who'll buy my fine flounders, and dabs, who'll buy?"
Poor flounder, he heaves up his fin with a sigh,
And thinks that *he* has most occasion to cry;
"Ah, neighbour," says dab, "indeed, so do I."

Buy my nice and new Banbury Cakes!
Buy my nice new Banbury Cakes, O!

BANBURY CAKES.

Buy Banbury Cakes! By fortune's frown,
 You see this needy man,
Along the street, and up and down,
 Is selling all he can.

Buy my Lavender! Sweet blooming Lavender!
Sweet blooming Lavender! Blooming Lavender!

LAVENDER.

Lavender! Sweet blooming lavender,
Six bunches for a penny to-day!
Lavender! sweet blooming lavender!
Ladies, buy it while you may.

Live Mackerel! Three a-shilling, O!
Le'ping alive, O! Three a-shilling O!

MACKEREL.

Live Mackerel, oh! fresh as the day!
At three for a shilling, is giving away;
Full row'd, like bright silver they shine;
Two persons on one can sup or dine.

Buy my Shirt Buttons! Shirt Buttons!
Buy Shirt Hand Buttons! Buttons!

SHIRT BUTTONS.

At a penny a dozen, a dozen,
  My Buttons for shirts I sell,
Come aunt, uncle, sister, and cousin,
  I'll warrant I'll use you well.

Buy my Rabbits! Rabbits, who'll buy?
Rabbit! Rabbit! who will buy?

THE RABBIT MAN.

"Rabbit! Rabbit! who will buy?'
Is all you hear from him;
The Rabbit you may roast or fry,
The fur your cloak will trim.

Buy Rue! Buy Sage! Buy Mint!
Buy Rue, Sage and Mint, a farthing a bunch!

THE HERB-WIFE.

As thro' the fields she bends her way,
Pure nature's work discerning;
So you should practice every day,
To trace the fields of learning.

Apple Tarts! All sweet and good, to-day!
Hot, nice, sweet and good, to day!

APPLE TARTS. APPLE TARTS.

Apple Tarts ! Apple Tarts ! Tarts, I cry !
They are all of my own making,
My Apple Tarts ! My Apple Tarts, come buy !
For, a honest penny I would be taking.

Ripe Strawberries! a groat a pottle, to-day,
Only a groat a pottle, is what I say!

RIPE AND FRESH STRAWBERRIES.

Ripe strawberries, a full pottle for a groat!
They are all ripe and fresh gathered, as you see,
No finer for money I believe can be bought;
So I pray you come and deal fairly with me.

Any Knives, or Scissors to grind, to-day?
Big Knives, or little Knives, or Scissors to grind, O!

ANY KNIVES OR SCISSORS TO GRIND.

Any Knives or Scissors to grind, to-day?
I'll do them well and there's little to pay;
Any Knives or Scissors to grind, to-day?
If you've nothing for me, I'll go away.

Door-Mat! Door-Mat, Buy a Door-Mat,
Rope-mat! Rope-Mat! Buy a Rope-Mat.

Rope Mat. Door Mat.

Rope Mat! Door Mat! you really must
Buy one to save the mud and dust;
Think of the dirt brought from the street
For the want of a Mat to wipe your feet.

Clothes Props! Clothes Props! I say, good wives
Clothes Props, all long and very strong, to-day.

CLOTHES PROPS, CLOTHES PROPS.

Buy Clothes Props, Buy Clothes Props!
Pretty maids, or pretty wives, I say,
I sell them half the price of the shops;
So you'll buy of the old man, I pray.

Come take a Peep, boys, take a Peep?
Girls, I've the wonder of the world.

THE RAREE-SHOW.

Come take a Peep, each lady and gent,
My Show is the best, I assure you;
You'll not have the least cause to repent,
For I'll strive all I can to allure you.

Water Cresses! Fine Spring Water Cresses!
Three bunches a penny, young Water Cresses!

WATER CRESSES. FRESH AND FINE.

Young Cresses, fresh, at breakfast taken
 A relish will give to eggs and bacon!
My profit's small, for I put many
 In bunches sold at three a penny

Mutton Pies! Mutton Pies! Mutton Pies,
Come feast your eyes with my Mutton Pies.

WHO'LL BUY MY MUTTON PIES?

Through London's long and busy streets,
This honest woman cries,
To every little boy she meets,
Who'll buy my Mutton Pies?

Please to Pity the Poor Old Fiddler!
Pity the Poor Old Blind Fiddler!

THE POOR OLD FIDDLER.

The poor old Fiddler goes his rounds,
  Along with old Dog Tray;
The East of London mostly bounds
  His journeys for the day.

Muffins, O! Crumpets! Muffins, to-day!
Crumpets, O! Muffins, O! fresh, to-day!

THE MUFFIN MAN.

The Muffin Man! hark, I hear
His small bell tinkle shrill and clear;
Muffins and Crumpets nice he brings,
While on the fire the kettle sings.

Oysters, fresh and alive, three a penny, O!
When they are all sold I sha'n't have any, O!

OYSTERS. FINE NEW OYSTERS.

They're all alive and very fine,
So if you like them, come and dine;
I'll find you bread and butter, too,
Or you may have them opened for a stew.

Buy fine Kidney Potatoes! New Potatoes!
Fine Kidney Potatoes! Potatoes, O!

POTATOES, KIDNEY POTATOES.

Potatoes, oh! of kidney kind,
Come buy, and boil, and eat,
The core, and eke also, the rind,
They are indeed so sweet.

Buy Images! Good and cheap!
Images, very good—very cheap!

BUY MY IMAGES, IMAGES.

Come buy my image earthenware,
Your mantel pieces to bedeck,
Examine them with greatest care,
You will not find a single speck.

Buy 'em by the stick, or buy 'em by the pound,
Cherries ripe, all round and sound!

ALL ROUND AND SOUND, MY RIPE KENTISH CHERRIES.

Who such Cherries would see,
And not tempted be
To wish he possessed a small share?
But observe, I say small,
For those who want all
Deserve not to taste of such fare.

Buy a Mop! Buy a Broom! Good to-day!
Buy a Broom! Buy a Mop, I say!

BUY A MOP OR A BROOM.

Ye cleanly housewives come to me,
And buy a Mop or Broom,
To sweep your chambers, scour your stairs,
Or wash your sitting room.

Golden Pippins, all of the right sort, girls!
Golden Pippins, all of the right sort, boys!

GOLDEN PIPPINS, WHO'LL BUY?

Here are fine Golden Pippins;
  Who'll buy them, who'll buy?
Nobody in London sells better than I!
  Who'll buy them, who'll buy?

Wash Ball, a Trinket, or a Watch, buy?
Buy 'em, all cheap and all good!

WASH BALL, TRINKET. OR WATCH.

Do ye want any Wash Ball or Patch.—
Dear ladies, pray, buy of me;—
Or Trinkets to hang at your Watch,
Or Garters to tie at your knee?

Past twelve o'clock, and a cloudy morning!
Past twelve o'clock; and mind, I give you warning!

THE CITY WATCHMAN

Past twelve o'clock, and a moonlight night!
Past twelve o'clock, and the stars shine bright!
Past twelve o'clock, your doors are all fast like you!
Past twelve o'clock, and I'll soon be fast, too!

Young Lambs to sell! Young Lambs to sell!
Young Lambs to sell! Young Lambs to sell!

YOUNG LAMBS TO SELL.

Young Lambs to sell! Young Lambs to sell!
Two a penny, Young Lambs to sell;
If I'd as much money as I could tell,
I wouldn't cry young Lambs to sell.

Buy my sweet and rare Lilies of the Valley?
Buy of your Sally—Sally of our Alley?

LILIES OF THE VALLEY.

In London street, I ne'er could find,
A girl like lively Sally,
Who picks and culls, and cries aloud,
Sweet Lilies of the Valley

Buy my young chickens! Buy'em alive, O!
Buy of the Fowlman, and have 'em alive, O!

BUY CHICKENS, YOUNG CHICKENS

Buy my young Chickens, or a Fowl, well-fed,
And we'll not quarrel about the price;
'Tis thus I get my daily bread:
As all the year round my Fowls are very nice.

Green Peas, I say! Green Peas, I say, here,
Hav'em at your own price—here! here!

GREEN PEAS! BUY MY GREEN PEAS?

Sixpence a peck, these Peas are sold,
Fresh and green, and far from old;
Green Marrows, it is quite clear,
And as times go, cannot be dear,

Hat Box! Cap Box! Boxes, all sizes;
All good, and at very low prices.

HAT-BOX; CAP BOX.

Hat or Cap Box! for ribbons or lace,
  When in a Box, keep in their place;
And in a Box, your favourite bonnet
  Is safe from getting things thrown on it.

Eels, fine Silver Eels! Dutch Eels!
They are all alive—Silver Eels!

EELS; FINE DUTCH EELS.

Eels, alive! fine Dutch eels, I cry,
Mistress, to use you well I'm willing,
Come step forth and buy—
Take four pounds for one shilling.

Plumbs, ripe Plumbs! Big as your thumbs!
Plumbs! Plumbs! Big as your thumbs!

PLUMBS; RIPE PLUMBS.

Plumbs, for puddings or pies,
This noisy woman bawls;
Plumbs, for puddings or pies,
In every street she calls.

Buy a Purse; a long and a strong Purse!
A good leather or a strong mole-skin Purse!

BUY A PURSE.

Buy a Purse; a long and strong Purse,
They'll suit the young—they suit the old!
To lose good money, what is worse?
Yet it's daily done for the want of a purse.

Kettles to mend! any Pots to mend?
Daily I say as my way I wend.

KETTLES OR POTS TO MEND!

Kettles to mend! any pots to mend!
You cannot do better to me than send;
Think of the mess when the saucepans run,
The fire put out, and the dinner not done.

The Jolly Tinker.

My daddy was a tinker's son,
And I'm his boy, 'tis ten to one,
Here's pots to mend ! was still his cry,
Here's pots to mend ! aloud bawl I.
Have ye any tin pots, kettles or cans,
Coppers to solder, or brass pans ?
Of wives my dad had near a score,
And I have twice as many more :
My daddy was the lord—I don't know who—
With his :—
Tan ran tan, tan ran tan tan,
For pot or can, oh ! I'm your man.

Once I in my budget snug had got
A barn-door capon, and what not,
Here's pots to mend ! I cried along—
Here's pots to mend ! was my song.
At village wake—oh ! curse his throat,
The cock crowed so loud a note,
The folks in clusters flocked around,
They seized my budget, in it found
The cock, a gammon, peas and beans,
Besides a jolly tinker. Yes, a jolly tinker—
With his—
Tan ran tan, tan ran tan tan,
For pot or can, oh ! I'm your man.

Like dad, when I to quarters come,
For want of cash the folks I hum,
Here's kettles to mend : Bring me some beer !
The landlord cries, " You'll get none here !
You tink'ring dog, pay what you owe,
Or out of doors you'll instant go,"
In rage I squeezed him 'gainst the door,
And with his back rubb'd off the score.
At his expense we drown all strife
For which I praise the landlord's wife—
With my
Tan ran tan, tan ran tan tan,
For pot or can, oh ! I'm your man.

Fine China Oranges, sweet as sugar!
They are very fine, and cheap, too, to-day.

FINE CHINA ORANGES.

If friends permit, and money suits,
The tempting purchase make;
But, first, examine well the fruit,
And then the change you take.

FINE RIPE ORANGES

Here are Oranges, fine ripe Oranges,
  Of golden colour to the eye,
And fragrant perfume they're dispensing,
  Sweeter than roses; come then and buy
Flowers cannot give forth the fragrance
  That scents the air from my golden store,
Fairest lady, none can excel them,
  Buy then my Oranges; buy, I implore.

Here are Oranges, fine ripe Oranges,
  Golden globes of nectar fine,
Luscious juice the gods might envy,
  Richer far than the finest wine.
Flowers cannot give forth the fragrance
  That scents the air from my golden store,
Fairest lady, none can excel them,
  Buy then my Oranges; buy, I implore.

ROUND FOR FOUR VOICES.

SIR. J. STEVENSON.

Come buy my cherries, beauteous lasses;
Fresh from the garden pluck'd by me;
All on a summer's day, so gay,
You hear the London Cries—"*Knives ground here by me.*"

Fine apples and choice pears,
Eat, boys, forget your cares;
All on a summer's day, so gay,
You hear the London Cries—"*Sweep, sweep, sweep.*"

Fruit in abundance sold by me,
Fruit in abundance here you see;
All on a summer's day, so gay,
You hear the London Cries—"*Parsnips, carrots, and choice beans.*"

Whey, fine sweet whey,
Come taste my whey;
All on a summer's day, so gay,
You hear the London Cries—"*Fine radish, fine lettuce, sold by me.*"

PRIMROSES.

Come who'll buy my roses, Primroses, who'll buy?
They are sweet to the sense, they are fair to the eye;
They are covered all o'er with diamond dew,
Which Aurora's bright handmaids unsparingly threw
On their beautiful heads: and I ask but of you—
To buy, buy, buy, buy.

The sun kiss'd the flowers as he rose from the sea bright,
And their golden eyes opened with beauty and glee bright,
Their sweets are untasted by hornet or bee—
They are fresh as the morning and lovely to see—
So reject not the blossoms now offered by me—
But buy, buy, buy, buy.

Nay, never refuse me, nor cry my buds down,
They are nature's production, and sweet ones, you'll own;
And tho' torn from the earth, they will smile in your hall,
They will bloom in a cottage, be it ever so small—
And still look the lovliest flowers of all!
So buy, buy, buy, buy.

[Pages 307 through 336 do not exist]

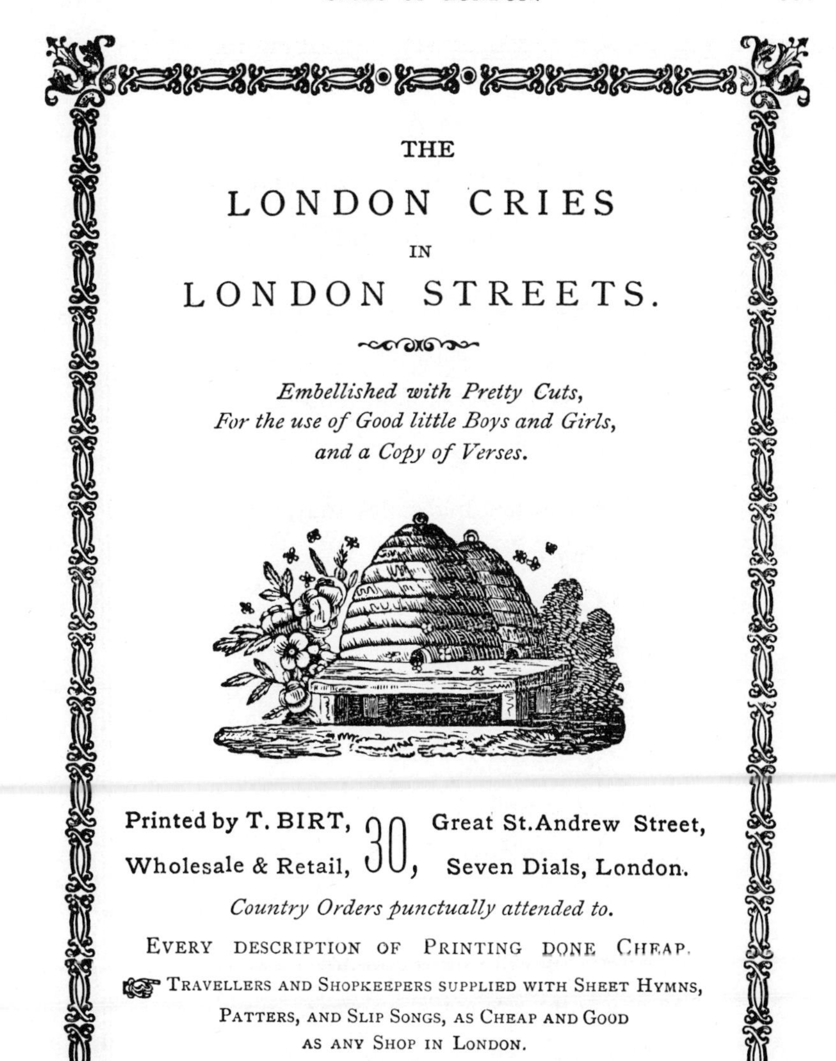

THE

LONDON CRIES

IN

LONDON STREETS.

Embellished with Pretty Cuts,
For the use of Good little Boys and Girls,
and a Copy of Verses.

Printed by T. BIRT, 30, Great St. Andrew Street,
Wholesale & Retail, Seven Dials, London.

Country Orders punctually attended to.

EVERY DESCRIPTION OF PRINTING DONE CHEAP.

☞ TRAVELLERS AND SHOPKEEPERS SUPPLIED WITH SHEET HYMNS, PATTERS, AND SLIP SONGS, AS CHEAP AND GOOD AS ANY SHOP IN LONDON.

T. BIRT.

To the Good Little Masters and Mistresses in Town and Country.

Here! look at the Cries of London town,
For you need not travel there;
But view you those of most renown,
Whilst sitting in your chair.

At Home—a hundred miles away,
'Tis easy now to look
At the Cries of London gay,
In this our little book.

Yes; there in quiet you may be,
Beside the winter's fire,
And read as well as see,
All those that you desire.

Or underneath the oak so grey,
That grows beside the briar;
May pass the summer's eve away,
And view each City Crier.

BUY A GAZETTE? GREAT NEWS!

In the Gazette great news, to-day:
The enemy is beat, they say,
And all arc cager to be told—
The news, the new events unfold.

COME BUY MY FINE ROSES.

Come buy my fine roses,
My myrtles and stocks;
My sweet smelling balsams
And close growing box.

BUY AN ALMANACK : NEW ALMANACKS.

My Almanacks aim at no learning at all,
But only to show when the holidays fall :
And tell, as by study we easily may,
How many eclipses the year will display.

Buy a Mop? Buy a Mop?

My Mop is so big,
It might serve as a wig
For a judge, had he no objection;
And as to my brooms,
They will sweep dirty rooms,
And make the dust fly, to perfection.

LOBSTERS AND CRABS.

Here's lobsters and crabs,
Alive, O! and good,
So buy if you please;
This delicate food.

MILK FROM THE COW.

Rich Milk from the Cow,
Both sweet and fine ;
The doctors declare ;
It is better than wine.

BUY A BASKET, LARGE OR SMALL?

Buy a basket? large or small?
For all sorts I've got by me,
So come ye forth, one and all,
If you buy once, another time you'll try me

BUY A CANE FOR NAUGHTY BOYS.

I've Sticks and Canes for old and young,
To either they are handy,
In driving off a barking cur,
Or chastising a dandy.

Hot Rice-Milk.

Hot Rice-Milk this woman calls—
   Behold her bright can,
As up and down the streets shc bawls
   Hot Ricc-Milk to warm the inner man.

PEACHES AND NECTARINES.

Nice Peaches and Nectarines
Just fresh from the tree;
All you who have money,
Come buy them of me.

HOT SPICE-GINGERBREAD.

Hot Spice-Gingerbread, hot ! hot ! all hot !
This noisy fellow loudly bawls,
Hot ! hot ! hot ! smoking hot ! red hot !
In every street or public place he calls.

Come, Buy my Spice-Gingerbread, Smoking Hot! Hot! Hot!

Come, boys and girls, men and maids, widows and wives,
The best penny laid out you e'er spent in your lives;
Here's my whirl-a-gig lottery, a penny a spell,
No blanks, but all prizes, and that's pretty well.
Don't stand humming and ha-aring, with ifs and with buts,
Try your luck for my round and sound gingerbread-nuts;
And there's my glorious spice-gingerbread, too,
Hot enough e'en to thaw the heart of a Jew.

Hot spice-gingerbread, hot! hot! all hot!
Come, buy my spice-gingerbread, smoking hot!

I'm a gingerbread-merchant, but what of that, then?
All the world, take my word, deal in gingerbread ware;
Your fine beaus and your belles and your rattlepate rakes—
One half are game-nuts, the rest gingerbread cakes;
Then in gingerbread coaches we've gingerbread lords,
And gingerbread soldiers with gingerbread swords.
And what are you patriots, 'tis easy to tell—
By their constantly crying they've something to sell.
And what harm is there in selling—*hem!*—

Hot spice-gingerbread, &c.

My gingerbread-lottery is just like the world,
For its index of chances for ever is twirled;
But some difference between'em exist, without doubt,
The world's lottery has blanks, while mine's wholly without,
There's no matter how often you shuffle and cut,
If but once in ten games you can get a game-nut.
So I laugh at the world, like an impudent elf,
And just like my betters, take care of myself, and my—

Hot spice-gingerbread, &c.

T. Birt, Printer, 30, Great St. Andrews Street, Seven Dials.

Marks Edition.

THE NEW LONDON CRIES
OR A
VISIT TO TOWN.

BUY A BROOM.

From morn till eve I rove along,
And joys my eyes illume,
If you but listen to my song,
And kindly buy a broom.

W

RIPE CHERRIES.

Cherries ripe four-pence a pound,
Come buy of me they're good and sound.

WATER CRESSES.

O you whom peace and plenty blesses,
Buy my fine spring water cresses.

YOUNG PEDLAR.

Threads laces bodkins here I cry,
Of a wandering orphan buy.

OYSTERS SIR.

My native oysters here I cry,
Gents and ladies come and buy.

OLD CLOTHES.

Daily streets and squares I range
Calling clothes to sell or change.

YOUNG LAMBS.

In London streets I'm known full well,
Two for a penny young lambs to sell.

DOLLS TO SELL.

Come buy a doll my little miss,
You'll find no time as good as this

GREENS CABBAGES HO.

London daily hears my cry,
Carrots Turnips who will buy.

Bonnet Box.

Buy a Box for hat and cap,
'Twill keep them safe from all mishap.

Flower Girl.

My basket daily I supply,
Come buy my nosegays buy who'll buy.

IMAGES.

My casts are form'd to get my bread,
And humble shelter for my head.

MILK BELOW.

At rise of morn my rounds I go,
And daily cry my milk below.

BALLAD SINGER.

Listen to my tunes so gay,
And buy a ballad of me pray

SWEEP SOOT HO.

Comfort from my toil you reap,
Then pray employ a little sweep.

London : Printed and Published by S. MARKS & SONS, 72, Houndsditch.

THE

CRIES OF LONDON.

FLOWERY WARE—ALL HOT!

Here's taters hot, my little chaps,
Now just lay out a copper,
I'm known up and down the Strand,
You'll not find any hotter.

LONDON:
GOODE, BROS.,
WHOLESALE STATIONERS AND TOY BOOK MANUFACTURERS,
CLERKENWELL GREEN.

CHERRIES, MY PRETTY MAIDS.

Here's cherries, oh ! my pretty maids,
My cherries round and sound ;
Whitehearts, Kentish, or Blackhearts
And only twopence a pound.

FINE HAMPSHIRE RABBITS.

Here I am with my rabbits
Hanging on my pole,
The finest Hampshire rabbits
That e'er crept from a hole.

HEARTHSTONE! HEARTHSTONE.

Hearthstones my pretty maids,
I sell them four a penny,
Hearthstones, come buy of me,
As long as I have any.

DUST OH ! DUST OH !

Dust or ash this chap calls out,
With all his might and main,
He's got a mighty cinder heap
Somewhere near Gray's Inn Lane.

BUY A BONNET BOX OR CAP BOX

Bonnet boxes and cap boxes,
The best that e'er was seen,
They are so very nicely made,
They'll keep your things so clean.

ALL A GROWING AND A BLOWING.

Now ladies here's roots for your gardens,
Come buy some of me if you please,
There's tulips, heart's-ease, and roses,
Sweet Williams, and sweet peas.

Any Old Pots or Kettles to Mend?

Any old pots or kettles,
Or any old brass to mend?
Come my pretty maids all,
To me your aid must lend.

ANY OLD CHAIRS TO MEND?

Any old chairs to mend?
Any old chairs to seat?
I'll make them quite as good as new,
And make them look so neat.

The London Street-Markets on a Saturday Night.

Mr. Henry Mayhew has painted a minute yet vivid picture of the London street markets, street sellers and purchasers which are to be seen in the greatest number on a Saturday night :—

" Here, and in the streets immediately adjoining, the working classes generally purchase their Sunday's dinner; and after pay-time on Saturday night, or early on Sunday morning, the crowd in the New-cut, and the Brill in particular, is almost impassable. Indeed, the scene in these parts has more the character of a fair than a market. There are hundreds of stalls, and every stall has its one or two lights; either it is illuminated by the intense white light of the new self-generating gas-lamp, or else it is brightened up by the red smoky flame of the old-fashioned grease-lamp. One man shows off his yellow haddock with a candle stuck in a bundle of firewood; his neighbour makes a candlestick of a huge turnip, and the tallow gutters over its sides; whilst the boy shouting " Eight a penny, stunning pears !" has rolled his dip in a thick coat of brown paper, that flares away with the candle. Some stalls are crimson with the fire shining through the holes beneath the baked chesnut stove; others have handsome octohedral lamps, while a few have a candle shining through a sieve; these, with the sparkling ground-glass globes of the tea-dealers' shops, and the butchers' gaslights streaming and fluttering in the wind, like flags of flame, pour forth such a flood of light, that at a distance the atmosphere immediately above the spot is as lurid as if the street were on fire.

A STREET-MARKET ON SATURDAY NIGHT.

The pavement and the road are crowded with purchasers and street-sellers. The housewife in her thick shawl, with the market-basket on her arm, walks slowly on, stopping now to look at the stall of caps, and now to cheapen a bunch of greens. Little boys, holding three or four onions in their hands, creep between the people, wriggling their way through every interstice, and asking for custom in whining tones, as if seeking charity. Then the tumult of the thousand different cries of the eager dealers, all shouting at the top of their voices, at one and the same time, is almost bewildering. "So-old again," roars one. "Chesnuts, all 'ot, a penny a score," bawls another. "An 'aypenny a skin, blacking," squeaks a boy. "Buy, buy, buy, buy,—bu-u-uy!" cries the butcher. "Half-quire of paper for a penny," bellows the street-stationer. "An 'apenny a lot ing-uns." "Twopence a pound, grapes." "Three a penny! Yarmouth bloaters." "Who'll buy a bonnet for fourpence?" "Pick 'em out cheap here! three pair for a-halfpenny, boot-laces." "Now's your time! beautiful whelks, a penny a lot." "Here's ha'p'orths," shouts the perambulating confectioner. "Come and look at'em! here's toasters!" bellows one with a Yarmouth bloater stuck on a toasting fork. "Penny a lot, fine russets," calls the apple woman: and so the Babel goes on.

One man stands with his red-edge mats hanging over his back and chest, like a herald's coat; and the girl with her basket of walnuts lifts her brown-stained fingers to her mouth, as she screams, "Fine warnuts! sixteen a penny, fine war-r-nuts." A bootmaker, to "ensure custom," has illuminated his front-shop with a line of gas, and in its full glare stands a blind beggar, his eyes turned up so as to show only "the whites," and mumbling some begging rhymes, that are drowned in the shrill notes of the bamboo-flute-player next to him. The boy's sharp cry, the woman's cracked voice, the gruff, hoarse shout of the man, are all mingled together. Sometimes an Irishman is heard with his "fine ating apples," or else the jingling music of an unseen organ breaks out, as the trio of street singers rest between the verses.

Then the sights, as you elbow your way through the crowd are equally multifarious. Here is a stall glittering with new tin saucepans; there another, bright with its blue and yellow crockery, and sparkling with white glass. Now you come to a row of old shoes arranged along the pavement; now to a stand of gaudy tea-trays; then to a shop with red handkerchiefs and blue checked shirts, fluttering backwards and forwards, and a counter built up outside on the kerb, behind which are boys beseeching custom. At the door of a tea-shop, with its hundred white globes of light, stands a man delivering bills, thanking the public for past favours, and "defying competition." Here, along side the road, are some half-dozen headless tailors, dummies, dressed in Chesterfields and fustian jackets, each labelled:— "Look at the prices," or "Observe the quality," After this a butcher's shop, crimson and white with meat piled up to the first-floor, in front of all the butcher himself, in his blue coat, walks up and down, sharpening his knife on the steel that hangs to his waist. A little further on stands the clean family, begging; the father with his head down as if in shame, and a box of lucifers held forth in his hand—the boys in newly-washed pinafores, and the tidyly got up mother with a child at her breast. This stall is green and white with bunches of turnips—that red with apples, the next yellow with onions, and another purple with pickling cabbages. One minute you pass a man with an umbrella turned inside up and full of prints; the next, you hear one with a peepshow of Mazeppa, and Paul Jones the pirate, describing the pictures to the boys looking in at the little round windows. Then is heard the sharp snap of the purcussion-cap from the crowd of lads firing at the target for nuts; and the moment afterwards, you see either a black man half-clad in white, and shivering in the cold with tracts in his hand, or else you hear the sounds of music from "Frazier's Circus," on the other side of the road, and the man outside the door of the penny concert, beseeching you to "Be in time—be in time!" as Mr. Somebody is just about to sing his favourite song of the "Knife Grinder." Such, indeed, is the riot, the struggle, and the scramble for a living, that the confusion and the uproar of the New-cut on Saturday night have a bewildering and sad effect upon the thoughtful mind.

Each salesman tries his utmost to sell his wares, tempting the passers-by with his bargains. The boy with his stock of herbs offers "a double 'andful of fine parsley for a penny;" the man with the donkey-cart filled with turnips has three lads to shout for him to their utmost, with their "Ho! ho! hi-i-i! What do you think of us here? A penny a bunch—hurrah for free trade! *Here's* your turnips!" Until it is seen and heard, we have no sense of the scramble that is going on throughout London for a living. The same scene takes place at the Brill—the same in Leather-lane—the same in Tottenham-court-road—the same in Whitecross-street; go to whatever corner of the metropolis you please, either on a Saturday night or a Sunday morning, and there is the same shouting and the same struggling to get the penny profit out of the poor man's Sunday's dinner.

Since the above description was written, the New Cut has lost much of its noisy and brilliant glory. In consequence of a New Police regulation, "stands" or "pitches" have been forbidden, and each coster, on a market night, is now obliged, under pain of the lock-up house, to carry his tray, or keep moving with his barrow. The gay stalls have been replaced by deal boards, some sodden with wet fish, others stained purple with blackberries, or brown with walnut peel; and the bright lamps are almost totally superseded by the dim, guttering candle. Even if the pole under the tray or "shallow" is seen resting on the ground, the policeman on duty is obliged to interfere.

The mob of purchasers has diminished one-half; and instead of the road being filled with customers and trucks, the pavement and kerbstones are scarcely crowded.

The Sunday Morning Markets.

Nearly every poor man's market does its Sunday trade. For a few hours on the Sabbath morning, the noise, bustle, and scramble of the Saturday night are repeated, and but for this opportunity many a poor family would pass a dinnerless Sunday. The system of paying the mechanic late on the Saturday night and more particularly of paying a man his wages in a public-house—when he is tired with his day's work, lures him to the tavern, and there the hours fly quickly enough beside the warm tap-room fire, so that by the time the wife comes for her husband's wages, she finds a large portion of them gone in drink and the streets half cleared, thus the Sunday market is the only chance of getting the Sunday's dinner.

Of all these Sunday morning markets, the Brill, perhaps, furnishes the busiest scene; so that it may be taken as a type of the whole.

The streets in the neighbourhood are quiet and empty. The shops are closed with their different coloured shutters, and the people round about are dressed in the shiny cloth of the holiday suit. There are no "cabs," and but few omnibuses to disturb the rest, and men walk in the road as safely as on the footpath.

As you enter the Brill the market sounds are scarcely heard. But at each step the low hum grows gradually into the noisy shouting, until at last the different cries become distinct, and the hubbub, din, and confusion of a thousand voices bellowing at once, again fill the air. The road and footpath are crowded, as on the over-night; the men are standing in groups, smoking and talking; whilst the women run to and fro, some with the white round turnips showing out of their filled aprons, others with cabbages under their arms, and a piece of red meat dangling from their hands. Only a few of the shops are closed; but the butcher's and the coal shed are filled with customers, and from the door of the shut-up baker's, the women come streaming forth with bags of flour in their hands, while men sally from the halfpenny barber's, smoothing their clean-shaved chins. Walnuts, blacking, apples, onions, braces, combs, turnips, herrings, pens, and corn-plasters, are all bellowed out at the same time. Labourers and mechanics, still unshorn and undressed, hang about with their hands in their pockets, some with their pet terriers under their arms. The pavement is green with the refuse leaves of vegetables, and round a cabbage-barrow the women stand turning over the bunches, as the man shouts "Where you like, only a penny." Boys are running home with the breakfast herring held in a piece of paper, and the side-pocket of an apple-man's stuff coat hangs down with the weight of halfpence stored within it. Presently the tolling of the neighbouring church bells break forth. Then the bustle doubles itself, the cries grow louder, the confusion greater. Women run about and push their way through the throng, scolding the saunterers, for in half-an-hour the market will close. In a little time the butcher puts up his shutters, and leaves the door still open ; the policemen in their clean gloves come round and drive the street-sellers before them, and as the clock strikes eleven the market finishes, and the Sunday's rest begins."

As it was in the beginning of our book and in the days of Queen Elizabeth :—

"When the City shopkeepers railed against itinerant traders of every denomination, and the Common Council declared that in ancient times the open streets and lanes had been used, and ought to be used only, as the common highway, and not for hucksters, pedlars, and hagglers, to stand and sell their wares in"—

so it is now, in the Victorian age, and ever will be a very vexed question, and thinking representative men of varied social positions materially differ in opinion ; some contending that the question is not of class interest but that of the interest of the public at large; some argue in an effective but perfectly legal and orderly manner for the removal of what they term a greivous nuisance; others ask that an industrious and useful class of men and women should be allowed their honest calling. They protest against the enforcement of an almost obsolete statute which conduces to the waste of fruit, fish, and vegetables, in London and large towns, which practically maintains a trade monopoly, and discourages an abundant supply. They claim for the public a right to buy in the cheapest market, and plead for a liberty which is enjoyed unmolested in many parts of the kingdom, and protest against a remnant of protectionist restriction being put into force against street-hawking.

By the side of this temperate reasoning, let us place the principal arguments which are so often reiterated by aldermen, deputies, councillors, vestrymen, and others, when "drest in a little brief authority," and come at once to the *gravamen* of the charge against the hawkers, which we find to consist in the nuisance of the street cries.

London, as a commercial city, has numbers of visitors and residents to whom quiet is of vital importance. The street cries, it is alleged, constitute a nuisance to the public, particularly to numbers of day-time-alone occupants, to whom time and thought is money. It is the same thing repeated with many of the suburban residents, in what is generally known as quiet neighbourhoods. Discounting duly the rhetorical exaggeration, it is to be feared the charge must be admitted. Therefore, the shopkeepers argue, let us put down the hawking of everything and everybody. But this does not follow at all. Not only so, but the proposed remedy is ridiculously inadequate to the occasion. Admit the principle, however, for the sake of argument and let us see whither it will lead us. At early morn how often are our matutinal slumbers disturbed by a prolonged shriek, as of some unfortunate cat in mortal agony, but which simply signifies that Mr. Skyblue, the milkman, is on his rounds. The milkman, it is evident, must be abolished. People can easily get their breakfast milk at any respectable dairyman's shop, and get it, too, with less danger of an aqueous dilution. After breakfast—to say nothing of German bands and itinerant organ grinders—a gentleman with a barrow wakens the echoes by the announcement of fresh mackerel, salmon, cod, whiting, soles or plaice, with various additional epithets, descriptive of their recent arrival from the sea. The voice is more loud than melodious, the repetition is frequent, and the effect is the reverse of pleasing to the public ear. Accordingly we must abolish fish hawking: any respectable fishmonger will supply us with better fish without making so much noise over it; and if he charges a higher price it is only the indubitable right of a respectable tradesman and a ratepayer. Then comes on the scene, and determined to have a voice—and a loud one,too,in the morning's hullabaloo, the costermonger—Bill Smith, he declares with stentorian lungs that his cherries, plums, apples, pears, turnips, carrots, cabbages, *cow*cumbers, *sparrow*-grass, *colly*-flow-ers, *inguns*, *ru-bub*, and *taters*, is, and allus vos rounder, sounder, longer, stronger, heavier, fresher, and ever-so-much cheaper than any shopkeeping greengrocer as ever vos: Why? "Vy? cos he don't keep not no slap-up shop vith all plate-glass vinders and a 'andsome sixty five guinea 'oss and trap to take the missus and the kids out on-a-arternoon, nor yet send his sons and darters to a boarding school to larn French, German, Greek, nor playing on the pianoforte." All this may be very true; but Bill Smith, the costermonger, is a noisy vulgar fellow; therefore must be put down. Mrs. Curate, Mrs. Lawyer, Mrs. Chemist, and Miss Seventy-four must be taught to go to the greengrocer of the district, Mr. Manners, a highly respectable man, a Vestryman and a Churchwarden, who keeps :—

PLATE, WAITERS, AND LINEN FOR HIRE.

N.B.—EVENING PARTIES ATTENDED.

As the morning wears on we have :—" I say !—I say ! ! Old hats I buy," "Rags or bones," " Hearthstones," " Scissors to grind—pots, pans, kettles or old umbrellas to mend," " Old clo ! clo," " Cat or dog's meat," " Old china I mend," "Clothes props," " Any old chairs to mend ?" " Any ornaments for your fire stove," " Ripe strawberries," " Any hare skins,"—rabbit skins," " Pots or pans—jugs or mugs," " I say, Bow ! wow ! and they are all a-growing and a-blowing—three pots for sixpence," and other regular acquaintances, with the occasional accompaniment of the dustman's bell, conclude the morning's performance, which, altogether is reminiscent of the "Market Chorus" in the opera of *Masaniello*; and if the public quiet is to be protected, our sapient Town Councillors would abolish one and all of these, dustman included. One of the latest innovations upon the peace and happiness of an invalid, an author, or a quiet-loving resident, is the street vendor of coals. " Tyne Main," or " Blow-me-Tight's," Coals ! " C-o-a-l-s, *one and tuppence a underd—see'em weighed.*" This is the New Cry. Small waggons, attended by a man and a boy, go to our modern railway sidings to be filled or replenished with sacks containing 56lbs. or 112lbs. of coals, and then proceed to the different suburban quiet neighbourhoods, where the man and boy commence a kind of one done the other go on duet to the above words, which is enough to drive the strongest trained one crazy. All the great coal merchants seem to have adopted this method of retailing coals, and have thus caused the almost total abolition of coal sheds, and the greengrocer and general dealer to abandon the latter part of his calling. Our afternoon hours, after the passing of the muffin bell, are made harmonious by public references to shrimps, fine Yarmouth bloaters, haddocks, periwinkles, boiled whelks, and water*creases*, which are too familiar to need description; and our local governors in their wisdom would bid us no longer be luxurious at our tea, or else go to respectable shops and buy our "little creature comforts." Professing an anxiety to put down street cries, our police persecute one class out of a multitude, and leave all the rest untouched. It is not only an inadequate remedy, but the remedy is sought in the wrong direction. The fact is, that the street noises are an undoubted evil, and in the interests of the public, action should be taken not to put them down, but to regulate them by local bye-laws, leaving the course of trade otherwise free. It is a plan adopted in most of the greater towns which have in any way dealt with the subject.

THE DEMONS OF PIMLICO.

[From *Punch*.]

Edwin is a Young Bard, who has taken a lodging in a Quiet Street in Belgravia, that he may write his Oxford Prize Poem. The interlocutors are Demons of both Sexes.

EDWIN (composing). Where the sparkling fountain never ceases—
Female Demon. "*Wa-ter-creece-ses!*"

EDWIN. And liquid music on the marble floor tinkles—
Male Demon. "*Buy my perriwinkles!*"

EDWIN. Where the sad Oread oft retires to weep—
Black Demon. "*Sweep! Sweep!! Sweep!!!*"

EDWIN. And tears that comfort not must ever flow—
Demon from Palestine. "*Clo! Clo!! Old Clo!!!*"

EDWIN. There let me linger beneath the trees—
Italian Demon. "*Buy, Im-magees!*"

EDWIN. And weave long grasses into lovers' knots—
Demon in white apron. "*Pots! Pots!! Pots!!!*"

EDWIN. Oh! what vagrant dreams the fancy hatches—
Ragged Old Demon. "*Matches! Buy Matches!*"

EDWIN. She opes her treasure-cells, like Portia's caskets—
Demon with Cart. "*Baskets, any Baskets!*"

EDWIN. Spangles the air with thousand-coloured silks—
Old Demon. "*Buy my Wilks! Wilks!! Wilks!!!*"

EDWIN. Garments which the fairies might make habits—
Lame Demon. "*Rabbits, Hampshire Rabbits!*"

EDWIN. Visions like those the Interpreter of Bunyan's—
Demon with a Stick. "*Onions, a Rope of Onions!*"

EDWIN. And give glowing utterances to their kin—
Dirty Demon. "*Hare's skin or Rabbit skin!*"

EDWIN. In thoughts so bright the aching senses blind—
Demon with Wheel. "*Any knives or scissors to grind!*"

EDWIN. Though gone, the Deities that long ago—
Grim Demon. "*Dust Ho! Dust Ho!!*"

EDWIN. Yet, from her radiant bow no Iris settles—
Swarthy Demon. "*Mend your Pots and Kettles!*"

EDWIN. And sad and silent is the ancient seat—
Demon with Skewers. "*Cat's M-e-a-t!*"

EDWIN. For there is a spell that none can chase away—
Demon with Organ. "*Poor Dog Tray!*"

EDWIN. And a charm whose power must ever bend—
Demon with Rushes. "*Chairs! Old chairs to mend!*"

EDWIN. And still unbanished falters on the ear—
Demon with Can. "*Beer! Beer, any Beer!*"

EDWIN. Still Pan and Syrinx wander through the groves—
She Demon. "*Any Ornaments for your fire stoves!*"

EDWIN. Thus visited is the sacred ground—
Second Demon with Organ. "*Bobbing all around!*"

EDWIN. Ay, and for ever, while the planet rolls—
Demon with Fish. "*Mackerel or Soles!*"

EDWIN. Crushed Enceladus in torment groans—
Little Demon. "*Stones! Hearthstones!*"

EDWIN. While laves the sea, on the glittering strand—
Third Demon with Organ. "*O,'tis hard to give the hand!*"

EDWIN. While, as the cygnet nobly walks the water—
Fourth Demon with Organ, "*The Ratcatcher's Daughter!*"

EDWIN. And the Acropolis reveals to man—
Fifth Demon with Organ. "*Poor Mary Anne!*"

EDWIN. So long the presence, yes, the MENS DIVINA—
Sixth Demon with Organ. "*Villikins and his Dinah!*"

EDWIN. Shall breathe whereso'er the eye shoots—
Six Dirty Germans with— "*The overture to Freischutz!*"

Here—EDWIN GOES MAD

AND OUR WORK COMES TO A TIMELY

END.

INDEX.

CRIES OF LONDON—Ancient and Modern. Alphabetically Arranged.